0 901 65 64 555

Who Do We Think We Are?

Yasmin Alibhai-Brown

WHO do WE THINK we ARE?

Imagining the New Britain

ALLEN LANE
THE PENGUIN PRES

This one is for you, Col. For the robust love, the coffee in bed every morning, the unwanted attention you pay to my punctuation and for challenging any lazy thoughts I try to slip by you.

ALLEN LANE
THE PENGUIN PRESS

Published by the Penguin Group
Penguin Books Ltd, 27 Wrights Lane, London W 8 5 T Z, England
Penguin Putnam Inc., 375 Hudson Street, New York, New York 10014, USA
Penguin Books Australia Ltd, Ringwood, Victoria, Australia
Penguin Books Canada Ltd, 10 Alcorn Avenue, Toronto, Ontario, Canada M 4 V 3 B 2
Penguin Books (NZ) Ltd, Private Bag 102902, NSMC, Auckland, New Zealand

Penguin Books Ltd, Registered Offices: Harmondsworth, Middlesex, England

First published by Allen Lane The Penguin Press 2000
10 9 8 7 6 5 4 3 2 1

Set in Linotype Sabon and Trade Gothic
Typeset by Rowland Phototypesetting Ltd, Bury St Edmunds, Suffolk
Printed in England by The Bath Press, Bath

A CIP catalogue record for this book is available from the British Library

ISBN 0-713-99413-4

We live in a world of niches, where each individual is separated from, wholly indifferent to and even hostile to the values, interests and wishes of those in other niches.

A good society must offer the concept of citizenship that relates to others, sees citizens in the round, and adds what they have in common to what they are entitled to have for themselves.

John Tusa, Independent, 30 January 1997

Contents

A Note on Terminology

I have shed the terms 'ethnic minority' and 'racial minority' for this book except when I am quoting other people. I feel these words no longer describe the state of this country. If they ever did. In some inner-city areas more than 60 per cent of the inhabitants are from the visible communities. They are still referred to as 'minorities'. For decades there has been no questioning of these carelessly used terms. They depend on the absurd assumption that all whites are part of the same homogeneous group and that by definition they have power propelled by prejudice. There has never, to my knowledge, been any research to break down this whiteness or to study the diversity within white British communities in the name of multiculturalism. As Alastair Bonnett says:

> Whiteness has been tended to be approached by anti-racists as a fixed, asocial category rather than a mutable social construction . . . as a static, ahistorical, aspatial 'thing': something set outside social change, something central and permanent, something that defines the 'other' but is not itself subject to others' definitions.[1]

Such essentialism is an affront to reality which I acknowledge at least in spirit, although in a book such as this, it is almost inevitable that 'white' is used in a generalized way because at present we don't have the detailed information needed to do otherwise.[2]

Instead of 'ethnic minorities' I prefer to use descriptions such as 'British black', 'British Asian,' 'Chinese British', because I feel that the British identity is now an umbrella term which gathers under it a large number of bi-racial and combined ethnicity people, as well as all kinds of ethnic and religious groups including the English, Scottish, Welsh,

Irish, Polish, Turkish, Jewish, Chinese, and a host of other people. One day soon it will become commonplace (I hope) to use 'English British' or 'Scots British' too which would finally make us all equal at least in name.

This makes sense too of our position in Europe. Within the European Union there are no majority groups, so the usage of 'minority' to describe people of colour is again inaccurate and unhelpful. Throughout this book I also use 'visible communities' and 'immigrants' where appropriate. The latter is of crucial importance because this country has not yet accepted that it has been a country of immigration for centuries and that immigrants, far from being a burden, have contributed immeasurably to the vibrancy and the making of the nation. It is disheartening that this lack of honesty and generosity has led so many children of immigrants to despise that expression too, and to spend their lives asserting that they are 'British' – as if that makes them self-evidently better than immigrants, or as if the two terms were mutually exclusive.

Since there has been so much incontinent talk of 'floods' of immigrants, it is useful to see just what the numbers are of visible communities in Britain. This is based on the 1991 census. The figure for whites includes Irish, Italian, Polish, Spanish, Jewish, English, Scots, Welsh and many other groups. The category 'other' may or may not include mixed race Britons because some prefer to describe themselves as 'black'.

Population groups and sizes 1991

White	51,874,000
Black Caribbean	500,000
Black African	212,000
Black Other	178,000
Indian	840,000
Pakistani	477,000
Bangladeshi	163,000
Chinese	157,000
Other Asian	198,000
Other	290,000[3]

Accurate demographic figures for immigrants and their descendants also need to be clarified especially as they are classified according to countries of birth for both white and Black communities. Looking at these it becomes crystal clear how the manufactured panic over immigration has been an excuse for racism. It is not the numbers of people who have been coming to this country who are a problem for this nation, it is the colour of their skins, as the figures below prove. In general, over the years, more people have emigrated from, than have immigrated into Britain.[4]

Country of birth and size of community in Britain

Irish Republic	592,000
India	409,000
Northern Ireland	245,000
Pakistan	234,000
Germany	216,000
USA	143,000
Jamaica	142,000
Kenya	112,000
Bangladesh	105,000
Italy	91,000
Cyprus	78,000
Poland	74,000
Australia	73,000
Hong Kong	73,000
South Africa	68,000
Canada	63,000
Middle East	57,000
France	53,000
Uganda	51,000

There needs perhaps to be a brief historical explanation of how terms to describe the visible communities in this country have evolved. After the war, people who arrived in this country were known as immigrants. But whereas Italian, Polish and Jewish immigrants who came here were able to overcome some of the prejudices unleashed in this country against 'aliens' (the official term for immigrants which had been established in 1906 and which persisted until the 1970s) black and Asian immigrants were caught in a flood of racism which was encouraged and orchestrated by racist or cowardly politicians who, from 1948, raised the cry against such 'coloured' immigration.

The children of the empire who arrived from various parts of the world had less in common with each other than would have been expected from people with a shared history of being colonized by Britain. Indeed the colonial system had divided and ruled them impeccably. But the experience of racism here on this island began a movement which brought together the activated ex-colonial subjects under the common term 'black'. This served us well for at least a decade. writers such as A. Sivanandan and Stuart Hall were our brilliant leaders and re-educated us. We fought against the National Front, against Thatcher, against police brutality, under that banner and that defiant identity.

Today they seem halcyon days. But only in part. Much of what we built was resting on rocky foundations. There were many in all the visible communities – especially in the older generations – who were unhappy with the term 'black', feeling it did not properly represent their deepest cultural and religious affiliations. Others objected because they had not unlearnt the inter-communal and racial prejudices imbibed before independence. These divisions have become even worse in recent years – not just between black and Asian Britons but within those groups too.[5] This has led to the growth in cultural politics where the focus is no longer on equality but on difference, diversity and complexity. The label 'black' is now rejected by many Asians and reclaimed by many Africans and Afro-Caribbeans who feel that the word relates to a common history of slavery. This showdown has not been painless and it continues. 'Asian' and 'black' have become the used currency. Or had, until the Rushdie crisis when British Muslims felt so alone, so isolated – no black Britons and hardly any other Asians supported their cause – and so particularly targeted that they began to describe themselves as British Muslims with many among the young vociferously rejecting the term 'Asian'. Their argument is that this identification best describes how they think about themselves and that it releases them from the Indian subcontinent, leaving them free to develop a European Muslim identity.[6] Their parents and grandparents are still tied culturally to the old countries. For the younger generations this is now only a mythical connection, or one which makes little sense.

These debates and developments have caused a weakening of unity and, as Sivanandan says, have led to people fighting one another over 'issues that transgress their identities and therefore their allegiances, rather than opposing the larger tyrannies of the state which affect them all'.[7] But it has also liberated people from the constraints of single identities imposed upon them by others and assumed to be static. We are more than simple political creatures, and culture and religion have a more central position in people's lives than those on the left have ever understood. These issues are further developed in the main text. The terms I will be using, therefore, are as follows:

> **British Asian** – Hindus, Muslims, Sikhs, Chinese, Vietnamese, Sri
>   Lankans, Indians, Bangladeshis, Pakistanis
> **British black** – Afro-Caribbeans and Africans
> **Black** – meaning the political term embracing all non-white groups
> **Mixed race/bi-racial** – people of mixed ethnic or racial origins.

Where appropriate I also use **British Muslims, British Hindus, British Jews,** etc., and **Afro-Caribbean, African, Indian,** etc. At times, I have also used **visible communities, immigrants** and **Black Britons.** Since we do not have the necessary information about how white Britons wish to be described, I have used **white** as a generic description although this is obviously unsatisfactory.

I have allowed my interviewees to decide how they wish to be described. Names have been changed where requested.

Introduction

> When victims stop seeing themselves as victims and discover the
> powers of transformations, forces are born on this planet. The
> possibilities of a new history depend on it. What is done with these
> possibilities depends on how wisely we love. And ultimately we are
> bound in fate with whoever the other may be. We are bound in the
> fact that we have to deal with one another. There's no way round that.
> The way we see the other is connected to the way we see ourselves.
> The other is ourselves as the stranger.   Ben Okri,
>   'Leaping out of Shakespeare's terror: five meditations on *Othello*', 1988

This is a book about New Britain and what we make of it. Incredible transformations have taken place in this country during the latter half of the twentieth century. From being a settled place in terms of class definitions (which the two world wars did shake up, but only in limited ways so the class *structure* was not even chipped) and culturally static, this country has become less fixed because of class mobility and more mixed in terms of its population, values and cultural identity.

It is more than half a century since the large-scale migration of visible communities into this country, a movement which brought not only the excitement of new foods and music, but ideas, art, different social functions and formations and a sense of history. Most immigrants came without a proper sense of class deference, although some brought with them an even longer and less mutable tradition of caste inequality. Indigenous Britons are still grappling with the implications of these altered contours of British society, of how this convergence affected those who came in the end to stay, their descendants and British society as a whole. Cognizance has not yet caught up with actual and irreversible developments. Integration and change have surpassed understanding. In a speech a decade ago, James Lynch of the World Bank said at a conference in London:

> If we consider the overlapping dimensions of Britain's diversity; racial, religious, linguistic, regional, ethnic, gender, social class and more recently caste, we cannot avoid the conclusion that not only are 4.5% of the population so called ethnic minorities, but that the population as a whole manifests a rich diversity across a large number of overlapping cultural factors and dimensions, representing a pluralism of pluralisms which are not usually embraced within the academic and political discourse about diversity in this country.[1]

In the 1950s and 1960s we had overt discrimination, with notices which said 'No Coloureds, No Dogs' on windows of lodging houses. In the 1970s a fifth of black and Asian men with degrees were in manual work. Successive Race Relations Acts from 1965 to 1976 made direct and indirect discrimination unlawful. Today discrimination continues to be a barrier and there is serious under-representation of black and Asian people in the top 10 per cent of jobs in the country (see Chapter 4). The Stephen Lawrence Inquiry Report[2] concluded that institutional racism was a feature in all our major institutions. Yet it cannot be denied that some visible groups are achieving higher levels of success than white people.[3] The picture is therefore more complicated than it has ever been. It makes as little sense, therefore, to say that this is a society totally in the grip of racism as it is to say that, give or take a few rotten orange pippins, this is a supremely tolerant country.

In Britain, in some local areas over 60 per cent of the population is from the minority populations. Mixed race relationships are among the highest in the western world. Fifty per cent of all British-born black men have a white partner as do a third of Asian men. Half the adult Caribbean and a third of the Indian population were born in this country, and over 78 per cent of children from all minority communities are British by birth.[4] Islam is the fastest growing religion in the UK and some minority groups are dramatically over-represented in professions

such as medicine, nursing and accountancy.[5] Even though their proportion in terms of the population is only 6 per cent, South Asian
Britons make up 20 per cent of hospital doctors, most of whom came
fully trained and have saved the NHS £300 million as a result. In
business South Asian Britons own 70 per cent of independently owned
neighbourhood shops and local newspaper outlets.[6] There are approximately 1.5 million women who are from the visible communities. Of
young women in this group 47 per cent are in full-time education.
Seventy per cent of black and Asian women work full time compared
to 54 per cent of white women.[7] Other facts are equally impressive
though as yet generally unknown. Indian food now has a turnover
which is higher than coal, steel and ship-building combined.[8] A growing
band of rich Asians appears in the *Sunday Times* annual list of the
richest people in Britain.

The number of black and Asian MPs in parliament has increased
to nine, slow but real change. The House of Lords has had an impressive
injection of black and Asian peers since Labour won the election in
1997 and we have, for the first time ever, a Muslim Baroness, Pola
Uddin, who has spent most of her life on housing estates in the East
End of London. John Agard and Benjamin Zefaniah; Meera Syal,
Hanif Kureishi and Sanjeev Bhaskar; Hugh Quarshie and Frank Bruno
are as proud Britons as the Spice Girls and Damien Hirst. Most white
Britons, however, would find it hard to say so, lost as they are in the
mists of a past of scones and teas and easily won cricket games. And
even when there is an embrace, racial hatred remains unaffected.
Impossible contradictions constantly present themselves. We may have
billionaires who are brown-skinned, but unemployment among Afro-
Caribbeans, Pakistanis and Bangladeshis is substantially higher than
the national average. The nation's favourite news-reader is Trevor
McDonald, but in recent times there have been up to 250,000 racially
motivated incidents[9] every year in this country on black people, many
of whom look just like him.

Academics have, admittedly, been occupied with exploring these
issues for some time, but they are largely people who recoil from any
democratic obligations to make their work accessible or inclusive; their
themes have played out in ivory towers and their state-funded wisdom
has not filtered into daily life. Educators, politicians, editors, even artists

have not, on the whole, been able to answer the need to comprehend and engage with the massive transformations or interpret the complex realities within our nation. This is an unforgivable abdication of responsibility and opportunity which, if taken up by our leaders, would have enabled the distinct and changing communities of this country not simply to 'tolerate' one another but to interact in more robust ways and perhaps to create a country that is more optimistic and more at peace with itself. It is telling to realize that there is less optimism today about the future of a multicultural Britain than there was in 1968.[10] For all the wishful talking of sanguine, metropolitan adventurers such as the Director of the ICA, Philip Dodd, author Mike Phillips and journalist Darcus Howe, who talk up the extent to which throbbing diversity and irreversible hybridity have become the identity of this country (and how I wish they were as right as they believe they are), Britain is still a cultural archipelago. That contemporary prophet and intellectual giant Michael Ignatieff was able to assert in 1998 – fifty years since the arrival from Jamaica in 1948 of the *Empire Windrush*, the ship that brought the first batch of immigrants, beginning the flow of postwar immigration from the colonies – that 'multicultural discourse implies that we now live together. In fact, notwithstanding the rise in intermarriage, most of us continue to live apart.'[11]

And now we face other challenges which are likely to encourage clannish tendencies and magnify the fear that, as the centre cannot hold, things will fall even further apart. Understandably. Tribes provide shelter and a way of coping with globalization and other trans-national developments, unstoppable American *puissance* and the apprehension felt by some over a Britain dominated by Brussels. Devolution is both a response to these tendencies and a further cause of discomfiture and fragmentation. Political and economic homogeneity (*The End of History* etc.)[12] has ushered in security as well as insecurity; people in all walks of life express fears of personal and cultural annihilation. These are common experiences which we do not yet share with each other. We never have. We don't know how to. Yet many of the feelings being experienced by the English today – the loss of their cultural roots – have been our fears for decades. I have this impossible image in my head. A group of Sikh, Muslim, English, Irish, Afro-Caribbean pensioners are ruminating in a park in Southall. They are discussing the erosion of their old ways and the careless young who have foolishly cast off so much of value. They might laugh ruefully. When they don't understand they lean towards each other and try again. They touch the odd elbow in an act of natural intimacy. A Sikh war veteran opens a tiffin and brings out some pakoras. Drinks appear from another bag. The women talk to each other about the rising cost of M&S cardigans. Maybe somebody shuffles a pack of cards . . .

Why does this seem absurd even to imagine? Why is it so much easier to conjure up pictures of white elders sitting stiffly, fearfully, clutching their belongings tight when they find themselves next to their black and Asian compatriots on buses and park benches? It has been thus since the different races met on this soil. But we can no longer delude ourselves that we can carry on living as islands within a too small island. As Ben Okri says above, needing each other is an indispensable component of our condition. Knowing each other is another. It is time to talk.

Maybe this book can begin that important conversation. But in order to do that, conventions will have to be sacrificed. This is extraordinarily difficult but worth it because of the liberation and exhilaration which can follow. In 1998, after much persuasion and negotiation and some fairly abject persistence, I was given the opportunity by BBC Radio 4 to present a series of programmes which brought together intellectuals, artists, other key *and* ordinary people from the various British communities, white and black, to talk about major issues of our times. Called *Diverse Perspectives* we got the *Any Questions* slot in the summer, which was remarkable in itself. What was even more extraordinary, though, is that this was the first such programme in the British broadcasting media, as far as we were able to ascertain. Those who listened and those who were part of the programme felt that this was not only a radical departure, but an essential one. As the *Guardian* columnist and author Jonathan Freedland, one of the panellists, who is convinced that we need to break out of old modes of thinking, put it:

> **It's up to us to change the way we think. Of course it's much harder and much scarier than not changing . . . the programme is right to be called *Diverse Perspectives*, because we are diverse. [And when we**

discuss things] there will be clashes, there will be overlappings, people won't stay in their labelled communities, it is all very fluid. But that's the process we must begin.[13]

Cheyenne Indians believe you must never enter another's territory without bearing a gift. I came to this country more than a quarter of a century ago, bringing with me not much cash (£20 I think), but copious hopes, ideas, thoughts, desires, much knowledge and immense curiosity. Many others – black, Asian, Chinese, Jewish, Polish and countless more people – had done the same before me and mine, bearing the priceless gift of diversity. Like that dusky King in Bethlehem, except that our offerings, with the exception of foods, were not generally well received. We, the New Commonwealth immigrants, also believed that the colonial experience had given us certain entitlements (we were here after all because they, you, were there) and much in common with the British. When I was young, living precariously in a household with no steady income and with uncertainty stalking every corner of our lives, my father would tell me: 'You will go to England one day. You will be someone big. They have the best education. See how they rule the world. I'll take you myself.' (It was England which carried this meaning for us, not Britain.) I was not close to him. In fact when I was born, late in the marriage, all the rooms in his heart were already closed down or occupied. He spoke little, and then too much about education and England.[14] My mother, Jena, could barely speak English, but she too loved the thought of England. Traces of this love linger on and it has survived the stones thrown at her by young white boys one Christmas. You can see it when she plies my English husband and friends with affection and food. Like others in our community Jena flung herself, when she could afford it, with pitiful enthusiasm into learning English cooking ('repairing' it too so that it was edible); into buying Cadbury's Milk Chocolate because it had one-and-a-half glasses of real milk (and good English companies would never lie), and making smocked Alice in Wonderland frocks and pinafores. She, like my father, encouraged me to read so much English literature that I could think of little else. Thus were scuppered more sensible ambitions; to be a doctor, lawyer or accountant. My head-master – an anti-imperialist – bellowed with pain when I told him that

I wanted to carry on with Eng. Lit. So innocent was this love that even *A Passage to India* could not dispel it. I did, however, scribble 'ONLY CONNECT' in caps on the cover of my autograph book, which had lovely ice-cream-coloured pages and which had been presented to me by my favourite white teacher for quoting from the essays in literary criticism by Lord David Cecil in my exams.

And so it was over here. I recently reread a yellow and brittle copy of *To Sir With Love*, an autobiographical novel by the black writer E. R. Braithwaite written in 1958, ten years after the first arrivals from the Caribbean. He, like me, was a lover of this land and its words. He describes, with unseemly awe, the 'fantastic' phenomenon which led to different races and cultures 'assiduously identifying themselves with British loyalties, beliefs and traditions'. He then goes on to show how these profoundly *British* colonized people had that identity kicked out of them, us, bit by bit. Norman Tebbit, who insists that we should be forced to learn British values, would be more convincing if he was better educated on recent history himself.[15] The hero of *To Sir With Love* is so shocked by the unexpected racism he suffers that there is a moment when he cannot bear to look at his own, black image. Those who came after him used other ploys to avoid recognizing their exclusion. I dressed in mock Victorian clothes and did not walk too close to relatives with 'bad' accents. Others changed their names. Balwinders became Babs. We taught ourselves to forget how to eat rice with our hands and grappled foolishly with chicken legs as they flew off our forks. How Peter Sellers laughed. Thus we became adept at chiselling off any bits that might cause offence, trigger off painful rejections. But they came anyway. To add insult, the more we tried to belong the less we were respected. As one of the interviewees in this book, a retired teacher, says:

> I talked in English, proper convent English. To my colleagues this meant that I was a fraud, not a real Indian. I wore saris to school and my head told me it was a health hazard so I had to wear trousers. This same head then went to India on tour and came back with all his souvenirs of the 'real' India. He never promoted me, treated me like I was nothing and the harder I tried, the harder he became. It was just so difficult for us. What were we to do?

In many ways it is still thus for intellectuals from the visible minorities. The Kurdish British journalist Hazir Teimourian did a moving series of talks on BBC Radio 4 in 1998 in which he described his love for this country, its history and fables. In the final part of his last talk he said this:

> The Thames made Londinium and Londinium made England and England made Parliament and Parliament made Britain and Britain changed the world. Britain also made me, for better or worse . . . Thank you once more then England.[16]

Such affection has either been ignored or forever misunderstood. Perhaps this explains partly why we withdrew, started mistrusting and stereotyping all whites. Prejudice rose to salvage pride. Our true lives were thereafter to be known only by our own. Fear of ridicule means that even our languages are spoken in private, as that wonderful writer Meera Syal describes in her novel *Anita and Me*:

> I felt strange to hear Punjabi under the stars. It was an indoor language to me, an almost guilty secret which the elders could only share away from prying eyes and ears. On the street, in shops, on buses, in parks, I noticed how the volume would go up when they spoke English, telling us kids not to wander off . . . They switched to Punjabi and the volume became a conspiratorial whisper. 'That woman over there, her hat like a dead dog . . . the bastard is asking too much, let's go.'[17]

We developed public faces and intensely private lives. Our expectations of loyalty and conformity became fortresses which kept out light but kept us warm. Embattled, reclaimed self-regard has no sweetness. It is a peculiar beast which has grown in time to something more ferocious which, like an untamed guard dog, stands at the door keeping the 'west' out, so the south and the east can remain clean and pure. As if. Here is one aunt expressing these views, a fairly typical example of what is said:

> Never let their ideas poison your minds, East is best. Our girls and boys know modesty, they don't need dirty things like sex before marriage. Their civilization is finished. Just mind our own business and don't have much more to do with them.

Meanwhile white Britons, especially in metropolitan areas, started developing conflicting attitudes to the changes in society. They opened up their stomachs and their sensory organs, but not, on the whole, their hearts or heads. Subtle moments, light racisms flutter in and out of your face so often you barely notice. The evidence of prevailing discrimination, racial violence and abuse piles up daily. Intermarriage is increasing but attitudes towards it are still fairly negative.[18] Ethnic food is eaten with such joy, and with such pride, it makes you wonder what could happen if politics, the arts, academia, the media and education were to be transformed in an equally positive way. I remember watching a young white British woman on television explaining why she had to leave her Sicilian husband and return to Britain. She missed home, she said, and especially British food, 'like curries and pappadoms'. But, even here, the style gurus, who fall over themselves to elevate French and Italian food (even when it is second rate and malevolent), denigrate oriental food partly because it is not European and partly because it is the food of ordinary people. If our society was better understood and communicated our vision would be dramatically altered. As Professor Bhikhu Parekh told me:

> **Cultural difference is an invaluable national asset. [These differences] widen the range of lifestyles open to all its citizens, enabling them to borrow from others and enrich their lives. They stimulate experiment, ideas, and a creative interplay between different traditions.**

You can see the possibilities of this most profoundly in the way literary books and language have been injected with this cosmopolitan energy.

On the whole, though, appreciation seems to come most readily when there are singular, undeniable success stories. Individuals are rewarded and encouraged not only for being talented, but for being different and talented. Salman Rushdie, Trevor Phillips, Paul Boateng, Keith Vaz, Anish Kapoor, Jazzie B., Oona King, Shobhana Jeyasingh, Lenny Henry, and hundreds of others have made it big in Britain. But to what extent does this represent merely the fact that, like cream, you can't hold down exceptional people in any society, and how much does this reveal that genuine cross-fertilization is taking place? That the spaces between our lives are narrowing?

In the early 1980s, Salman Rushdie himself wrote a scathing essay entitled 'The new empire within Britain' which was broadcast on Channel 4. He said:

> **Britain is now two entirely different worlds and the one you inherit is determined by the colour of your skin . . . very few white people, except those active in fighting racism, are willing to believe the descriptions of contemporary reality offered by blacks. And black people . . . grow increasingly suspicious and angry.**[19]

And if Ignatieff (p. 4) is even half right, the story continues. All these years on, although the rich mix has leaked out and coloured the fabric of British society, and individually some bonds have been forged, we have, as yet, not managed to trade secrets, nor to tap into the inner landscapes, the ways of living and being, dreams. And it is not just the ignorant who are ignorant. I remember reading Charles Moore, the editor of the *Daily Telegraph*, describing in the *Spectator* his next-door neighbours, who are British Muslims. He admitted they were good folk who have done his family many acts of kindness, but he confessed that their presence evoked in him fears of the 'hooded hordes' over-running his beloved country: 'Britain is basically English speaking, Christian and white and if one starts to think it might become basically Urdu speaking and Muslim and brown one gets frightened.'[20] Clearly, for Mr Moore, next door lay the terror that other Moore felt in the Malabar Caves. With ample apologies for patronizing such a pillar of the establishment, I ask whether it is not tragic that such a highly educated man should display such xenophobic delusions?

Lest we start to believe this is a sickness of the right, let us move the knob to the (new) left. As the designer Stephen Bayley leaves the Dome project, he arrogantly makes mindless assertions about voodoo sacrifices in Brixton.[21] Asked why so few Asians are in any powerful position within New Labour, I am told by a chap 'close to the government' that it is because we are culturally so baffling. It will, he announced, take a good many more years to bring us into the fold. Explaining to him that we use toothpaste too did not reassure him or convince him otherwise.

This is truly depressing and, worse, foolish. And it gets worse the more you look at the bigger picture. As the enormous structural changes caused by political realignment, economic and social upheavals, and technological revolutions engulf the country, leaving us all at sea (see Chapter 1), theorists have risen out of the fog in unprecedented numbers to explain all. But they do so as if they still speak to a homogeneous country, with a bedrock of shared and understood values and experiences. Politicians pronounce, think tanks think, writers describe, media folk reflect, and others in the establishment confer and thrash out ideas which are almost always unsustainable because they are based on such limited views and visions about who we are. And this is as true of those who are considered experts on the gender issue and feminism as of any other area of public discussion. How can pundits carry on the way they do without a glance in our direction, the black and Asian Britons, many of the key, if unrecognized, agents of change in the past fifty years?

Take just one example. How can it be acceptable that in 1996 we had a survey-based publication called *What Women Want*, which had nothing at all to say in the introduction about black and Asian women in Britain? There was a brief section on third world women which claimed that 'Women in the UK do not face the levels of discrimination and hardship suffered by women in many other countries.'[22] This may be true on the whole, but within this country, on this island, there are women who are worse off than their counterparts in the third world. You only have to see the misery of young Bangladeshi wives living in appalling conditions in Tower Hamlets to confirm this. TB is spreading in this community; poverty combined with high birth-rates (there is a clear relationship between the two) blights their lives. Low education levels, a patriarchal system, lack of resources and racism add to their burdens. To be fair, some views of black and Asian women do appear, but there is an overwhelming impression left by this book that it is driven by and for the white women of Britain.

Look through the various key publications on the family, the democratic deficit, health education, other areas of social policy and regeneration, and the same invisibility persists. Even Demos, our bright young think-tank, which has produced some of the most creative ideas on diverse Britain, cannot break free from the persistent idea that four 'nations' make up this country. The rest are simply 'minorities', fringe people, living on the swampy edges of society.[23] What *we* do and think would change so much of what *they* – the great and the good –

philosophize about, if only they connected with our lives. And unless they can make these connections how can any of them claim with any authority at all that they speak universal truths?

But we, black and Asian people in positions of influence, are guilty of the same processes. Professor Michael Dummett once said that white Britons were wilfully, rather than 'innocently', ignorant of black people.[24] It is a habit we have picked up also. We, too, dismiss white people and their ideas, pass them by as if they have no relevance whatsoever to us. Most, if not all, of us have certainly convinced ourselves that our lives are so particular, so specific, so defined by race and ethnicity that no white people can or should try to understand them.

We may be distinct in many and significant ways (and remember many are not; they are only seen that way) but as diverse people living in a hegemonic culture, we would have to be dead and buried not to be affected by the world around us. This is why I am not setting out, in this book, to create a separate space for black and Asian Britons to talk in comfort to one another and to assert this as an act of defiance and separation. I do appreciate the need many feel to do this. In the 1960s and 1970s, African-American writers used the concept of separate development with great effect in the United States. Writers such as Alice Walker, Nikki Giovanni, Maya Angelou and others ran writers' circles to sustain one another and to grow within their own communities. In part they were reacting to exclusion. They ended up with something far greater than revenge or 'equal opportunity'. Their writing blossomed first within those safe spaces and it was only then that their irresistible dynamism was able collectively to force itself upon the consciousness of black men and white Americans, and in time the whole world. We don't yet have our Toni Morrison or Maya Angelou, writers who can blend the scents of politics and literature and diffuse their thoughts through the atmosphere, affecting the very way we *all* breathe. In part this is because good writing by those not white still has to struggle to be seen and heard in Britain. Duncan Campbell described in the *Guardian* how black writers such as the explosive Ferdinand Dennis, for example, are 'unsung' because they are not 'deep in the literary loop'.[25] Inevitably, therefore, 'black spaces' are present in this country, too, albeit in a much quieter way.

But if reactive, self-imposed exile is the only response to our feelings of exclusion, that itself raises new problems and this is one of the themes of this book. Until recently I myself saw this as the only feasible option open to us. Now, it increasingly feels like all we are doing is playing marbles in the ghetto. Humiliated though it makes us feel, hard though it is, some of us at least must try and relocate ourselves and ensure that the relocation is as near as possible to the centre. And we must do it without assimilating, apologizing, posturing or setting ourselves up as saints.

What we think and believe would be rattled (and what a very good thing that would be) if we stopped seeing ourselves only as racial or ethnic creatures; if we followed and understood the debates and placed our lives within that wider context. Instead of this, having waited so long to be invited to the party, we now feign indifference or outrage or (worse) pretend that we are a species apart. 'You are becoming too English' is a comment with which my more 'authentic' cigarette-smoking female Asian friends frequently dismiss me as we grapple with the problems of fat upper arms, relationships, jobs, talkback children, lack or otherwise of fulfilment, and so on and on.

This is emphatically why I have chosen not to write a book which is a cosy confab with sisters and brothers of colour. It is not a book, either, which sets out to explain us to you or us to them. We are you; they are us. We can and must learn from one another. But first perhaps we must know ourselves. People who dominate discourse have been told this often enough (and they still will not listen), but those who have been invisible or marginalized sometimes cultivate their own brand of arrogance and think it is beneath them to communicate with the wider population. We cannot have it both ways. We must make a choice. It seems to me dishonest to say that we are being rendered invisible and then refuse to engage with those few who are trying to break down the barriers and who often find that we, in the meantime, have sunk behind our own barricades. We are so carried away these days by a sense of grievance that we have failed to see real possibilities. The writings of Germaine Greer in the past decade have been astonishingly broad, passionate and inclusive. Much (not by any means all) of what she has said in her own inimitable way is what many of the interviewees I spoke to for this book were also saying. In 1985, in *Sex and Destiny: The Politics of Human Fertility*[26] she challenged the anti-child views of western feminists and had the humility to look around at other 'developing' societies in order to learn and not to teach or gloat. So why have we, black and Asian feminists, not given her proper credit? Because she is white she cannot possibly be right, and even if she is we must keep our approval down because we believe that the only way we will be given our space is if we carry on griping.

Knowing each other and having respect for different world views is surely an inescapable responsibility in this complicated world. When a social environment undergoes extensive change, the 'horizon of expectations' is disturbed, says Professor Parekh, habitual assumptions are challenged and the tacit self-understanding of a community proves inadequate.[27] For fifty years we have not had the positive leadership which would have enabled people to rebuild their security and develop their understanding. As Isaiah Berlin said once, before he himself appeared to give up the effort in the years before his death:

> To judge one culture by the standards of another argues a failure of imagination and understanding. Every culture has its own attributes, which must be grasped in and for themselves. In order to understand a culture, one must employ the same faculties of sympathetic insight with which we understand one another, without which there is neither love nor friendship, nor true human relations.[28]

Here is a useful example of what I am attempting to argue in this book. In 1996 Polly Toynbee wrote, in her distinctive, authoritative style and tone which harbours no self-doubt, that Muslim schools should not be state funded in this country because:

> Eventually a high proportion of Britain's 400,000 Muslim children could end up isolated in sectarian schools. Does it matter? It means that the state will educate children to believe women are of inferior status, one step behind the divine order of things. The state will acquiesce in the repression of young girls, putting their parents' cultural rights above the duty to educate all British girls equally.[29]

Soon after this came out an English journalist, who periodically consults me on 'ethnic' or Muslim issues, rang up and asked me what I thought of this controversial topic. Her words to me were:

'Am I right in thinking that someone like you would probably agree with Polly Toynbee?'

'No and yes,' I said.

'You're not turning fundamental [*sic*] are you? Would you send your daughter to a Muslim school?'

'No,' was my reply to both new questions.

So what was my response?

Well, I explained, displaying patience I do not have, never have had. I didn't have one response. Part of me was put out. I wanted to know how many Muslim women or girls Polly Toynbee knew or consulted before penning her piece. I have hundreds of white friends and acquaintances. Many of my closest relationships are with white Britons. I can therefore pronounce upon their world with some knowledge that has not just come to me via third-hand sources. Do such feminist columnists have that same intimate knowledge of *our* lives? If so, they would then have the right to comment and would bring something fresh and insightful. Bill Bryson writes as an outsider intimately conversant with this country, and this is why he is so good. Somebody like the Irish travel writer Dervla Murphy too is respected for her outsider's view of Bradford Muslims because she comes to them with an open mind filled not with stereotypes and apprehension but real, sometimes brutal curiosity.

What would Polly Toynbee say if I told her that in my Muslim community, way back in 1951, our Imam issued an edict, which was immediately followed, that every family should educate their daughters first and then their sons because the world was male and the boys would find a way of making it? Or that today, in some Muslim communities, the proportion of university educated women is significantly higher than the national average? Our Imam also told all fathers that if they beat their daughters thorns would grow on their hands when they went to the nether world and that that would be their punishment for eternity, but that if they looked after their daughters properly they would go to paradise. Overnight girls became so coveted that my ex-mother-in-law actually dressed her fourth son as a girl, ribbons and all, until he was six.

But it would be easy if all I felt was indignation on behalf of my misunderstood people. I don't. I admire and envy the originality and passion of Polly Toynbee's writing. Together with Jill Tweedie, Lynne Segal and other British feminists, she taught me, amongst others, how to think about gender difference. I cannot simply dismiss a perceptive observer like her as someone who 'doesn't understand us' or who is suffering from Islamophobia. To make matters even more complex, I actually share some of her misgivings about Muslim schools but for reasons that are somewhat different from hers. There is an indisputable case, on grounds of justice, for the right of Muslims to have their own schools if we have Christian and Jewish state-funded establishments. Nevertheless, I believe that if we did get these schools, that would, in the end, make our exclusion and demonization even more compelling for an uncomprehending anti-Islamic society. I worry too that some parents, afraid of the world as it has become in the late twentieth century, might use the schools to rein in girls and their talents.

But yet, I have myself met confident and ambitious girls at private Muslim schools who tell me that being in a safe environment where they are not subjected to verbal humiliation has enabled them to blossom. It is also a remarkable fact that in the 1998 league tables, one Muslim girls school, the Mohammad Zakaria school in Bradford, out-performed Eton in the A level results.[30]

We accept that all-girl schools as opposed to mixed schools are good for girls. Muslim schoolgirls at comprehensives have the added burden of their teachers curtailing their aspirations because they are convinced that the girls would all be forced into marriages anyway. One white anti-racist teacher in Bradford confirmed this to me: 'Many of us feel why make these girls even more unable to live with their culture? I think my responsibility is not to create fissures in the family but to give some education to the girls which is relevant to their needs.' With so little trust or real awareness between teachers and parents it is little wonder so many parents are opting for separate education for their daughters.

Thirty years ago, white working-class parents went through similar confusing emotions about school life and their own values. Education did nothing to create pride in working-class life and instead imposed alien middle-class values on working-class children. There are so many other questions raised by this one debate. What about the fact that there are many white British women who are now happy to surrender their freedoms and opt instead for some of the most uncompromising forms of Islamic life? As a columnist for the *Independent*, I get dozens of letters from such women asking for help to get on the road to conversion. If we are that worried about the education girls in this country need and deserve, why the silence on how girls are brainwashed about abortion and sex in many Catholic schools? We could go on. What is seen as a story about the backwardness of one alien ethnic group becomes instead a symbol of wider debates which involve all of us, whoever we are.

This is but one example of how complex and connected our lives and needs now are and it is the aim of this book to crack open some of the circumscribed ways we have so far chosen to interpret them. We should stop falling back on stereotypes as relief from the hard work it takes to dismantle them. We need to reveal and analyse how the diverse groups of people in Britain interact and how we might deepen that relationship, make it more equal and honest and perhaps enhance the way we negotiate the problems and opportunities we are facing. The interactions will not be easy or polite. As Carol Gilligan, Professor of Education at Harvard, says, the subjects of race, sexuality and class never are, because:

> **Unvoiced they act like a slow burn. Voiced they bring conflict into the open, where it can be talked about and seen. A relational psychology is a talking/listening cure. The greatest difficulty is finding a way to speak that does not silence others by insult, by violation.**[31]

As we reach the end of the twentieth century and shuffle into the next millennium, people of all backgrounds will need to broaden their ideas if only to survive the seismic changes that have started already. We must learn humility to look beyond our own worlds, obsessions and interpretations. Somehow we need to break away from the foolish idea that we are all forever fated to remain disconnected; to shout across ravines and canyons at one another or gripe amongst ourselves about those on the other side. Maybe one day we will find the courage and wisdom not to deny, in the face of truth and all evidence, that our lives overlap, and that they share most of what it means to be human.

Over 120 people have been interviewed for this book, over the course of two years. I can't name them all, so I will not name any, but, as is often said, without these conversations, books like this cannot be written. Many of my interviewees were people who grapple daily with many of the themes of this book but are ignored by those who so often pontificate on social and political truths. Bea Campbell shows us how not to do this. For years she has, with consummate skill and commitment, consulted disenfranchised communities continuously and not just for the few months it takes authors to research books. In order to have that continuity of contact, a large number of my interviewees were people I already knew in some capacity. A journalist has that advantage. I have wearied friends, my lover, colleagues and many others by constantly bringing them round to discussing these ideas – even when all they wanted was a shallow chat about good wine or yet another collapsed marriage. Many times these conversations ended up being noisy, unpleasant bouts. I have read every word Bhikhu Parekh has written in the past five years. He is arguably the most extraordinary commentator we have in this country, and I hope he will forgive me for taking many of his lofty thoughts and turning them into slightly more accessible forms. Claire Longrigg, Sally Weale, Hilly Jane and the late Ruth Picardie, as commissioning editors of the *Guardian* and *Independent* at various times, often allowed me space to write on some of these issues – something I needed to do from time to time if only in order to convince myself I was neither mad nor some irrelevant, soft-centred liberal who believed in beige-coloured piano keys.

For the first time in a long time, I have included the voices and thoughts of black and Asian women whose lives and views have not been adequately chronicled and who are never taken as seriously as they deserve to be. The majority of my white interviewees, also, were women. The reason for this is that both ethnic minority women and white women have confronted multiculturalism in more enterprising ways than men. Remember that the immigrants who came also left behind homogeneous, settled values which they could take for granted and which had remained unchanged for generations. Like white Britons, they too had delusions that they could move across the seas and nothing fundamental would need to change. In many communities the women were expected to keep the culture warm and uncontaminated. Many did not make the choice to move. They had to because the men made the decision to migrate or because their families chose for them husbands who lived in Britain. Black women have for years been at the front line of the battles for equality and justice. The women had to adjust to diversity and complexity. They had to deal with their children growing up here and getting more and more confused about their identity and the split between the values of the home and the wider society; for the first time they had to work, and most have changed much more radically as a result of their encounter with the west than men have. White women have always had attitudes to black migration different from those of white men. Since the seventeenth century, they have found it possible, in spite of their own racial prejudices, to love, have sex with and even cohabit with 'immigrants'. They have often been made to suffer for this. And since this book was to provide an enlarged, more inclusive view of what this country could be, white women's views were of some importance.

You cannot write such a book, however, without talking to men. It is they who hold the power and the key to any future progress. I talked to over fifty black and Asian men and fifty white men, including members of the British National Party, the Socialist Workers Party, Tories, Labour and Liberal Democrats. White men were some of the most thoughtful interviewees. Even the laddish ones broke their own constructed stereotypes. Yes, they spoke with bravado about sex and women and beer, but, pushed gently to talk on, they revealed terror and longings which moved me. Peter – big, hairy, unemployed – was very angry when I first met him. His wife had left him and their three young children and gone off with the lorry driver next door who had more cash than Peter could ever imagine having. That was his story. It was his Asian neighbour, Shanu, who told me more about him. She could not begin to understand how a mother could do this to her children. Sheila, the wife, did indeed confirm Peter's version of events. He was a broken man who said to me: 'How can this be right? I am telling you, please don't go the way of these women. Asian men are lucky. Shanu here would never do this to her kids.' For the first time ever, I heard such sentiments from someone I would have expected to have more sympathy with Enoch Powell's views. Shanu, whose maternal and feminine instincts were utterly engaged by this, was completely on his side, as was her husband, Rehman. Together the three of them discussed the end of real womanhood in ways that indicated how new alliances are forming all the time. It was striking that none of them was willing to try to understand why the woman did what she did, or what she had said in her defence.

I have tried to include interviewees whose experiences and memories span the many decades since the *Empire Windrush* arrived in 1948. This material is quoted, when relevant, in the various chapters. A word of caution. A book such as this necessarily has to rest on a degree of generalization. But certain trends are discernible and were confirmed by the many interviews I carried out. This is not to deny the fact that we are all primarily individuals. It has been one of our battles as black and Asian people not to be seen as part of the herd but to be recognized as distinct individuals. I would wish to extend that same respect to white people. Through a large number of serious conversations and discussions, qualitative interviews and other research, much became clear for me, and I learnt more than I ever thought possible. As a journalist, I was forced to confront how superficially we illustrate information and how our increasingly strident writing styles cover up a terrible lack of groundwork.

Almost everyone I talked to had a sense that the old world was collapsing, that certainties were disappearing, and that what was needed to fill the void was still up for grabs. The book looks at politics, the media, feminism and other broad issues, asking how inclusive they have been in recent times and how well or otherwise they have responded to the changing landscapes. For example, in the great womanization of politics at Westminster, where are we, the women of colour? One and a half (Oona King is half African American) – admittedly very able and feisty women – represent over two million of us in Parliament. White women can of course represent our interests, but they will not necessarily do so. And when they do take on our causes, as the very brave MP Anne Cryer has done on the issue of forced marriages, they face astounding obstacles from the conservative members of the Asian community, most of them middle-aged men, or young men who are even more traditional than their fathers.

Every subject I scrutinized revealed a wide, untapped source of ideas and opinions, and unexpected fresh things happened all the time. Older Asian women were more likely to be militantly against male oppression than were many of the twenty-somethings. Why? Is the younger generation too conservative and conformist, or is it because they are afraid of the implications of bitter battles?

The final part of the book concentrates on the private sphere. On families, love, sex, and the self. I passionately disagree with those, such as Natasha Walters, who would say that the personal is not the political. The political has transformed the personal and continues to do so. There can be no separation between them, no excuses either. Whether we are looking at the role of religion in our country or the decision of a white British woman to convert to militant Islam, the political becomes the personal.

A few years ago, that deep writer Aamer Hussein said: 'In your cities . . . lie invisible cities where things merge, blend, metamorphose. Find them. A blueprint for your future perhaps.'[32] I hope dearly that this book can begin to excavate those buried, hidden treasures in our soil. A note to booksellers. Please do not place this under 'Race and Multiculturalism' or 'Feminism'. Is there a more suitable category? The British Nation perhaps?

The Context: Gales of Change

The lives of British women and men today need to be seen in the context of what is happening in the west at the end of the twentieth century. These are strange, uncertain times for us all. Some of what many of us are feeling may be connected to the end-of-millennium angst which is exaggerating to our inner selves the awful state of the world. In that interesting collection of essays *The Age of Anxiety*, the editors, Sarah Dunant and Roy Porter, describe how portentous we could make our times sound. We might, they suggest, put it like this:

> **The world was full of omens of its own destruction. New plagues swept across the globe; people died in agony, some shrivelled to skeletons, some pouring blood and fluids from every orifice. Children began to wheeze and choke on the very air they breathed. A heart of a pig was found to beat in the body of a man . . .** [1]

But these are not simply fears and fantasies generated by a mood that has come upon us because of a certain change to date. Such very real problems *are* afflicting the world, and at moments, for the first time since the Enlightenment, Man (yes, especially Man) may be feeling more helpless and less in control before larger forces. About the environment in particular there is, together with a sense of urgency, a quiet hysteria that it is all too late already. And Dunant and Porter are wholly erroneous when they claim that, except for American fundamentalists, people see these disasters not as God's work but as Man's mismanagement. Millions of people in this country – stable, decent, rational creatures – do believe that an angry God has had a hand in these punishing times.

People of faith were once seen as sad folk who were incapable of being free spirits. Today these freedom-loving children of the sixties are flocking to church. Our local Church of England school could not fill its places in 1985 when my son started there. These days people would kill (if they didn't fear it would appear un-Christian) to get their children in. These are young parents, caught up in the moral panic about values, God and the bad young. In a speech he made at a meeting to discuss Islam and the West, Prince Charles put his finger on it:

> **My belief is that in each one of us there is a distant echo of the sense of the sacred, but that the majority of us are terrified to admit its existence for fear of ridicule and abuse. This fear of ridicule, even to the extent of mentioning the name of God, is a classic indication of the loss of meaning in so-called western civilization.**[2]

This tentative moving towards the spiritual is perhaps no bad thing following decades of complacency and human arrogance, but, as ever, these desires can lead to unpredictable outcomes. It is no accident that Christian, Jewish and Hindu extremism is on the rise at this time or that in 1998 a quarter of a million folk marched on London to assert their country lifestyle which supposedly goes back hundreds of years. Seventy thousand people, including Madonna and Ringo Starr, see an Indian woman living in Germany who calls herself 'Mother Meera' as a divine incarnation of God on earth.[3] Glen Hoddle gets lost with a misleading map navigating the theology of reincarnation and is sacked from his job as the English football manager for talking about disabled people having to atone for past mistakes. This is not to suggest that the resurgence of religion or 'ruralism' is something necessarily to be feared or derided. These are important reminders that western capitalism is not the heaven earthlings have been pining for; that we are more than what we eat or own or wear. But it is indisputable that even the benign manifestations of these movements symbolize a search, discomfort and the lack of a clarity which is no longer available or fashionable. It is interesting, though, that – as the Black Environment Network has indicated – almost all conservation trusts and organizations in Britain remain nearly all white.[4] Those unable to hurl themselves into over-reaching ideologies respond to their unease by worshipping crystals or animals, falling for Feng Shui, sitting on trees with unwashed hair, offering themselves up for regimented body-forming systems orchestrated by thin, disciplinarian schoolmistresses who run health farms or write bestsellers on the subject. The truly vulnerable among us resort to counselling – the biggest growth industry of our times – which reveals the extent perhaps of the pain we are in and the desperate belief in planned solutions.

Is there anything new in this? Are such alternatives, causes and enclaves not always with us? I would argue that these might indeed be cyclical and recurrent themes, but also that there is something particular going on at the present time. In the sixties when George Harrison and co. fell into kaftans and guru worship, they were doing so for optimistic reasons and as spoilt children of the west who had never had it so good and simply wanted more. Some of this is still going on if one listens to the well-fed and homespun philosophies of people such as the re-invented Lynne Franks, for instance. But many others on the search for The Meaning of Life in the nineties are more confused and disconsolate. Those seeking alternatives are doing so because they are seeking a centre, a core to their lives. Reena, a young Asian woman who does Indian oil body massage, says she has never had so many disillusioned white Britons on her books as now:

> They come for the massage. But really they are coming for something else. They always ask me about my life, my religion, my culture. So many say that their lives are empty. Two men have asked me to marry them for silly reasons like I have eastern values. It is just rubbish. I was born here; my values are not from Mars. But I have to play the part otherwise I think I will break their tender hearts. I just see so

> many sad people. It is strange. We think that they [white people] have
> everything. But if they don't think it makes them happy, what is the
> use? It was not like this before. When I started doing this in 1985, my
> clients came because they had a pain or they wanted beautiful skin.
> Now it is for other reasons. So often they cry. The other day a young
> man from the City started crying. I had to give him an extra half hour.
> I sometimes feel like their mother.

Then there is the political and economic positioning across the globe
where similarity is breeding not only contempt but real as well as
simulated resistance. As one of my interviewees, Sunil, a history student
at the University of London, put it:

> Every barrier, every safety net, every assumption – all the frameworks
> we need in order to predict what tomorrow might look like, they are all
> gone. Our solutions are creating bigger problems than they are solving
> and meanwhile we are all swimming in oceans instead of small safe
> ponds. Why do you think *Captain Corelli's Mandolin* is such a success
> in London? Because we yearn for the simplicity of rural love and wars
> we can understand.

Our world is indeed so protean, capricious and volatile at present
that it is making us all – not just those once steadfast and self-assured
white, conservative men like Worsthorne – feel giddy and unsteady,
not knowing how to respond. Globalization – economic and cultural
– is perhaps one of the most pervasive and bewildering of these changes.
We don't know how to understand what is going on but we know
that it cannot possibly be all unremitting good news. People like
Anthony Giddens would tell us that the international flow of capital
and technology and the consequent loss of national sovereignty are
not issues to lose sleep over. Maybe some problems are created, but on
the whole the news is good because we have international communities
who understand each other.[5] Such economic cheerfulness is an affront
to those across the globe whose lives have sunk even further into
poverty and chaos.

In 1998, the massively successful 'Tiger' economies of the east were
seen shattering. Night after night intelligent journalists appeared on
television to tell us this and then, with indecent haste, to reassure us

that all was still well with *our* world, because (so far) the British economy was largely unaffected. These professionals have no language to illuminate for us the realities of one-world economics, so they revert to an imperial model. And yet, is it at all sensible to pretend that what happens in Malaysia, Indonesia, Hong Kong and China is of little consequence to us? At the most mundane level, what about the Hong Kong Chinese British citizens who live in this country? How much of their money was invested in businesses in Hong Kong? We have Thai people in this country too. And even if we didn't have these direct connections, should we not care that millions have lost their money, resulting in even more imbalance between the west and the rest? Writing in the *Guardian*, Salman Rushdie powerfully asserts that, unless we deal with this imbalance both in reality and in our knowledge of it, the next century will be catastrophic and the whole globe will be destabilized. He writes: 'The Debt must be wiped out unless we want a third millennium marked by the resentment, violence, fanaticism and despotism that must be the inevitable effects of this global injustice.'[6]

Forced migration is a problem which affects both the poor and the rich nations: on the one hand, the suppliers who often lose their best and most talented and enterprising people, and, on the other, the paranoid recipients who never grasp this fact. Most of us know that we should broaden our awareness of what is going on and this is why these over-confident journalists and smooth-talking politicians, pundits and business people fail to convince us that everything is all right, leaving us with unspoken fears as they move to the next story or exotic market-place.

There are many other examples. The bombings in 1998 by the USA of sites in Iraq and Sudan have been interpreted with as little sophistication as in the days of the oil crisis in the seventies, when the west had to wake up to the fact that oil-producing countries actually owned their oil and had the right at least to try to manage the asset. Our middlemen and women, those whose mission it is to explain, were left floundering then. More than thirty years on, the same old words and attitudes were used to describe a very complex modern situation. There is barely a handful of journalists who can explain the perils of a world dominated by a hegemonic superpower and who also understand how this creates extremism even within the west. Robert

Fisk is one of them. He managed to get through real evidence about what had been happening in Iraq since the Gulf War, in order to explain the causes and effects – beyond the US and British designer truths – of the bombings in Iraq. He also exposed the hypocrisy of US presidents who, just before they bomb their victims, tell them how great they really are, and described how these empty words on the 'greatness of Islam' fool nobody in the two-thirds world any more.[7] When Hutu rebels went on a killing rampage in a Ugandan national park in February 1999, only two newspapers and hardly any radio or television programmes gave the names of the Ugandan victims.

Meanwhile, as homogeneity is diffused across the globe, other forces are unleashed. Fundamentalists of all kinds flourish and nourish the hunger not just for simple loves and wars as Sunil sees it, but for simplistic tribal or religious identities and cravings for uncomplication. Added to this are our internal demons which again seem less easily placated or persuaded to behave. Empirical evidence is emerging all the time to show how the west is in some trouble. A report by the Medical Health Foundation in 1999 found that 1.5 million British children have serious mental problems and that three out of a hundred girls are expected to attempt suicide in their teenage years. Anorexia, Chronic Fatigue Syndrome, depression are all on the increase among the young, and prescriptions for Prozac for six- to twelve-year-olds shot up by 300 per cent between 1995 and 1996.[8]

Figures show that levels of depression among adults have steadily increased. The figures for violent crime have gone up in England and Wales from 6,000 in 1950 to 239,000 in 1996. Marriage break-ups, school exclusions, stress-related medical conditions, all indicate serious problems. The psychologist Oliver James confirms that this malaise is infecting society at an unparalleled level:

> There is little doubt that, compared with 1950, Britons are unhappier. This is broadly true of people throughout the developed world despite unprecedented growth of incomes . . . advanced capitalism fails to meet our need for status; and it is destructive to the stable relationships to which we are instinctively drawn – driving a wedge between mother and father, parent and small child, elderly parents and their offspring.[9]

James adds that the way we live creates a permanent state of failure as we strive to match impossible ideals fed to us by the media and others. These descriptions are powerful and persuasive, but do not apply in the same way to those who are still removed from the heart of British society. We, in the visible communities, have been denied equality and significance in the spaces where it is all happening, but, as later chapters will reveal, some of us might in fact have been spared through this exclusion. Mental illness rates are appallingly high among second- and third-generation black men, those born and raised here. Suicide rates among young Asian women are twice the national average. These are not migrants who might be expected to sink under the strain, but their children who were expected to reap the fruit of the great sacrifices their parents made. But as yet we don't suffer from the kind of general angst and interminable greed which defines so many middle-class white folk. We still retain the sense that we should be grateful for a life which is just good enough. We still dream within our means.

Political extremism also begins to appeal during periods of incertitude. The backlash against change gains a foothold. Again we appear to be on harsher if more 'productive' terrain than before. The environmental costs and the social devastation created by liberalized economies – now apparently the only answer across the world – have left many feeling at sea and with the smallest of logs to cling to while they work out their bearings. Alternative economic theories are emerging through the ideas of people such as Will Hutton and others, but at the moment the battle seems all but won by the right. And as the struggles over economic ideology have become more or less settled and emulated, other ideological battles are becoming more clamorous and uncompromising. Many of the conflicts are now arising in the areas of culture, religion and values. Without two superpowers fighting it out in the world arena, a new cultural hubris fed by economic might begins to prevail. The end of history has been announced by the United States, which has become the great cultural aggressor, and Britain hangs on to the tail of this great power in spite of the fear of being demolished by it. There can be little doubt now that, as Ziauddin Sardar puts it: 'the global theatre is a strictly western theatre, a personification of western power and control.'[10] Not since the glory days of the European

29

empires has there been such a patent display of might and right playing off one another.

The massive western conceit, in turn, produces strange retaliations. There was a breathtaking illustration of this on *Start the Week*, BBC Radio 4, in October 1997. Nawal El Saadawi, the well-known and highly regarded Egyptian feminist, has fought long and brave battles against the forces of barbarism in the Middle East, often risking her own life and those of her loved ones. Having led, along with many other women, the fight against female circumcision in her own country, she felt unable, she said, to support a US senator who wanted to tie US aid to the forced eradication of the practice in Egypt. This was a new kind of 'colonialism', she said. Countries must not be coerced to take the right path by big western powers. Talk to some African and Muslim women in Britain and they too defend the right to cultural sovereignty, no matter what, because they see this resistance as an essential strategy for survival in a world owned now by multinationals and determined by western values. This is how muddled life has now become. Appalling violence against small girls cannot be condemned outright by those whose instincts to do so are held back by global power games. All across the world and in the many small worlds here you hear similar cant. In a memorable essay, Arundhati Roy describes the insanity and vulgarity of dividing the 'west' and the rest up as if it is the ultimate battle between Evil and the Angels. Attacking the Indian government for the nuclear tests which shook up the subcontinent in 1998 (and which were sold to Indians partly as an act of equality and partly on grounds of cultural integrity), she asked whether the drive to authenticity and rejection of all things western would mean that, among thousands of imports, India would be giving up the aeroplane, train, mobile phone, chillis (they were brought over from Mexico) and the English language.[11]

This encounter between the west and the rest (some of whom live in the west) is giving rise to increasing clashes over the definition and desirability of progress and of the politics of identity.[12] This too adds to the unease felt by a society which can no longer cohere in the way it once did. Maybe. Before the *Empire Windrush* arrived perhaps; but more importantly, before we, black and Asian Britons, stopped being the mimic men and women described by V. S. Naipaul and lost that

awe and obsequiousness which was and is still, for some, a condition
of our presence. Or before barrow boys could make their mark on
world markets by enlisting in the City. Or when men were men and
women the pups at their heels. Or when children imbibed early the
rules of life and knew their place in the home. Or when we were
all going forwards, with the welfare state and industrial progress
supporting us under each arm.

Modernity was the only desirable destination then. But now even
the future king of the United Kingdom wonders if this is wise. In the
contemplative speech quoted above he says: 'Modern materialism in
my humble opinion is unbalanced and increasingly damaging in its
long-term consequences.'[13] The rest of us mortals are also questioning
whether relentless, unsustainable progress and development is the devil
in our midst. If Oliver James is even half right, why should we, those
still relatively unscathed by many of the problems of post-industrial
societies, rush to embrace this so-called progress and the fiends it brings
with it?

Sonara is a thirtysomething optician whose parents came from India
in the fifties. A highly articulate woman and mother of two, she looks
at white British society and asks:

> Is this progress and do I want it? Why is their present my future? My
> parents' generation were completely uncritical of Great Britain as they
> call it. People like me are the opposite because we have grown up
> here and we see through their façade. They carry on destroying the
> world. I see them drowning in drugs, divorce and depression. I see
> them unable to control their children. I see them producing filth and
> violence and claiming it is some kind of freedom. I see love between
> men and women evaporating. They fight each other like bears in a
> ring. Why should I take this same road in the name of progress? I may
> gain some independence, but I will enter a jungle where nobody owes
> anybody anything. At present I have a choice. I feel uncontaminated.
> And maybe some things will happen anyway even if I say no. But I
> have something they don't have and I will fight to keep it. It is my way
> of belonging too, otherwise who am I?

Many beyond the margins are also questioning their sense of belonging,
the way western society has been going and where it may end up. Sonara

is one of the fifty-eight interviewees, including white middle-class men, who expressed similar anxieties. As the critic Kenan Malik describes in his book on race:

> Western society feels ill at ease with its politicians, its institutions, its governmental policies, its social values. There is in society a lack of vision, an absence of purpose, a failure of will . . . The most pervasive mood today is that of disenchantment. This sense of disenchantment has been exacerbated by the economic crisis which seems to suggest that politicians have no answers to the problems which most people face. The ideologies which bound together or gave a sense of purpose to society have either collapsed or lost their credibility . . . old bonds that held society together are dissolving. New ones have yet to be forged.[14]

The crisis may be futile because, whatever we might feel about it, the disintegration of previously held bonds is now an essential and inevitable component of contemporary life. Knowing that there is no way back or out surely only adds to the panic. There is no answer, however much grief ensues. Michael Ignatieff describes this inevitability beautifully:

> Certain social anxieties are an inescapable part of the experience of being modern. One of these concerns is the possibility of belonging. Is it possible to feel a sense of belonging to societies which change as rapidly as modern ones do, which are as explicitly divided – by race, class, gender and religion – as modern ones are and which are driven by the power of money as capitalist modernity has been?[15]

But even he accepts that this national and international anxiety needs to be treated seriously.

> If the legitimacy of politics is in question at the end of the 1990s it is because we don't seem to be able to devise policies to prevent the apparently unstoppable erosion of community, cohesion and a sense of belonging.[16]

Much research among the young in recent years has indicated that young people are not impressed by what adults have created around them and that many are expressing poignant longings for a stable family life and job security and that an enormous number of them feel isolated and dislocated from any community and political party or even political activity.[17]

Race politics was one area of almost forced simplicity once. Today many of us are too confused or too sophisticated to fall in line. As the brilliant human rights activist, now a lawyer, Unmesh Desai told me:

> We must recognize that our response to communities today cannot be a blanket one. We have remained fossilized in our thinking and, if anything, communities have moved ahead of single-issue community activists and, dare I say, local race and equal opportunity advisers. And in the process the anti-racist movement has lost its moorings. We have to rescue this issue from the intellectual and political ghettos to which it has been confined and reassert its primacy in the debate around building a new modern Britain. Reactive, knee-jerk actions and policies have got to be discarded, and more strategic, solid solutions sought in recognition of the complexities of the issues we are dealing with.

Daniella, a mixed-race women in her forties who designs and makes clothes, believes all this is having a profound impact upon the ethnic minorities in very specific ways.

> We are as caught up in feeling unsure of our future, of not sharing the faith that sustained our parents, of wanting more and more and never feeling even a moment of satisfaction because we're so so afraid it will all go before we have even begun to smile with pleasure. Why are black women so frantic about material success? It is of course because we have been denied our rights for so long. But it's more than that. We must collect our pile and hide it away before it all collapses. We want our men to change and become more feminine but are worried that this will take away their strength so we let them pretend that they can carry on being cave men.

A researcher into ethnicity believes that these trends must be taken seriously:

> Why do we suddenly get a burst of identity politics now? So everyone wants to define themselves in smaller and smaller, simple tribal

groupings? What we are feeling is exactly what the Scots, English, and Welsh are needing to do. Somehow grab back past ancestral connections, be different in the sea of sameness. Then we know exactly who we are and we are only one thing. Once we were all happy to be called black. Then we became black and Asian. Now it is Muslims, Sikhs, Hindus, Guyanese, Trinidadians, Nigerians, and so on. Suddenly gender politics which talks about black women and white women seems laughably old-fashioned. Difference is sexy, even the Commission for Racial Equality thinks so. And not all of this is necessarily bad news. So much of what we simply accepted is being questioned and we are now reaching that grown-up point where we can disagree and we are freer to react in non-formulaic ways to white society, to what is happening out there and to our own lives.

Underlying uncertainty is present in very real ways in the environment as well as in practical areas such as increasing job insecurity, the gradual erosion of the welfare state, rampant consumerism, new trading blocks. The domestic and the international pictures are that of divided societies where those who can, with impunity and without a conscience, accumulate more than they will ever need, while those who are disenfranchised are destined to remain on the outside and regarded with contempt. Remember it was our Labour Prime Minister who said, soon after winning a landslide election victory in 1997, that he does not give money to beggars.

Morality has become another obsession of our times. When the most powerful man in the world has his sordid sexual habits put on world display, that old wall between public and private morality can no longer stand up. People endlessly talk about moral relativism, which simply mirrors confusion instead of providing an answer. There are unresolved tensions between rights and responsibilities. Our world is in the grip of the media which appears to influence everything from intimate sexual behaviour to the criminal justice system. Journalists and politicians have taken on the mantle of the priest, while priests concentrate on becoming more lovable by not condemning any immorality at all. Melanie Phillips, Janet Daley, Jack Straw, Polly Toynbee, Tony Blair, and many, many others have joined in the fray for the soul of modern Britain. It is when you try to talk to people who are not part of this priesthood, which has set itself up to decide what life is and what it ought to be, that we get the most illuminating descriptions of this malaise. For example, when nothing can be taken for granted any more, even relativism seems intrusive for someone like Mariyam (previously known as Mary White, devout daughter of a butcher in Northfields), who converted to Islam three years ago:

> I did it because I could not stand the way everything was unsure. We can't bring up our children with any clear direction because all is 'what if?', 'but' and things like that. That is not a way to live. Yet even the bishops have lost their nerve. And those who decide our values have made a virtue of their own confusion. So to be unsure is the only way, the only value. This is rubbish. You ask me why I chose to put myself into this position where I have less choice, because too much choice and too many questions destroy the spirit. If you are in a place where everything is upside down, inside out, the wrong way round, do you look for comfort in getting even more lost, or do you seek some simple straight direction?

It would be simplistic to dismiss Mariyam's decisions as simplistic. They explain our times more accurately than all the ramblings of overblown newspaper columnists. But although tempting, this in the end is not an adequate answer for our troubled but plentiful times.

Life was easy when we taught ourselves to think in hierarchical categories, allocating simple attributes to men and women, blacks and whites, the godly and the ungodly – whichever God that may be. The break-up of many of the old ways is making spaces which will have to be filled. Some very encouraging shoots have appeared on these spots. Britain is less stuffy and formal, is certainly freer with emotional expression, and is learning not to be automatically deferential. If even the Queen can be forced by public opinion to behave like an ordinary human being, things must have moved on.

In spite of all the terrors we are feeling, we might just consider that this is a moment when we are witnessing the final passing away of old, irrelevant structures, relationships and ideologies. The election may have been the first indication of this. It remains unclear whether the voters who supported New Labour were doing so for reasons of disillusionment or hope; whether they found the Tories irrelevant to their needs or Labour better able to meet them. But there can be little doubt that Tony Blair skilfully tapped into the angst and the expectations, and although one now tires of his use of 'New' it captured the imagination of the public. It is obvious too that the deconstruction and reconstruction of the nation is part of the Blairite project and that this is in part a response to the national unease, although the way this is mapping out leaves much to be desired.

Fragile and trembling as it still is, that change of direction did start up with the election and was confirmed in the most operatic way by the death of Diana, like Blair an encapsulation of a fundamental shift in the way we want to be. The despair which was displayed by millions of buttoned-up people when Diana died felt like some preternatural phenomenon. A year on Andrew Marr wrote, in a wonderfully perceptive essay:

> Something had changed [that day] in the country and Diana's death crystallized it, more so than the general election a few months before. Britain suddenly stared at itself in the mirror and didn't quite recognize the face looking back. No longer was the expression tight-lipped, white, and drawn with reticence. Diana was the queen of another country, a multicultural, more liberal, emotionally open Britain . . . Diana was only a symbol of social changes already happening.[18]

I saw gents clutching tired flowers with tears streaming down their faces; loud sobs I have never yet heard at an English funeral. Even more staggering was the obvious anti-establishment sentiments on the many cards and letters plastered desperately on walls, on trees, on gates, even on the door of the public toilets in Kensington Gardens. Many were written with blood red ink. Millions of flowers strained menacingly against the gates of the palaces. It could have been bodies pushing and pulsating. Weapons whose scent combined with the fury in the air. A popular insurgence in the name of a royal who was denied her special place, as a royal. Only in England perhaps. Final frontiers of behaviour, decorum, deference were being broken here. And not before time.

One thing I have never understood in all the years I have lived here is why the majority of white Britons have so unquestioningly accepted a settlement which so grossly privileges the two top classes over the others. I have looked on with disbelief at the pride expressed by those at the bottom about how this class edifice and their compliance provides and explains continuity and stability. I have frequently said to my English husband that this placidity lay at the heart of many of *our* problems as minorities who came to stay. How could we bang on about equality and huge structural changes when the working classes are so content and accepting because change would cause such impolite disturbance? It seemed impossible to imagine that this was the country which gave the world Tom Paine and John Locke.[19] But now suddenly, unexpectedly, something was unravelling. It became clear that the People had not been that content after all, not recently, not since Diana came along and started misbehaving by not accepting. Depressingly, the floral revolutionaries soon went back into their classes, grabbing back form and conservative certainties, grovelling now more than ever before a fossilized royal family. But, for a while, this felt like a youthful, brave country with a people actually demonstrating discontent. They were mourning the person who enabled them to confront these feelings of dislocation while at the same time using her presence as a palliative for them. But, paradoxically, although she looked quintessentially English, Diana was also thoroughly un-English and this is what made her so appealing to black and Asian Britons. The significance of the frequently relayed images of strong black men in T-shirts and diminutive women in saris breaking down is not yet understood by most white Britons. We saw in her a challenge to the old ways and to British hubris. Through her and the whispered tales of the dark House of Windsor, we knew that all was not well with the nation. We sensed that from these rumblings could come something else; that she, and only she, could lead the nation away from where it was dug in. She demonstrated, as Andrew Marr believes and Martin Jaques wrote in the *Observer*:

> that public life could be different, that public institutions did not have to be aloof, male, stuffy, the preserve of the Great and the Good. She indicated the possibility of renewal. And she did this in a way that everyone could understand . . .[20]

There were other reasons why we loved her and the depth of that love only surfaced at the moment of her death. In spite of my strong republicanism, I felt compelled to go to Kensington Palace because for me, like Emma (below, p. 39), she seemed to provide some way out of the constant sense of fear and anxiety that so many black and Asian people have learnt to live with. We identified profoundly with her pain and rejection too. As we displayed our anguish at the palaces, or stood with our candles in Southall praying for Diana, she represented the tragedy of womanhood as only we understood it. (Older women like my mother felt her to be, like so many they know, a fragile young woman deliberately used and destroyed by a bad arranged marriage, a duplicitous husband and unsympathetic in-laws.) We also loved her for the respect which she gave us without effort, from the heart. No other white person in the political arena or the traditional establishment has ever made ethnic minorities feel such a natural and essential part of this country. She chose one of us for her *Panorama* interview; her closest friendships were with women like Jemima Goldsmith, who had carried out her own revolutionary act in marrying Imran Khan in spite of the xenophobic hysteria which rose out of her decision. To top it all, Diana fell in love with an Arab and his affection made her shine as never before. Most of the hundreds of cards and letters that I read mourned the loss of Dodi as well as Diana. He may have been an Arab, from a group the white public have been programmed to loathe, but here, during this time, most thanked him for his love for their princess. Her life marked out the start of new possibilities for white and non-white British people. For this, in spite of being moralistic people, we were easily able to forgive her indiscretions and weakness for cads.

Rosa, unemployed and still in mourning for her Diana, says this:

> She was one of us. They didn't deserve her, they knew not how to treat her. They treated her like they have treated blacks for so long. She be a victim like us. Jesus saved her. But I never think that I can love a white woman like I loves her. I never have a white friend in school, or now. But she was my friend. When she smile at that black man dying in hospital, when she hold his mother's hand, you know, she is one of us.

The English idolized her for other reasons too. As Elton sang, they cried. She was *their* rose, the only symbol and object of English pride they had had for an awfully long time. As Emma, a thirty-five-year-old mother and a solicitor with two homes, said to me:

> I know there is much that we as a country should feel proud of, but these days we don't or can't. Suddenly Diana changed all that. We were great in the world again because we had her and nobody else did. I used to show my children all her pictures and stories as she travelled. It made me feel like, I don't know, that we weren't finished as a nation; that we could feel good about something homegrown. Not imported you know. Diana was ours. She was English and we lost her.

In front of an event of such colossal significance the traditionalists failed utterly. Shame on those who organized the funeral which was designed to expunge cruelly every trace of this, the greatest gift of Diana to the nation, to stuff it into the coffin of narrow Englishness. They, who wish to get the country back to what they believe it should be, to what it can never again be. They, who would not allow the world to see that this English rose (like many before and since) had chosen to break out of her station and race and embrace New Britain.

The adoration of Diana shows just how lost the English are at present. These once proud people are feeling under assault because of devolution (which might lead to independence for Scotland and which is obviously going to affect the union and the demands of patriotism) and further European integration. Many on the right and left see this as a crucial issue for all our futures. When Ann Leslie, Melanie Phillips, Anthony Barnett, Billy Bragg and I write on this theme in roughly similar terms there must be something going on. And there is. I believe that a positive English (not synonymous with British) identity needs to be encouraged if only to give the English an equal (not better, not worse) place among the firmament of identities which are now defined as British. This is not only fair but essential. Most clearly put by Bernard Crick, the argument goes like this: 'We English must feel secure in our Englishness if we are not to lapse back into a super-nationalism fuelled by rancid imperialist nostalgia.'[21] When Decca Aitkenhead, the *Guardian* columnist, showed contempt for these feelings, the letters page was packed out with angry voices upset at this indifference to what is clearly a deeply felt crisis among the English.[22] As Clive Aslet writes in his excellent book, *Anyone for England?*: 'Our cultural insecurity and self-doubt are evident and in this weakened state of morale, we have been particularly vulnerable to the homogenising tendency of Europe.'[23] And we must take it seriously. Research by Roger Hewitt,[24] the Home Office[25] and Les Back[26] has begun to show how important cultural esteem is to people and how a lack of it or a discouragement of it can turn to foul hatreds. As this is being written, football hooligans have expressed this disgracefully at World Cup matches in France.

As Diana's impact fades away and fin-de-siècle mutterings are all in the air, creating a mood both of discomfort and self-interrogation,[27] where do we go from here? Hard though it is with all pillars trembling precariously, we are being forced to think through the many, often lazy assumptions of the past and the consequences of voting in the people we did, of too many people choosing to live as fattened mice instead of grown-up men and women, and of not challenging what was being done to our country. As John Tusa wrote in the *Independent*: 'A good society believes in integration and togetherness; the market thrives by fragmentation, by differentiation, through exclusivity rather than inclusivity. You are no longer a citizen; you are a marketing target group.'[28] Caught in these bonfires of uncertainties, we must give up facile assumptions and embrace confusion. Yes, racism, sexism, the oppression of the weak and powerless continue to destroy lives and things have not got better in the way we all hoped. But these days many of us have accepted that men, even white men, are not universally the enemy. What's more, we do have to think again if evidence shows that boys are doing worse than girls at school. Although economic differentials and other gender inequalities do persist, the loss of job security for working people is making that picture less clear-cut. Men and boys are going through a crisis of their own – not that much understanding is being put their way as yet by women, who have fought so long for some progress of their own. Talking about the double jeopardy for black women makes less sense than it once did given the way young black men are among the most alienated and excluded people in this country, sometimes even despised by thrusting black women these days.

There are bad, ineffective, self-serving black and Asian men and women too and it is not racist to say so. Some of our top Asian businessmen are being shown up to be among the worst employers in the kingdom. Their workers have no rights, are paid disgracefully low wages, have no holiday or sickness cover. The experience of racism has taught the fat cats little about injustice. Other 'truths' do not bear up to the slightest scrutiny. Middle-class black and Asian women in certain situations have more clout than never-employed, under-educated white women. The very women who have and have long had the power and influence to determine the feminist agenda are those most readily and vociferously accused of failing women who do not share their class, or their post-Enlightenment, Christian, western herit-age. And yet many among these women too are less sure of what their own beliefs are.

All of us have to confront difficulties in balancing work and home life, though it helps immeasurably if you have money. Relationships between men and women in all communities are more exacting than ever before. This is of course because roles are becoming fluid and we want more. But it is also because men (all right, some men) are now getting used to the idea that they need to become more responsive. Both men and women have raised their expectations to such a level that perhaps eternal disappointment can be the only consequence. We may not have it all, but women certainly feel they have to be it all: from career woman to whore, from the perfect River Café cook to mother, and caring, sharing partner. If that were not exhausting enough, women have also signed up to promising never to age or grow fat, to be understanding even if dumped for another. Yet another friend of mine has just been delivered that blow which seems to come to too many of us as our new men rediscover the pleasures of old ways – then called 'adultery', a word which seems as old-fashioned as 'corset'. While she is going through the searing pain of being abandoned by an equal and loving partner, she frets about whether she is allowed to express that pain, to shout and rage, whether maybe to try and scare him by swallowing (not too many) aspirins. Or is she supposed to be civilized and think of the children (which he does not and is not expected to do because his artistic spirit is simply unwilling or unable to resist the magic lure of a young vagina and other such poetic stuff) and try to be friends with him? Other questions rack her. Did she let herself go? Should she have tried harder to be the perfect woman? As a young professional woman, should she not be drinking champagne with the sisterhood instead, loving her liberation? Her husband is white; she is black. He has left her for, she says, 'one of his own. A nice English girl who won't throw her feelings about like I did.' Fifty years ago, thirty years ago, how different would have been the situation and the responses. And what are we going to do with that troubling dilemma that even some highly intelligent, independent women have rather old-fashioned ideas about what constitutes a real man. Sophie, one of my white interviewees who works in human resources, exemplifies this in its crudest form:

> We all love a bastard. We think we can change them. We lick up to them when they treat us like shit. I had a nice man in my life and I dumped him for Daryl who is not worth a second of my time. I have a great job, I know I look good so why am I doing this? My own mother – a working-class woman without much education – tells me I don't respect myself. Daryl hits me, speaks to me like I am nothing. Then he'll take me to bed or buy me something and I am all his. The thing is we say we want a good man but what we love is a cool, dangerous guy. We don't respect the really nice men.

Meanwhile, fathers are going through dilemmas of their own. Fathers and fatherhood, as Adrienne Burgess and Sandy Ruxton say in their book on the subject, 'are on the agenda as never before. All over the developed world, questions are being asked about their role, status, rights and responsibilities: where have all the daddies gone? Can unemployed men be "proper" fathers? What are fathers for?'[29] Unfortunately, as this book shows, the market-place and society in general do not accommodate the changes that are now needed for fathers to alter the part they play in the lives of their children – even those fathers who no longer want to enjoy the benefits of the *status quo*.

Children are in part the beneficiaries, in part the victims of many social changes that have already happened. With both parents working, or a working mother, materially and in terms of their own horizons, children gain an enormous amount. But something is getting badly distorted when ambitious women do or have to work so long and so hard that their children barely see them. This is not a plea for women to get back into their gingham-apron roles. But it is self-deluding to claim that what is good for us has been good for our children to the same extent. And what previously seemed appealing – the chance to be just like men – is now quite rightly being shunned as the way forward. According to Germaine Greer the problems faced by women today come out of the fact that they settled for equality.[30] The world for many white women is not at all well. They are the ones presumably rushing out to buy *Bridget Jones's Diary*. Almost all the black and Asian women interviewed for this book said they did not want to get to the positions that high-flying white women had got themselves into with this. A few years ago these women were looking across at their white privileged sisters longingly, enviously, angrily. Today they want to be treated without discrimination but are much less sure that they want to be the same as either men or their high-flying white sisters.

Sex and sexuality, individualism and the demands of the family and community, rights and responsibilities, marriage and cohabitation, divorce, shame and guilt, social opprobrium and freedom, discipline and self-discipline, childbirth and child-rearing – all these subjects are unsettled, under discussion, embattled. Minority voices are raised increasingly not in terms of defending their rights, but more assertively in the belief that their ways have much to offer if only those consumed by cultural racism could bear to look in their direction. Black and Asian people are also more committed to changing aspects of their own culture. Fluidity seems to be replacing rigidity here too.

The next chapters trace the route taken by contemporary history and examine some of the key institutions and (more importantly) the central concepts which define a nation and its fundamental character-istics and values, in order to assess whether they are enabling us to interpret our flickering lives and the way we live.

2
Long in the Root

I came to Britain from Uganda in the troubled summer of 1972 when
the island of Great Britain, under Captain Heath, seemed to be heaving
and flailing about just to keep itself from drowning in its own chaos.
In 1971 my first husband had arrived in Oxford to find himself in the
midst of a series of crises which were to dominate life until the general
election in 1974 when the Tories lost two general elections in a year.
The interim years had witnessed a major energy crisis, miners' strikes,
the passing of a new Industry Act which created an unworkable
statutory incomes policy, several policy U-turns, wage restraints, the
three-day week and a country plunged into darkness and inaction for
long periods during the winter months. The population seemed to be
disorientated as the political leadership showed itself unable to take
real charge and map out a new destiny for a country which had
been through a number of fundamental changes without necessarily

44

understanding the implications. The Empire had come home and was striking back. But that was not all. The country had experienced wounds to the class system after the two world wars and was attempting to accommodate the moral and social upheavals of the sixties. Parallel to this, massive economic and political challenges – the European Common Market, for example – were presenting themselves thick and fast. One of the most alarming of these was the Ugandan Asian crisis – of which more later. With the exception of 10,000 Vietnamese refugees who were taken in by Margaret Thatcher in the eighties because her hatred of communism was greater than her fear of 'swamping' multiculturalism, and the half-hearted gestures made towards some Hong Kong British passport holders in 1997, we were the last wave of the so-called immigration floods to sweep into this island.

What is mostly unrecognized, though, is that the first gentle ripples had already come in 500 or more years before. The historian Peter Tryer claims in his seminal book *Staying Power*[1] that there were Africans in this country before the English got here. There are records dating back to 250 AD of their presence in this country. They were soldiers in the Roman army of occupation and there were enough of them to form an entire 'division of Moors' and to be given the responsibility of defending Hadrian's wall.[2] I went to the famous-for-being-good Oratory School in London in 1999 to talk to sixth-formers and their teachers. None of them knew any of this early history of black people in this country.

This book, which is mostly about contemporary Britain, will only make sense if at least some of this early history of our encounter and the continuity and reciprocity of that association can be presumed. We, black and Asian Britons, are here because you, white Britons, did not resist the temptation to go out to the rest of the world, to see and trade and conquer. Knowing our common historical bonds – even if they were ultimately based on inequality – is a contractual responsibility. It also provides a core around which a new national identity can be layered. The various tribes of Britain have not yet reached the understanding which would enable them to see that such a history makes mutuality a real possibility and that to assume a 'natural' antagonism or genetic cultural purity is wishful nonsense. That great historian Christopher Hill asked in his Conway Memorial Lecture back in 1989:

'Have we come to grips with the horrors in our past as German historians are trying to come to grips with Nazism?' The answer has to be no. Hill quoted Nietzsche, who said: 'History keeps alive the memory of the great fighters against history – the blind power of the actual.' The past is always going to exert power over our lives and thoughts, but it needn't be, as Hill says, blind.[3]

In the aftermath of the publication of the Lawrence Report, there was an unprecedented consensus among people, including Conservatives such as Michael Portillo and the columnist Matthew Parris, that racism was still a pernicious problem in this society.

There needs to be a greater awareness of the consequences of decisions taken by rulers on behalf of populations, and how these set down our collective destiny. Those in denial are akin to flat-earth folk or creationists. Black and Asian immigration and multiracial Britain are facts. They happened. They cannot be willed or locked away from memory for ever. One day I hope some body in this country will carry out mass DNA testing of the white British population to show us just how racially impure this nation is. Such excavation of historical knowledge would immeasurably benefit people like the kind gentleman from Kent who wrote me a sweet letter at the end of 1998 telling me that, although he loved the way I wrote, he felt threatened when too many coloured folk came to town. It was to do with queues he said, and other 'British ways' which we disrupt because 'as natives from a lower civilization' we can never know how to act 'naturally' like our betters.

This is not meant to be cheap mockery. It is astonishing that there are highly educated Britons, white and black, who do not know that the presence of black and Asian people in Britain goes back centuries, and (much worse) who cannot accept that this was an inevitable consequence of an insatiably ambitious seafaring nation which had ventured forth to trade with and then take over large chunks of the globe. I nearly lost a close friend recently because he, in his whiteness, refused vehemently to believe that the history of black Britons in this country goes back as far as it does. In order to preserve a valuable friendship I sent him extracts from Henry Mayhew's monumental survey, *London Labour and the London Poor*, published in 1861, in which Mayhew described Indian jugglers, street musicians, sellers of religious tracts and herbalists such as Dr Bonkanki, the hero of the sick and poor. What helped change his mind, or at least induce some useful self-doubt, was the 1998 dramatization of *Vanity Fair* on BBC2, in which black servants and coachmen appeared as a natural part of the landscape.

Sadly, but perhaps understandably, most black Britons were just as ignorant of this history until very recently. It is only in the past two decades, thanks largely to the admirable scholarship of people such as Peter Fryer,[4] Rozina Visram,[5] Kusoom Vadgama,[6] James Walvin,[7] Ron Ramdin,[8] A. Sivanandan[9] and a few others, that this lost history has been reclaimed and retold in a form which is not only incontestable but accessible.

We know now that long before June 1948, when the *Empire Windrush* arrived bringing 492 Jamaicans to Tilbury Docks, black and Asian Britons had arrived and claimed small spaces for themselves all across the island. In 1555 one John Lok brought with him five slaves into Britain. By the end of the century, Negro servants were a common sight both among the nobility and among merchants and sailors. Shakespeare was acutely aware of the dynamics of such an explosive cultural confluence, and you see this not only in *Othello* but in his much earlier *Titus Andronicus*, written in 1589 and an extraordinary play with utterly modern discussions about the children of mixed relationships and their identity. The famine of 1590 created a context in which began the official scapegoating of blacks. Elizabeth I launched an anti-colour immigration panic, a policy path faithfully followed to this day by every single British government. In a letter to the mayors of major cities in Britain, Elizabeth declared:

> there are of late divers blackamoores brought into this realme, of
> which kinde of people there are allready to manie consyderyng howe
> god hath blessed this land with great people of our nation as anie
> countrie in the world . . . those kinde of people [blacks] should be
> sent forth of the land . . .[10]

This exhortation did not have much effect, so in 1601 she issued a Proclamation which empowered certain seamen to ship black people out of this country. None of this had any impact on the black population, which carried on growing.

47

There are records of black entertainers in the courts of Charles II and James I and many accounts of these individuals participating in Lord Mayors' pageants in London and elsewhere. Through the seventeenth and eighteenth centuries advertisements would appear in newspapers giving notice of runaway slaves or of forthcoming auctions in coffee houses of redundant slaves. The slaves were often children. In 1690, for example, 'a Negro boy, about 8 years old, named Jack, straight limb'd . . .' who had 'strayed away' was sought.[11] In the same year Dryden, writing satirically, suggested that English soldiers fighting in Ireland should:

> Each bring his Love, a Bogland Captive home,
> Such proper Pages, will long Trayns become;
> With Copper-Collars, and with brawny Backs
> Quite to put down the Fashion of our Blacks.[12]

In 1665 when Pepys visited the affluent merchant banker, Sir Robert Vyner, he was shown the oven-dried body of a slave on display in an ornamental box.[13] Indians were also brought in as servants and slaves. When those who owned them had no further need of these possessions they would pass them on. On 1 February 1775, for example, this advertisement appeared in the *Daily Advertiser*:

> Any lady going to the East Indies, having occasion for a maid servant may be advantageously supplied with one who is lately come from thence; she is a Slave girl, and the mistress who brought her over having no occasion for her will give her over to any Lady to attend her in the passage to India and to serve her for three years after arrival there without wages, provided the lady engages at expiration of the Term to give her freedom. She is a good servant, perfectly good natured and talks English well.

Although there are many who dispute the fact that slaves were owned on British soil, there is substantial evidence to show that there were. In the various legal judgements on this issue which went on throughout the 1700s in this country, judges contradicted one another, making the rights of slaves at best ambiguous. By 1669 the black servant had become the fashion statement for those who set the trends and those who desperately aspired to be amongst the people who mattered. Pepys indulged in the trend too, writing in his diary for 5 April 1669: 'For a cookmaid we have, ever since Bridget left, used a black-moore of Mr Batlier's, Doll, who dresses our meat mightily well.' After the American War of Independence, the numbers – which had been growing since the 1670s – increased even more dramatically. The treatment of these servants and slaves was shameful. As Fryer describes:

> **Black people fortunate enough not to be struck on the head, whipped, or otherwise brutalized were nevertheless denied elementary human dignity. Their own African names filled with meaning were taken away from them. It was the fashion for black slaves owned by titled families, by high class prostitutes and by others with social pretensions to be given high-sounding Greek or Roman names . . . the commonest was Pompey, which by the 1750s, had virtually become a generic name for a black servant.**[14]

Those who busy themselves denying that slaves existed in this country and that they were seriously maltreated are also most reluctant to admit the very real, tangible benefits of slavery to this country. In the eighteenth century 20 million guns were made in Birmingham, creating thousands of jobs. Most of the guns were for the control of slaves or the payment for them in kind to those Africans who were suppliers of the human cargo. Companies in Bristol and Liverpool were just as actively involved in the horrendous business and much of the prosperity of these cities was built on it. Yet it is only in the 1990s that the two cities have finally started the public conversations which acknowledge this and which tell the story of their bloody early prosperity. Even so, in early 1998, the City of Bristol felt able to erect a monument to an eighteenth-century merchant venturer, Edward Colston. He is described as 'one of the most virtuous and wise sons' of the city because he made vast donations to good causes. But his money in part came directly from the slave trade, as violent graffiti on the statue remind the world.

It is important to record, though, that relations between Black and white Britons were not only restricted to those of master and lackey. There were some extraordinary stories of how conventions were broken by both sides. Ignatius Sancho, the first black prose writer published in this country, was born a slave. He transformed his life by teaching himself to read and write and then leaving the house where he was a servant to become part of fashionable literary circles. He became a friend of Garrick and was painted by Gainsborough.[15] He remained popular in spite of being openly critical of Britain which, he said, had been 'uniformly wicked' in the West Indies and elsewhere by pursuing wealth at any cost and by encouraging local tyrants too. From the beginning of black people's presence in this country, sex has been another point of contact. Hogarth's drawings show black and white couples in sensuous embraces. Shakespeare, as has already been described, dealt with the effect of this among the upper echelons of society and the whole business of inter-racial sex has been a national obsession through the centuries. In the eighteenth century and the first quarter of the nineteenth there were many stories and scandals about these relationships, although the tolerance displayed in earlier periods puts the present to shame. One concerned the Duchess of Queensbury who had a passionate attachment to her servant Soubise from St Kitts. She educated him and enabled him to get respect and access to West End clubs, the Opera and upper-class society. He was said to be a fop among fops and a legendary lover, as good as Don Juan according to one of his well-satisfied ladies.[16] In the India Office in London there is a painting by Francesco Renaldi, done in 1786, showing a noble gentleman, William Palmer, with his Muslim wife Bibi Faiz Baksh and their children. The relationship of Queen Victoria to her beloved Indian servant, Abdul Karim, was so profound (she had his portrait painted and made him her Indian Secretary and Companion of the Order of the Indian Empire) that politicians and courtiers burnt all the written records of this 'friendship' after the death of the Queen. She was similarly close to John Brown, her Scottish servant. Many in the government were highly disapproving of both.

When it came to these relationships, however, the more common pattern was that of strong sexual attraction between black men and lower-class white women, a drama which was played out against a background of racist and sexist fury and panic. Edward Long, a plantation owner, wrote in his memoirs:

> **The lower class of women in England are remarkably fond of the blacks for reasons too brutal to mention; they would connect**

themselves with horses and asses if the laws permitted them . . . They have a numerous brood. Thus in the course of a few generations more, the English blood will become so contaminated with this mixture.[17]

This sexual attraction and the rampant disapproval that accompanied it set down a legacy which carries on to this day. In our book, *The Colour of Love*, Anne Montague and I explored these relationships from the forties to the nineties. They were not all negative stories of struggle against disapproval, but many were, and much of that heritage still remains and haunts even the best of relationships happening at the best of times for such choices.[18]

The early history of Asians, known to be in Britain from the seventeenth century onwards, is equally surprising and largely unrecognized, says the historian Rozina Visram: 'It is often forgotten that Britain had an Indian community long before the Second World War and that the recent arrival of Asian people in Britain is part of the long history of contact between India and Britain.' She claims with impeccable authority that Indian links with Europe go back 10,000 years, via trade routes. But it all took off in a significant way only after 1600, when the East India Company managed to obtain a charter to trade in India. This then grew into the lucrative venture which gave many in this country more wealth than they had ever imagined and which in time led to the covetous spirit and reality of the Raj. But trade is by definition a two-way process. There was no chance at all of the 'natives' staying put once the empire builders had entered their lives and their countries. Soon subject peoples were coming to the mother country.

Seamen were also arriving in Britain from various parts of the world. Seaport settlements – which have lasted to this day and are completely integrated into local populations – were the result of these seamen from Africa, India and the Caribbean setting down bases in these areas, mainly because they had no money to return home. Fortunes at sea were cruel and much more so if you were a sailor on starvation wages. By 1804 there was a steady flow of these lascars (barely paid sailors) and Chinese seamen. By 1836 the numbers had risen to over 3,000 per year. They were savagely treated on board and then dumped here when ill or when there was no work for them, or when they were without resources to return home. Like ayahs (female servants), these 'rejects' ended up in such abject poverty that Christians and some politicians felt obliged to establish homes for them in the 1860s.[19] This was three decades after a parliamentary inquiry had been set up to look into their plight. All around the East End of London you can see charity homes which were set up by various philanthropists to provide food and shelter for destitute servants and sailors from abroad.

Throughout the days of Empire you also had maharajahs, cricket players, students and religious individuals coming to Britain and making an impact on life here. The first woman law student in this country was Cornelia Sorabji, a beautiful Indian scholar who had already fought extraordinary battles to go to college in India. In 1889 she came to Oxford and enrolled for a law degree. She quite turned the head of Benjamin Jowett, Master of Balliol, who became her tutor and her friend. She befriended Florence Nightingale, who had contributed to a fund for her fees, and was granted special dispensation to appear in front of the Queen in a sari. She obtained her degree and after some years became one of the first women to be admitted to the Bar. By the first quarter of the twentieth century we had had three Indians elected to the House of Commons, including one Conservative, Sir Mancherjee Bhownagree, who was in the House for a decade. This did not happen again until the 1992 election when Nirj Diva won a seat (only to lose it in 1998). Shapurji Saklatvala, a communist, and Dadabhai Naraoji, Labour, were the other two Indian MPs, both famous for their impressive speeches, many of which were made arguing the case for Indian independence.

Millions of black and Asian people fought in the First and Second World Wars and, at least then, were much admired for their loyalty and bravery. It is important to remember that, even before these two defining wars for Europe, individuals of colour had often chosen to do their bit even when they remained unrecognized. The role of Mary Seacole, the Caribbean nurse who went to the Crimea with her own money to tend wounded soldiers, at the same time as Florence Nightingale, disappeared from history until two black British writers excavated her story in the 1980s. One Lieutenant wrote of her: 'She was a wonderful woman . . . all men swore by her, and in case of any malady would seek her advice and use her herbal medicines in preference to reporting themselves to their own doctors.'[20] Brighton Pavilion was made into a hospital for Indian soldiers in the First World War and you can still see the notices which show separate facilities for Hindus, Sikhs and Muslims, and notices in various Asian languages – something which is rare today even in our modern NHS hospitals. Special foods were imported so the wounded soldiers could eat appropriate diets. Indian doctors qualified here were used to treat the patients. There is an inspiring memorial in the South Downs to the role played by these soldiers. In 1921 the Prince of Wales unveiled this Chhatri memorial and said:

> **It is befitting that we should remember, and that future generations should not forget, that our Indian comrades came when our need was highest, free men – voluntary soldiers – who were true to their salt, who gave their lives in a quarrel in which it was enough for them to know that the enemy were the foes of their sahibs, their Empire and their king.**[21]

What he did not say was that in many of the battles the Indian soldiers were deliberately sacrificed before the British, something that has come to light in recent years through censored letters from Indian soldiers from the various fronts. The soldiers described how the 'black pepper from India' was all being used up and that much less 'red pepper' was being used. A German soldier wrote of these soldiers: 'Today we had to fight against the Indians and the devil knows those brown rascals are not to be underrated.'[22]

The role played by Asian and black soldiers in the Second World War was even more striking. Over 3.5 million volunteered even as independence struggles were gathering pace and Indian leaders were being detained by the British. Yet these men were prepared to give their lives. At Cassino and in Burma and the Middle East their bravery made such a mark that scores of monuments were built in their honour, in Italy and elsewhere too. Noor Inayat Khan was the descendant of Tipu Sultan – the ruler who hated the British so much he commissioned a life-sized wooden tiger with a British soldier in its mouth. Nevertheless Khan joined the resistance movement as a secret agent for the Allies and was in time arrested, tortured and executed in Dachau in 1944. Yet in May 1998, the highly erudite Chris Dunkley of the *Financial*

Times, and erstwhile presenter of Radio 4, wrote in response to the *Windrush* programmes on BBC television: 'Perhaps the remarkable number of West Indians who fought for the UK during the war was common knowledge to the British public, but it was news to me.'[23]

Our endless war memorial services have so neglected to reflect these sacrifices that in 1995 local authorities in London and the Midlands began special events to honour this record. You only have to go to the West Indian ex-servicemen's clubs to listen to the stories of bravery and sense the outrage that these remain invisible in a country which is arguably fixated in every other way on these war memories. In 1993 when a British National Party member won a seat in local authority elections in London's East End, I interviewed a number of black and Asian war veterans. One of them, Sergeant-Major Rajinder Singh, was beside himself over this:

> Can you imagine how we feel? I am a proud and loyal man, madam. We had so much faith in this country. In the war, I thought it is important to help Britain to save democracy and fight fascism. They don't remember what we did.[24]

Bill Nalty, who was in the RAF, was similarly shocked and disenchanted with the way this country had allowed racism – the very poison they had fought against in the Second World War – to so infect its own shores.

> To see this all in 1993, it makes you think. If that time was to repeat itself, there is no way, knowing what I do know, that I would have come to fight for this country or embarked on the journey to come here. We were so naïve. We truly had faith in the mother country, enough to want to die for her. And in return there has been little reciprocity, and rejection for too many of us.[25]

This particular contribution is central to our presence here and to the sense of common destiny that we need to foster between black and white Britons. It is important, not only because so little of it is known, but because it is a statement like no other which establishes our absolute right to be here. Again and again we are forced to hear comments about how the 'real' British fought in the war, as if this is the only valid qualification for belonging. The power of that particular historical recollection is still intensely strong and poetic. As a result, abject though it feels, we have to fall in line and repeatedly assert our role in the victory and remind those who won't listen what this means. There are obvious dangers in this. If some sections of the British public feel under pressure to explain, and present positive stories about themselves, they are not yet truly equal in this society. Black Britons have the right to be good *and* bad and our criminals are as much part of our narrative as our heroes and heroines. But this is not permitted, not yet anyway. So, conspicuous and unfair though it feels, we are obliged to wear placards and fading medals on our chests showing how, over the course of history, we have been an integral part of the progress made by this country. It is significant that Polish and Italian immigrants are not called upon to tediously state and re-state their contributions or the reasons why they are here, even though many of them landed in Britain in the same years as many Jamaicans and Trinidadians did. As George Brown, a black elder I interviewed, put it:

> It wounds me to wear my duty to this country all the time on my sleeve, like I always have to earn the right to walk these streets. My friend Gianni, he came here the same time as I did, but nobody expects him to remind people that he fought in the war or, like me, worked as a cleaner in the hospitals. But we must, it seems, carry on educating whites. As we move to the next century . . . as white racism grows in Europe because it is encouraged by white politicians who want to see a white fortress, these are the facts which will determine our rights to be here, to be European. The industrial revolution, capitalism across the Continent, the wealth generated over centuries, has come from our toil as much as it has from white Europeans. More, really, because we were exploited more. We are Europeans, British through and through because our history says so.

The tragic fact is that, after the war, historical amnesia seems to have set in so hard and fast. The postwar story can be described as our determined battle against this national forgetfulness but, unlike those in the first half of the century, at least we are empowered to do this. There was another difference too between the first half of the century and the second. After the fifties most of the people of colour who came here or sought to come here were not chattels of the Empire or even symbols of it, but free people seeking equality with those who still find the concept unpalatable.

Those who make history must take a lot of the blame for the state we are in. As the rest of this chapter will demonstrate, throughout the second half of the twentieth century, ordinary white Britons have been led astray by the actions of duplicitous politicians who have not given moral leadership. But those who interpret events have played their part too. This growing, changing nation has been failed by an ignorant, even at times a manipulative media[26] and an education service which is firmly on the road back to the future.

When the *Empire Windrush* landed at Tilbury on 22 June 1948, bringing 492 Jamaicans, the headline in the *Evening Standard* was: 'Welcome Home.' Local and central government moved fast to make these arrivals feel welcome and to find them jobs and accommodation. But even as they did this, some politicians had already begun the national panic over what could happen to this country if such expeditions were to be repeated. Knowing full well how urgent the labour needs were across the country, eleven Labour MPs wrote to Clement Attlee, on the day the *Empire Windrush* landed, expressing their concerns in stark terms which framed the debates that still continue over the issues of immigration and race relations: 'An influx of coloured people domiciled here is likely to impair the harmony, strength and cohesion of our public and social life and cause discord and unhappiness among all concerned.'[27] Attlee reassured his anxious colleagues that, if there was indeed 'a great influx of undesirables', he would take tough action. Interestingly, in that same year, the Conservative Sir David Maxwell Fyfe said: 'We are proud that we impose no colour bar restrictions. We must maintain our great metropolitan tradition of hospitality to everyone from every part of our Empire.'[28] These sentiments were an extension, of course, of imperial ambition and enterprise, but they were also an important demonstration of positive leadership which was attempting to influence the attitudes of the general population towards the early immigrants.

In these responses, as Kenan Malik points out, 'are contained many of the assumptions that have shaped both official and popular attitudes to post-war immigration'.[29] At the very point of arrival, black people were seen as potential agents of social friction, immigration was linked to race relations, and those arriving were represented not as an asset but as a burden. In contrast, white immigration to the United States and Canada, which had escalated after the war, was described mostly in affirmative terms. As the Canadian writer Margaret Cannon observes, after the Second World War record numbers of British citizens emigrated to Canada and were welcomed and accorded full rights.[30] The positive response to British immigration was the centrepiece of a speech made by Canadian High Commissioner Eaton on the occasion of the 125th anniversary of the proclamation of the Canadian Immigration Act.[31] In addition, what is largely ignored is the fact that fewer than 5,000 black immigrants were causing this fuss when at the same time hundreds of thousands of Irish, Italian and Polish immigrants were coming in to make new lives in mainland Britain. The largest 'ethnic minority' group in Britain today is actually Irish.

These official attitudes have, through the decades, sown a forest of shadows which have blocked off the light for black and white Britons. The consequences of seeing postwar black immigrants as a burden rather than an asset are still being felt. As the following brief history of arrival and settlement will show, the main migrations of black and Asian people fell into five phases, with each decade from the fifties to the nineties producing new challenges and old solutions.

The fifties brought Caribbean men, closely followed by Pakistani men and Caribbean women and children. These early arrivals were needed by both the public and the private sectors for the massive postwar national reconstruction project which included the new public systems that were to change health provision, welfare and transport services in Britain. People forget how weakened this country was through a massive loss of lives and assets. In 1951 the Conservatives came to power and the Cabinet papers of the time reveal that Winston Churchill and Anthony Eden both had serious anxieties about black immigration but that they did not want to sour relations with the colonies and ex-colonies, nor could they afford to cut off the supply of cheap and cheerful (at that time at least) labour. The expanding NHS was creating an enormous need for labour and many of these jobs were taken by immigrants. But even this was not enough to give policy a clear and honourable direction, and ambiguities continued under Harold Macmillan and beyond. Racial attitudes and hypocrisy formed the basis of the early immigration control laws. In 1955 Alec Douglas-Home, then in the Cabinet, said:

> On the one hand it would presumably be politically impossible to legislate for a colour bar and any legislation would have to be non-discriminatory in form. [But] we do not wish to keep out immigrants of good type from the old dominions . . . I understand that immigration officers could, without giving rise to trouble or publicity, exercise such a measure of discrimination as we think desirable.[32]

These shifty attitudes and mixed motives stopped governments in the fifties taking the responsibility to educate white Britons on the role and value of black immigrants, or to begin a public awareness process which would have helped to move the national mentality from imperial arrogance and xenophobia to proud multiculturalism. And because of the failure of this leadership and the way in which the arrival of black people was described, race relations did in fact begin to show signs of deteriorating soon after 1948. Paul Foot, who in 1965 wrote a seminal book about this early history, is convinced that matters could have been handled differently to create a much more settled and integrated society. He wrote:

> Commonwealth immigrants before they became the playthings of party politics, and despite a total lack of Government concern and planning, were greeted with general friendliness and hospitality. Of course there was colour bar in some pubs. Of course there was antagonism in some factories and bus garages. But these were exceptions. Overall the reaction was kind, even helpful. A considerate and co-ordinated effort by politicians to assist assimilation, to isolate and punish the racialist minority would have been decisive.[33]

Ivor, a white railway worker, described to me how he felt at the time when the colour of the workforce began to change:

> We believed we were better than the blacks and that is why we had the right to rule over them. Then they arrived to work with us on the railways. They were good men but you could not forget what you had

> learned about them all your life, that they could never be as good as a
> white Englishman. They came to live next to us and we were expected
> to live with that. They [the government] never asked us how we felt. I
> am not saying we should not have let them in, no Ma'am. My
> grandchild is half Jamaican and he's family. But our feelings were
> ignored then as they are now.

Ivor's grandchild, as it happens, has a black British father who has
never been to Jamaica. What is indisputable about this period of recent
history is that Caribbean immigrants, unlike the immigrants who came
from the Indian subcontinent and elsewhere, had nothing to divide
them from the indigenous British – neither religion, nor language, nor
education. The only problem with them was that they were black and
presuming to be as British as the rest. They were regarded as pretenders.
This was almost more unforgivable than being a cultural curiosity or
alien, which is how most Asians, including the Chinese, are still seen.
Ivor illustrates this perfectly:

> The thing was, you see, I thought that these people lived in trees and
> hunted for food. I was not ready for these men dressed like Frank
> Sinatra speaking English like, better than me. I remember this one
> guy Harold. He always had a Bible and Dickens in his lunch bag and
> he would sit away from us and read every day after the sandwiches.
> We thought he was showing off. We gave him a right old time.

What added to the resentment was the fact that politicians never
properly informed their white constituents about the crucial role that
black workers were playing. Professor Zig Layton-Henry said they
needed to know and most still need to understand that

> [i]mmigration has contributed to economic growth and prosperity. It
> has acted as a check on inflation as migrant workers have been
> prepared to work long hours for low wages. They have also assisted in
> the upward social and economic mobility of indigenous British
> workers because, as a replacement labour force, they have been
> assigned the lowest positions in the labour and housing markets.[34]

Instead of explaining this, politicians of all parties began to play the
race card more openly as immigration accelerated from the Caribbean

and the Indian subcontinent. But though overt racism was in evidence everywhere, employers in factories would offer their 'coloured' workers jobs for their friends and families, even if it meant bringing them over from abroad. Middle-class people from many of the countries once or still under British domination also came over, as they had done in earlier decades, in order to go to British schools and universities and get what was assumed to be the best education in the world. As I was growing up I remember the bleeding, deep envy I felt when the rich folk sent their children off to boarding schools in places like Poole, and when during the summer months these brown toffs would arrive back and treat us locally educated kids like ants under their patent leather (bought, not just made in England) shoes.

The year 1958 was a turning point in this story. In September, terrible racial violence erupted in Nottingham and in North Kensington. Over 6,000 people were involved, the leaders being racist teddy boys and supporters of Oswald Mosley. The riots were partly triggered by the distaste felt by many white men that integration was revealing itself in a flagrant way.[35] Too many white women, it seemed, were too happy to be seen going with black men. The journalist Mervyn Jones reported that fascists were orchestrating the attacks. One of them told him: 'We're going to scare the hell out of the niggers.' Norman Manley, the Chief Minister of Jamaica, was concerned enough to fly to London. Lord Justice Salmon said that the attackers had brought shame on the areas affected and that their actions had 'filled the whole nation with horror'.[36]

The 1958 riots were orchestrated by known racists. Instead of roundly condemning them, politicians immediately started crowing about the need to halt immigration because immigrants were damaging race relations. Just as women cause hapless men to rape. A poll carried out in the *Daily Mail* immediately afterwards showed 80 per cent of white Britons supporting hard-line immigration policies. What is interesting, though, is that racism did not emerge a clear winner even at this tense time. White Britons were then still capable of resisting racist politicians. Paul Foot observed: 'In the predominantly working-class areas where the immigrants have settled they have encountered two contradictory reactions – on the one hand decency, hospitality and solidarity; on the other, resentment and xenophobia.'[37] British politicians opted to nurture the latter by arguing that the 1958 riots were a symptom of genuine anxieties felt by white Britons about 'coloured' immigration, and that therefore the solution lay not in re-educating the white population on the benefits of immigration or their civic responsibilities, but in stricter immigration controls. Tory and Labour MPs in Nottingham immediately called for a halt to all 'coloured' immigration. George Rogers, the local MP for Notting Hill Gate, and even Alec Douglas-Home, by this time Minister of State for Commonwealth Relations, put forward this view. Immigration control and 'good race relations' became even more knitted together.[38] A poll carried out for the *Daily Express* in the immediate aftermath showed 80 per cent of white Britons in support of immigration controls.[39] Some in the Labour Party however, appalled at the racial violence directed at black people, took a position of total opposition to immigration controls (showing that they did not understand the strength of feeling behind the riots) and the NEC began to declare openly their intention to introduce anti-discrimination legislation.[40] This, speculates Layton-Henry, may have been a miscalculation:

> they were unable to see that the strength of public opinion on coloured immigration would have to be appeased . . . the riots . . . seem to have prevented the Labour Party from developing a realistic policy on immigration which would have both reassured the public about the size and consequences of New Commonwealth immigration and at the same time been non-racist. The riots were regarded as ugly isolated incidents and not part of a rising trend of opposition to black immigration which might have growing political significance.[41]

Meanwhile, Conservative politicians such as Cyril Osborne stepped up a vocal campaign to keep out 'coloured' immigrants, asking whether it made sense to turn Britain into a multiracial community. Foot argued that such politicians had a particularly damaging effect on race relations:

> With no other issue are the attitudes struck by politicians more crucial. In the choice of economic priorities, the level of social services, the character of defence, the politicians play a minor role. The big decisions are made for them by civil servants, managing

> directors and the international rate of exchange. So irrational is race
> and colour propaganda that its exploitation by politicians has an
> effect proportionately far wider than political propaganda on other
> matters . . . Even conditions of substantial unemployment and
> poverty, though capable of provoking race resentment and
> antagonism, are unlikely to do as much damage to race relations as
> are the rantings of unscrupulous politicians.[42]

The year 1959 saw the first officially acknowledged racist murder
of a black man in this country when Kelso Cochrane was stabbed to
death in a North Kensington street. His killer was never found but an
overwhelming number of white people turned up at his funeral to
express their shock and horror at what had been done. It would be a
long time before we would such a reaction from white Britons to racist
violence. Maureen, an Irishwoman married to Ozzie, a black musician,
was one of the mourners:

> I was pregnant with my second child and I stood in line feeling the
> shame of my colour. Those near me were all white, all feeling that it
> was our fault for not stopping the poison. Ozzie changed from that
> day. He was so carefree when we met. I was a singer. He became
> dark, afraid even and sometimes he took it out on me. He saw me as
> white, not the woman he had fallen in love with. When he died, I was
> the only white person at the funeral. That was in 1970.

As time has gone on, even the mourning of those murdered because
of the colour of their skins has divided along racial lines.

But the battle for integration was not all lost. In the 1959 election
Oswald Mosley stood as a candidate in North Kensington, the very
area where the worst rioting had taken place. He lost his deposit. What
you saw in all the urban areas (and this too is something much rarer
today), were clubs and dance halls where black and white Britons of
all ages mixed freely and easily and where sexual relationships and
friendships could not be discouraged by the clouds of prejudice around.
But the goodwill should not be overstated either. White trade unionists
resisted the entry and promotion of black and Asian workers[43] and
some writers, such as A. Sivanandan of the Institute of Race Relations,
take the view that where black workers were welcomed it was only

because of the low-cost labour they provided which private and public employers could exploit at will.[44] In many areas they were not regarded as a threat because they were taking up the poorly paid and essential jobs that white working-class people did not want to do. So it was not genuine munificence but indifference which made life relatively easy for these immigrants. The fifties were a *laissez-faire* period in immigration and race politics which perhaps sat well with the economic boom of the mid-fifties and which facilitated the use of essential immigrant labour without causing too much discomfort to those running the country. This was of course the period when Enoch Powell himself, as Minister of Health, actively encouraged the recruitment of overseas nurses, doctors and ancillary workers into the expanding National Health Service. And so powerful was this economic imperative that when he met members of the newly formed British Immigration Control Association, he opposed their views.[45]

With hindsight, it is clear that the public responses to this early phase of settlement were complex but not fixed. Positive leadership had a role to play but even the Labour government chose not to take up the challenge. The 1950 Cabinet papers, for example, revealed that the Labour government did not believe that public education would reduce white prejudice.[46] That historical moment of real possibilities was all too brief, and the much-needed process of planned integration was neglected, says Layton-Henry.

> The response to colonial migration to Britain by politicians and policy makers in the 1950s was hesitant and ambiguous and little positive was done to assist their settlement, integration and acceptance . . . it was not welcomed as a response to manpower needs and a valuable asset in creating economic growth and sustaining higher living standards and prosperity . . . a more positive early lead by government and political leaders might have done much to assuage public anxieties.[47]

These positive messages were not given by the leaderships. Instead politicians of all parties soon used race as an election tool. They should rather have behaved more responsibly as immigration was picking up not only from the West Indies, but also from India and Pakistan where Partition and other political and natural disasters were creating push factors.[48] But in spite of the fact that their labourwas required, in the late fifties and through the sixties black and Asian immigrants were increasingly to experience overt racial antagonism.[49]

At a personal level, social mingling, especially between black men and white women, continued to flourish. Frank Crichlow owned the Rio Club in Notting Hill and he described the people who went there:

> It was amazing. White and black people socializing like you cannot even imagine today. Christine Keeler used to call me 'dad'. Colin McInnes, all sorts of arty types, they loved the spirit of the place and felt released from their own stiff culture. Darcus Howe was there and we would talk, drink, dance. The West Indian men were very popular with the ladies.

Mixed-race couples were jitterbugging away and many began to believe that the fears of politicians had been unfounded.

As the sixties progressed, this somewhat contradictory picture and political vacillation continued, as race relations got worse in some ways and better in others. When it came to race and immigration, public opinion (whether real or imagined) was thereafter going to lead politicians in a manner, says Paul Rich, untypical of the rest of British politics. This, he believes, had something to do with the fact that liberal opinion was losing confidence, in part because the old Commonwealth was rapidly disappearing. British national pride was thus at a low ebb and suffered further from the several rejections of Britain's attempts to join the European Common Market:

> There was a decline in the beneficent liberal spirit within middle opinion itself and 'race relations' became not the means of a confident promotion of policies of multiracial harmony . . . but an increasingly defensive assertion of liberal values on race which had formerly been attached to the Commonwealth idea but which were cut adrift on a hostile sea and on a boat with no clear instructions as to where it was to navigate to.[50]

Rich was right in his analysis. The emotional fallout of decolonization cannot be underestimated; its effects on white public confidence and attitudes were deep and long-lasting. The vacuum created by the end of imperial dreams (which the New Commonwealth concept could in no real way replace) and the racial antagonism which was manifesting itself made space both for the first strong immigration controls aimed at those from the Commonwealth and eventually for Powellism, arguably one of the most damaging developments for race relations since the war.

The context is significant if one is to understand what happened to British public attitudes in this period and the years that followed. The clamour for immigration control continued, and at the Conservative Party Conference in 1961 thirty-nine resolutions demanding restrictions were put up. The campaign for control itself increased the flow of immigrants at this time because of fears that the doors were about to close. The Commonwealth Immigrants Bill was published and had considerable public support. Only Commonwealth citizens born in the UK and those with passports issued by the UK government could, thereafter, enter the country freely. All others had to apply for Ministry of Labour vouchers. The long tradition of treating all Commonwealth people as British subjects with equal rights of citizenship ended with this Act and the racial implications were quite clear. That racial exclusion was the real aim of the 1962 Act is accepted by William Deedes who was Minister without Portfolio at the time: 'The Bill's real purpose was to restrict the influx of coloured immigrants. We were reluctant to say as much openly.'[51]

Were politicians at this time responding to public opinion or creating this opinion through their own actions? Samit Saggar believes that the first restrictions 'did not so much follow public sentiment as create it'.[52] But even during this period the political leadership could and sometimes did exert a benign influence. The fire and fury of the Opposition in the period which followed the announcement of the Bill took the government by surprise. Hugh Gaitskell made a devastating speech accusing the government of colour prejudice. The strategic onslaught by Labour had a marked impact on public opinion and a Gallup poll showed that public support for immigration controls immediately afterwards fell from 76 per cent to 62 per cent.[53] In 1963 Harold Wilson made a speech in Trafalgar Square on the need for public education and a change of attitudes towards immigrants. Later he appointed a junior minister to look into the possibility of a national public education programme and other strategies for integration. These were tentative steps in the right direction which were not taken forward.[54]

By the time of the general election in 1964, these attitudes had turned again. The most significant result was at Smethwick, where Patrick Gordon-Walker, the Shadow Foreign Secretary, was defeated by Peter Griffiths, whose campaign used the slogan: 'If you want a nigger neighbour, vote Labour.' This is seen as a turning point in British politics, says Layton-Henry, shifting everything further towards the politics of appeasement when it came to policies to do with race and immigration: 'It was a shattering result and a disaster for race relations as it appeared to show that racial prejudices could be effectively exploited for electoral advantage.'[55] Richard Crossman who had, in 1962, condemned the Commonwealth Immigrants Act, was writing just two years later, in 1964:

> **Ever since the Smethwick election it has been quite clear that immigration can be the greatest potential vote loser for the Labour Party if we are seen to be permitting a flood of immigrants to come in and blight the central areas of our cities.**[56]

In 1965, the newly elected Labour government, still reeling from the shock of the Griffiths victory, proposed further restrictive measures directed at Commonwealth citizens, by reducing the number of vouchers available under the 1962 Act. The White Paper was clearly targeted at New Commonwealth immigrants and was put through even though it meant going against economic good sense. The aims of imposing further restrictions were political and the White Paper was met with overwhelming public support. Richard Crossman admitted as much in his diaries:

> **We have become illiberal and lowered quotas at a time when we have an acute shortage of labour . . . nevertheless . . . if we had not done this, we would have been faced with certain electoral defeat in the West Midlands and South East. Politically, fear of immigration is the most powerful undertow today.**[57]

The next general election in 1966 was won by Labour and, so well had the Labour government placated people's fears and paranoia, that opinion polls revealed that the majority did not think immigration was a serious issue. But race relations were far from harmonious. A damaging bipartisan consensus had emerged on these issues: there were to be greater immigration controls and measures to ensure fair treatment for immigrants and minorities who were settling. The 1965 Race Relations Act came out of the cross-party accord. This Act outlawed discrimination in specified public places such as cinemas and transport facilities and made it illegal for anyone to publish and distribute written matter which deliberately stirred up racial hatred. A Race Relations Board was set up to co-ordinate and deal with complaints, but housing and employment were not covered. The spirit of this law was conciliatory; it urged people to do what was right instead of providing for strong punitive measures to stop people doing what was discriminatory. The Act aimed to pacify those angry about the increasing immigration controls introduced by Labour, and, by getting Conservative support, the principle was established that the law could be used to combat discrimination.

The idea was seeded which bound together race relations and immigration policies. They remain coupled to this day although there has never been any evidence to show that race relations have improved because of our immigration policies, nor that the fears of the white British public have been assuaged by an endless stream of new immigration laws and regulations, all justified each time with the same mantra. Even the most basic questions remain unasked. Why do we need new immigration laws so frequently? Is it an acknowledgement of failure? If so, could they please admit this. This coupling of two areas of public policy has meant that we have never been able to develop rational immigration policies based on need. Politicians are caught in the traps they have built and this means that in spite of the massive shortage of nurses in 1999, for example, the government is not free to advocate a specifically targeted needs-based immigration policy. This approach, says Colin Brown, encouraged rather than discouraged racism:

> **The 'race relations' justification for immigration control has not been publicly presented by the government as an accommodation of white racism, however; rather, it has been explained in terms of problems**

caused by the presence of black immigrants. It may be that by aiming
to appease white opinion by turning first to immigration rather than by
tackling racialism itself, the government has nourished and given
legitimacy to anti-immigrant sentiment; thus the outcome of the
appeasement policy may have been only a deepening of the racialist
currents in British society. It is difficult to analyse the extent to which
successive immigration controls have been responses to public
opinion simply because the government's introduction of those
controls may itself have been very influential in forming that
opinion.'[58]

Little wonder then that the 1965 Race Relations Act was seen as a sop
which pleased nobody. Just one year on from the Act a major study
by Political and Economic Planning (PEP) revealed that direct discrimination against ethnic minorities was still commonplace. Using discrimination tests, W. W. Daniel found that although excuses were made by
employers and house owners, they *were* denying black and Asian
people jobs and accommodation on the basis of their own racial
prejudices.[59] But even at this time many liberals felt that race relations
were still capable of being influenced positively. In their monumental
study *Colour and Citizenship*, Jim Rose and others concluded:

A forthright, unequivocating leadership would be a powerful factor in
allaying unfounded anxieties . . . Conversely there is a danger that in
the absence of leadership, anyone who wishes to play on the anxieties
of the majority . . . can move them towards prejudiced attitudes.[60]

Immigration raised its head again in 1968 as British Asians in East
Africa began to be put under pressure after independence. Africaniz-
ation policies and other steps taken by the Kenyan government caused
many of these Asians to leave Kenya and come to Britain to settle. As
British passport holders they were free to enter under the 1962 Act.
Enoch Powell and others were making increasingly vociferous anti-
immigration speeches. The government panicked and rushed through
a Bill imposing strict quotas and removing automatic entry to people
with British passports except those born here or descended from a
British parent or grandparent. It was seen by many as a betrayal of
principle and of a community who had retained their British citizenship

in good faith. The vigour with which Labour took up the politics of appeasement was condemned even by the right-wing Auberon Waugh who described the new measures as 'the most immoral pieces of legislation ever to have emerged from any British parliament'.[61]

It was partly to rescue its reputation from such accusations that, a few months later, the government passed the 1968 Race Relations Act. Some years later, in 1976, Liberal MP Alan Beith was honest enough to say that the first two Race Relations Acts were a 'counter-balance or accompaniment to new legislation restricting immigration', adding that it was wrong 'that the two things should be as closely associated, as this created suspicion and anxiety'.[62] The Act duly came into force, making it unlawful to discriminate on grounds of colour, race, ethnic or national origins, in housing, employment, and the provision of services. Displays of discriminatory notices were banned and the Race Relations Board was given powers to investigate cases if there were grounds to suspect that discrimination had taken place even if no complaint had been received. The emphasis was still on conciliation with legal redress seen as a last resort. Overt race discrimination was made unlawful and the new provisions covered the key areas left out by the previous Act, although there was concern that complaints against the police were left outside the remit of the new law. But even as the Bill was going through Parliament, it was clear that good race relations could not be promoted in an atmosphere of public hostility against New Commonwealth immigration which was simply being encouraged by increasingly draconian immigration controls.[63] Some politicians were also concerned that the public mind had not been influenced adequately to accept this new law.[64]

It was in the same year, 1968, that Enoch Powell made his apocalyptic speech:

> **We must be mad, literally mad, as a nation, to be permitting the annual inflow of some 50,000 dependants who are for the most part the material of the future growth of the immigrant-descended population. It is like watching a nation busily engaged in heaping up its own funeral pyre . . . As I look ahead I am filled with foreboding. Like the Roman, I seem to see 'the River Tiber foaming with much blood'![65]**

The result of this speech was immediate, says Layton-Henry:

> It made him the best loved and most popular member of the
> Opposition overnight and even a serious contender for the position of
> leader of the party. The popular support for Powell could be measured
> in the polls, the deluge of favourable letters he received and the
> public demonstrations of support.[66]

Opinion polls showed that up to 75 per cent supported him.[67] Later
he fine-tuned his views and began to argue that the only way to sustain
this nation was through repatriation because 'coloured' immigrants
could never, in his eyes, be Englishmen. He also planted the seeds of
suspicion among the white British population, claiming that the political elite did not understand them and that the true facts about immigration were not being made public. This tactic has since been used
intermittently by politicians, the latest example being Charles Wardle
who resigned as immigration minister in 1995 claiming that people in
this country were not being given the information about how many
'millions' of people would come into this country if European Union
internal border controls were scrapped.[68] The long and deep influence
of Enoch Powell continued to paralyse politicians and people in this
country for the next three decades in spite of all the mounting evidence
that *de facto* integration was taking place. Much emotion was wasted,
many possibilities surrendered as leaders lacking vision flopped around
doing little that was positive and reacting defensively against the power
of the negative.

Rebranding Britain and the Weeds of Multiculturalism

The Souls of nations do not change; they merely
    stretch their hidden range
Just as rivers do not sleep
the spirit of empire still runs deep.
Into a river many waters flow
the merging and conquest that is history's glow
A gathering of homely and alien streams
A tumble of turbulent and tranquil dreams
Classes overflow their rigid boundaries
slowly stirring mighty quandaries; Accents
    diverse ring from the land's soul
a richer music revealing what is whole; new
    pulsings from abroad shake the shores
troubling the sleep of the land's resonant bores.
But the gods of the nation do not change, their
    ways are deep and often strange.
History moves, and the surface quivers, but the
    gods are steadfast in the depth of the rivers.

Ben Okri, *Guardian*, 20 January 1999[1]

The wider turmoils of the early seventies discussed in the last chapter created an atmosphere of such panic in this country that scapegoating the 'other' became the national sport. With Powell still enormously popular at the time, anti-racists like that great and humane MP, Fenner Brockway, were as marginalized as Ken Livingstone is today. Once again the leadership succumbed to the appeasement of racially prejudiced white British citizens instead of cultivating a new spirit of pride in change. Once upon a time the people of this country were encouraged to see themselves as fine world seamen, brave and intrepid and, in spite of coming from such a small island, capable of exploring and later owning the world. Where were the spin doctors to tell them feel-good things about the internationalization of their nation? Even the most idealistic politicians from all the main parties were having to temper the messages they were giving out and ministers were under strict orders not to stray. Tony Benn's entry in his diary for 16 January 1974 reports that Harold Wilson instructed Labour politicians to 'ignore Enoch Powell, because last time the attack on him lost five seats'.[2] Liberal Tories became victims too of a xenophobic population they had helped to create. As Layton-Henry says:

> the government was on the defensive, desperately trying to hold the bipartisan consensus against the onslaughts of Enoch Powell and his friends with Edward Heath trailing behind Powell, but gradually moving the Conservative policies towards tougher and tougher controls.[3]

Leaders were acting as followers. Conservatives first and then Labour made themselves hostages to (often ill-informed) public opinion instead of influencing opinion to back policies which would improve race relations and benefit the country. Heath and Powell hated each other but a mutual dependency grew out of this with the result that the latter played a key part in Tory victory. This happened even though only a quarter of the Conservative candidates took up the issue of race and immigration during their campaigns. They were still perceived to be tougher on immigration. The 1971 Immigration Act replaced employment vouchers with work permits which did not give people rights of permanent residence or entry rights to dependants. People who were connected by birth or descent to the United Kingdom were free to enter. Should South Africa or Zimbabwe ever flare up in an unexpected way, floods of white immigrants could, perfectly legally, enter this country today. Many do today and with impunity. Like all previous laws since the late forties, the immigration law was intentionally racist. The rights of non-white Commonwealth citizens to settle in Britain ended with this Act. It helped to confirm the feeling that the Tory government could be trusted to keep this country safely and predominantly white.

This belief was to be shattered in 1972 with the Ugandan crisis. In August of that year Idi Amin announced the expulsion of the 50,000 Asians who had lived in the country for generations. The majority of them had British passports. This tested the reputation that Heath had established. Was he now going to be tough enough to reject calls to take responsibility for these citizens? Enoch Powell, the Monday Club and the National Front reacted with predictable hostility and insisted that the United Kingdom had no moral case to take in the dispossessed Asians. Ordinary Britons protested that they would not be prepared to admit the thousands who were affected by Amin's order. Local authorities in Leicester and Ealing paid for advertisements in newspapers asking Ugandan Asians not to move into their areas. In the end the government decided to honour their obligations and accept their citizens who were being threatened with incarceration in Ugandan concentration camps. In the interim months the government had tried to get other countries, as Heath said to me, 'to share the burden',[4] and tried in vain to negotiate with Amin. Instead of dealing with the situation with assertiveness and courage, the whole event felt badly managed, with panic dominating decisions. In the end Edward Heath did the right thing at a time when he was under intense pressure to capitulate to the anti-immigration lobby. But the decision could have been presented and communicated better. This was, after all, an example of a conscientious leader making an honourable, moral decision. The Ugandan Asians were educated, skilled people who would become a success legend within twenty years. The clumsy way public relations were handled meant that this event raised old fears among many white Britons and made ethnic minorities already settled in this country feel vulnerable and humiliated. I had arrived here only weeks before the expulsion order and a few months prior to the exodus. I was affected enough both to go into a reception camp where bedraggled Ugandan Asians were housed and helped (often by conscientious white Britons), and to use shameful tricks to avoid being linked to that group of pitiful people. Politically the scene was set for another major shift to the right.

One unique feature of this event was that once the Heath government had accepted responsibility for the Ugandan Asians, ministers went all out to convince the British people that this was something the country would benefit from. If one forgives the early vacillations, there is much left to admire. Walking away from the politics of cowardice was in the end a nail in his own coffin for Heath, but history should remember well what this curiously unattractive British leader did at a time when the country was deeply divided, lacking in confidence, terrified of us and proud to be prejudiced. When my people arrived, lost, bewildered and hopeful, unprecedented scenes of racial hostility greeted them outside the airports. You would not see this now. But then mothers with babies, pensioners, well-dressed punters, all felt they had the right to abuse us, to spit venom and tell us to go back where we had come from. A taxi driver refused to take my money when I told him where I was from. I threw the coins in his face. He had thick glasses on. It was a very satisfying moment.

In the face of all this Heath remained steadfast. Uganda's loss was 'our' gain, said Heath and others, and to his credit he also made resources available to enable successful integration. We, at least, have never forgotten our debt to him and to this day around the country his picture, garlanded with marigolds, is found in many Asian homes in the rooms which contain shrines to the gods and pictures of saintly earthlings.

Most white Britons have only the most superficial understanding of why we were in Africa and the reasons for our eventual presence in Britain. East African Asians were driven to come here between 1967 and 1972. They were all British passport holders who were put under increasing pressure by the governments of Kenya, Tanzania and Uganda, determined to Africanize their public services and the economic infrastructures after independence. Until the mid-sixties, although political power lay with black Africans, economic power was still in the hands of white companies or Asian businessmen. Racial tensions between black and Asian East Africans had not been resolved and black leaders found it easy to exploit anti-Asian sentiments to gain popular support. The situation for these British citizens was made impossible by the 1968 Commonwealth Immigrants Act. That was the year when thousands of Kenyan Asians with British passports had to flee Africa and come to an ever more xenophobic country.

President Idi Amin had taken control of Uganda in a coup in 1970. The British government had been more than a little encouraging. In fact, within hours the new government was recognized by Britain and all was felt to be rosy for the future. Most of us still believe that the coup was engineered by the USA, Israel and Britain.[5] The reasons for this were clear. The previous president, Obote, was felt by the west to be too pro-communism. Perhaps more importantly, Amin had been trained at Sandhurst; he loved the Queen and displayed her pictures proudly. In other words, he was smitten with his rulers like many of the rest of us. This is probably why he was perceived by the British establishment to be a potential puppet who would be willing to do the right thing by the west as long as they kept him happy with aid. It was a dangerous assumption and one that black Ugandans, more than anyone else, would have to pay for. By 1972 relations had soured because Amin's cruelty, unpredictability and most of all his profligacy had begun to trouble Britain and Israel, the two main players in the story at the time. He began by low-key attacks against Asians, then went into dramatic over-drive, threatening us with incarceration in concentration camps, blackmailing the British government in the hope of getting more money out of it, and finally throwing us all out in the autumn of 1972. I tell this story only as a single example of how complicit white Britain has been in what has happened in the ex-colonies and how this has led to displacement of people who have had to end up here. These truths and these responsibilities have never been properly acknowledged by the mother country and there is still the belief that the only reason so many non-indigenous people arrived here and continue to do so is because this is, in the words of Michael Howard, a 'honeypot'.[6]

Our pain and abject humiliation were compounded by shock that the people we had admired for so long were now incapable of managing even a small ship like the United Kingdom. Like many other ex-colonial people, who were still bound up in myths of British order and self-control, seeing this was as shocking (and perhaps as secretly pleasing) as finding out that your headmaster is a hopeless alcoholic. As one distant uncle put it:

> Hai hai. The greatest country in the world, even God could not defeat them. Today look at them. Sinking into the ocean. Wriggling like small fish inside the net of destiny. No discipline, no more the courage of the empire. No more the big ambitions. I don't know if I am more sad at losing beautiful Kampala or finding this destroyed country.

This exaggerated grief for our ex-rulers was in part insincerity masquerading as compassion, but the feelings, whatever they were, were real and powerful.

Even before our arrival the political elite had realized how appalling community relationships had become. But most failed utterly to recognize that they were largely to blame for the state of the nation. By the mid-seventies it had become clear that there was need for another tighter and more effective Race Relations Act. The 1968 Act was not respected by most black people and surveys by the PEP confirmed that although direct discrimination had been reduced, indirect discrimination was a significant factor in the social exclusion of racial minorities.[7] The Home Office itself produced a White Paper on racial disadvantage which recommended a 'fuller strategy' to combat discrimination and to ensure genuine equal opportunities for young black and Asian Britons born here. Roy Jenkins, the most visionary Home Secretary this country has ever had, made compelling speeches in Parliament saying that racism was morally repugnant and that the success of the legislation depended on the political leadership and the attitudes of society. Conservative MP Sir George Sinclair spoke in equally powerful terms about the Race Relations Acts and why they were important:

> Those of us who, on both sides of this House, supported those Acts hoped that by the bringing to an end of a wide range of discriminatory practices, attitudes would also change. It is one of the great myths that laws do not change attitudes.[8]

The Commission for Racial Equality was set up and when the Bill was going through Parliament, Alex Lyons – then Home Office Minister – said:

> It will be part of the task of the new Race Relations Commission to inform and educate public opinion on race relations . . . [there is a

**case for] the general education of society about the need to regard
ourselves as a multiracial society and to act accordingly.[9]**

The Commission was to be a vigorous law-enforcing body as well as
an institution with a promotional function. Over the years some people
have questioned this amalgamated function.[10] There are problems too
in leaving it to the Commission for Racial Equality to tell the country
how marvellous diversity is. But despite these reservations, the 1976
Act was undoubtedly an important development. Cases could be taken
to the county court or, in the case of employment, to industrial tribunals.
Legal definitions of discrimination were extended to cover organiza-
tional practices as well as individual behaviour. Indirect discrimination,
which meant discrimination in effect whatever the intentions, was also
made illegal.

This was also the time when extreme right-wing parties made substantial gains in recruitment and electoral victories. In the 1976 local
elections, the National Front and the National Party between them
captured nearly 44 per cent of the votes in Deptford. This was, Samit
Saggar believes, because immigration was still a burning issue for
many: 'The period between the mid seventies and the early eighties
witnessed an intense rise in domestic anti-immigration political sentiment.'[11] People also felt that political leaders were 'betraying' the white
population. This explosion of racism was partly to do with the fact
that these issues had been dealt with with such ambiguity by the two
parties for decades. Not much was done to counter the scaremongering
and other disturbing developments, says John Twitchin in the introduction to *Five Views of Multiracial Britain*:

> **the result of ignorance of the facts, rationalized by the 'leave well
> alone' approach, has been to leave the stage clear for those who,
> wittingly or otherwise, speak and act on racist assumptions to take the
> initiative both in public opinion leadership and in setting the agenda
> of public discussion.[12]**

Margaret Thatcher became leader of the Conservative Party in 1975.
She was among the forty-four Tories who were opposed to the 1976
Race Relations Act. She even threatened to order complete opposition
to the Bill but was prevented by liberal Tories who thought tough

immigration policies required the antidote of positive race relations policies and who were concerned that the party would be seen as racist.[13] She was, at heart, like many other disgruntled Little Englanders. And unfortunately the alarmingly ambitious and forceful Margaret Thatcher, daughter of Powell, acquired such power and mythological status that she was able to push this view and make it not only respectable but admired. She was thus able to stamp out any slight progress on multiculturalism that cautious but high-minded people such as Jenkins and Heath had tentatively been promoting. Nearly two decades were wasted by a woman of dubious national aspirations and a thunderous disregard for the cultural and political needs of a modern nation. We all, black and white Britons, lost out.

By 1978 Mrs Thatcher's hard anti-immigration views had become clear although the Tory Party was actively promoting itself as a party for ethnic minority communities. It was in that year that Margaret Thatcher on a *World in Action* programme justified cultural xenophobia by saying that she understood the British people's fear 'that this country might be rather swamped by people with a different culture'.[14] In this statement lie the roots of what was to come later: her own white and nationalistic version of Britishness and her rejection of the ideology of multiculturalism. Many saw her as a heroine, an honest politician unafraid to articulate what the ordinary white population was feeling, one who was moving from the elitist liberal consensus which had ignored and misled these people on immigration. The Party's ratings shot up by 9 per cent in the immediate aftermath of her 'swamping' speech. As the 1979 election approached Thatcher became calculatedly more divisive, upsetting many in her own party. A minority spoke up. Peter Walker honourably argued that winning votes was less important than the principles of a workable multiracial society: 'if you exploit people's worries in a way which shows hostility to minorities, you will do immense damage to racial harmony.'[15] But she heeded not.

The election of Margaret Thatcher in 1979 was, at least partly, the electorate's response to the still simmering problems around race and politics and the perceived lack of solid political leadership on these matters. Negative attitudes towards ethnic minorities persisted and Margaret Thatcher enjoyed tapping into these with great political acumen and in a way which appealed because it was so commonsensical. There is little doubt that she sought to re-establish a connection between populist views on race and the political leadership although, as Saggar says, there is disagreement over the motivations behind this:

> From 1976, the apparently orchestrated strategy was employed by the Conservative leadership to alter public perceptions of the party's position on immigration. Interpretations of these strategic moves however vary from those of supporters who emphasized the need to bring public opinion and policy commitments back into line to those of critics who asserted that it merely pandered to crude racism.[16]

In the eighties, Thatcher consolidated her position through messianic leadership, driving the nation with right-wing, free-market, conviction politics. She developed further her neo-Powellite view on English nationhood and British history. This was the cheap glue used to stick together the shattered fragments brought about by her radical economic structuring. So she told the people of this country, those with and without bicycles, as they were losing their jobs that they still had the best country in the world because of their glorious past. She was determined to put back the 'great' in Britain and this included pride in the Empire. She said this during her important speech in Bruges in 1991, when she asked her people to be proud that they had conquered and civilized the rest of the world.[17] Her nation was quite clearly still all white. Black Britons were hardly likely to applaud Imperial Britain. Yet in 1996 Tony Blair made similar statements at the pre-election Labour Party Conference. What Margaret Thatcher started up was in effect the battle for the British soul, says Philip Dodd:

> Mrs Thatcher's Britishness depended . . . upon a sustained process of *purification* and *exclusion*. In her British story, enemies were here, there and everywhere . . . Mrs Thatcher hardly invented such a strategy since Britishness has long worked on the principle of separating the inside sheep from the outside goats. Sometimes they have been Catholics, denied the vote, other times they have been Jewish people, and more recently people from the Caribbean or Asia. While the groups may change the principle does not – their presence threatens the historic identity of Britain.[18]

79

But looking at that period of history, it is notable that, in spite of the move to the right spearheaded by Thatcher, there were still many within the Tory Party who were convinced that even her brand of Conservatism, which defined national identity in the narrowest of terms, was not hard-line enough. For example, Harvey Proctor of the Monday Club – which has had the support of middle-of-the-road politicians[19] – wrote in a pamphlet:

> **Thirty years of mass immigration from the New Commonwealth and Pakistan and consequent demographic changes present by far the greatest threat to the future unity and common identity of our people and country upon which our parliamentary sovereignty depends. The fault lies not with the immigrants – all of whom should be treated equally before the law – but with politicians who allowed, even encouraged, the flow and who now seek to avoid but not avert its consequences by silence, evasion and humbug. The magnitude of the problem is increasingly hidden from the public's gaze.[20]**

Margaret Thatcher was not simply a racist. She was a shrewd politician who was capable of confounding those who regarded her as such. Her distaste for communism prompted her to admit Vietnamese refugees in the 1980s, her government providing resources for their settlement. The speeches made on this by the ruling party all focus on positive aspects such as the generosity of the British people and the skills of the refugees. This was a period when the twin-track approach to voters was also astutely developed. White voters anxious about immigration were placated; black voters in key areas were told that they were an indispensable part of the country and part of the Thatcher dream. The famous poster used by the Tories with a smart black man and a slogan saying 'Labour says he is black; Tories say he is British' is but one example.

But there can be little doubt that, unlike most other British leaders, she did not merely surrender to bigotry, but positively led it to respectability, and arguably was influenced by her own deeply felt attitudes just like Enoch Powell was. The end of the National Front was the result not of a left-wing victory but of a right-wing ideological coup. This validation of racial prejudice combined with the obvious leadership qualities of Thatcher and the extraordinary way she managed to control and carry the country through the massive reshaping in the eighties, put back the development of a new, easy multiculturalism for decades. Those who would worship this leader – including feminists – should remember this.[21]

Her effect on key state institutions was even more worrying; by far the worst of this was the hard-line and unaccountable policing tactics that grew under her rule and which have become so much a part of the policing culture which the Lawrence Report denounced. What was learnt in Brixton and Tottenham was then applied in Wapping and against the miners. A police officer with the Metropolitan police at the time explained the mood:

> **Thatcher let it be known to us, the police, that we could do anything to keep in control the enemy within. They were blacks, trade unionists, and people who did not agree with her views. I know that when I was on duty in Notting Hill Gate, I would go for the blacks more than I should have done, but you get into a kind of state, like you are in the army and the enemy is the enemy. No wonder the blacks never trusted us. They would be idiots to. By the time of the Poll Tax riots, even some of us couldn't handle this kind of thing.**

Hardly any white commentators then or now have sought to analyse the negative impact of Thatcherism on white Britons who, under false promises made by an iron lady they found irresistible, were led sheepishly away from where they needed to be in order to flourish in a competitive, global, cosmopolitan world. In the deluge of coverage which followed the end of Thatcher, not a single programme, book or article dealt with this, one of the most profound consequences of her reign.

Those who despised her brand of Britishness, like the Inner London Education Authority and the Greater London Council, became less self-controlled and at times almost as damaging to the cause too. Looking back it is almost farcical to see how the Thatcher government went into battle to prevent progress on equality initiatives and multi-culturalism. The Inner London Education Authority, the Greater London Council and some London Labour boroughs were particularly criticized by Conservatives for many of their equality initiatives. Nancy

Murray, in analysing these attacks, believes that the way they used race as a 'focus of cohering patriotism' had not been seen before: 'what is new is the emphasis on rolling back the gains of anti-racism in the name of traditional freedoms, national pride and the liberation of the white majority.'[22]

There was certainly a joint sense of mission which united Downing Street, the *Daily Mail*, the *Daily Telegraph*, and people such as Ray Honeyford – the Bradford headmaster who was sacked for publishing his views criticizing multicultural education – together with academics from right-wing think-tanks. Many of these think-tanks facilitated discussions and specific media initiatives backed by the Thatcherite wing of the Conservative Party.[23] The unity of purpose of these alliances and the way they put out messages was stunning. Indeed it stunned the left into dumb inaction.

This onslaught was being orchestrated at a time when equal opportunity policies were being crafted and used energetically by many local authorities to transform the racial composition of their workforce and to realize the obligations they had under Section 71 of the Race Relations Act. This was to 'make the appropriate arrangements . . . to promote equality of opportunity and good relations between people of different racial groups'. Many of the good ideas, particularly in education, were specifically targeted for criticism because they were beginning to have an impact, says Sammit Saggar: 'The more scathing attacks on multiculturalism have been reserved for the progressive LEAs which have been at the forefront of innovation and reform.'[24] Like faithful old dogs who follow any ghost of a stick, the right-wing press printed articles which sometimes had no factual basis and which were eventually proved to be complete fabrications. For example, articles which claimed that black binliners and 'Baa Baa Black Sheep' were banned by 'loony' Labour councils were later shown by researchers at Goldsmiths College to be untrue.[25] But the myths had entered public consciousness so effectively that in the 1997 Institute for Public Policy Research (IPPR) attitudes surveys, individuals were claiming that they were still subjected to this 'tyranny'. Interviewees said things such as, 'I could get the sack for asking for black coffee', and 'They are not allowed to sing "Baa Baa Black Sheep" at our school.'[26]

It did not help, though, that these right-wing attacks could not entirely be discredited. There is little doubt that many ideas that were implemented were ill thought out and resulted in even more public anger against racial equality initiatives.[27] Those responsible for finding ways to change the world were strangely indifferent to public relations, assuming wrongly that working on the side of the angels is all the publicity you need. There was also some shockingly bad practice. The London Borough of Brent, for example, had anti-racist inspectors going into schools to change the content and methods of teaching. The unit responsible for this was, by all accounts, Stalinist or perceived as such. And because there was so much bad practice in the name of good practice it became easy for white council staff and teachers who wanted to keep the *status quo* to reject all equality policies. Inefficiency meant that they had an excuse for their resentment and inability to accept how the country had changed.

Samantha, 'an English patriot', still can't see the point.

> I mean I was asked as a housing officer to make sure that there was all this counting of race and that. We couldn't do what had been done for years, let family members pass on the property to their families. I just used to ignore it all. It is our country. Whites should get more rights and I made sure I did my bit. I used to tell the local paper all kinds of made-up things to stop the council pushing all this equality stuff.

Recall too that the eighties were also a period of serious unrest in British cities.[28] Young black Britons took to the streets in Brixton and Toxteth in 1981. These were major riots which resulted in serious injuries and substantial damage to property. Triggered by the actions of police operating in these areas, the flashpoints were signs of deeper disaffection. This should have been a wake-up call for the country revealing the levels of alienation and racism afflicting inner-city black citizens. Police behaviour then, as now, was on trial and white Britons in power needed to make an honest assessment of how they had failed to create a cohesive nation. Black Britons, on the other hand, needed to look at how their young could be pulled back from self-destructive tendencies – which have only got much worse in some groups – whereby the experience of racism corrodes all sense of direction, self-esteem, even a sense of morality. All that we got out of this period of disorder was the tame Scarman Report which gave the useful *impression* that the British state was genuinely bothered about the deteriorating health of the nation.[29] The recent Lawrence Report has been received with howls by the right-wing press because it is so much bolder and less conciliatory than the Scarman document was.[30]

Naomi is fifty-five now. Her young son was involved in the Brixton disturbances as a very active participant. She feels that society failed to learn anything:

> My son was wild at the time. One reason was that he was a big child even at the age of ten. So if he played out on the streets, white people, the police, the traffic wardens all looked at him like he was a criminal. So he went with a bad lot and during the riots he set fire to cars, all that. He was lucky. He was not arrested. He saw his friends being kicked by the police and beaten up. But then I decided that racism or no racism, I should not let this boy rot his brain with the pain of it. So I sent him back to Jamaica for a few years where he learnt to like himself again. I told him never to use racism as an excuse because then he was really defeated. Today he is a social worker. Too many black parents let their kids get away with this kind of thinking. This is why our boys are excluded from schools and that. They and whites have learnt nothing for all these years. And the police don't want to learn anything, so that's that.

What was most important about these disturbances was that they destroyed black and white expectations. Wishful and naïve people make the silliest of assumptions about migration and the fable goes like this: the first generation works inhumanly hard, expects little, longs and plans for back home. The second generation learns to squander time and money a little more, partly because ease is setting in and back home is just a faraway dream resort. Their values shift; they get into terrible battles with the deepest values so carefully imported by their parents, but some kind of understanding is reached by both sides, partly because the older generation is also having to change in spite of itself. By the third generation, acceptance is complete, the problems are over. In Brixton and Toxteth we saw the searing disenchantment and alienation among those expected to belong because they were

British by birth. Previously, black community activists had themselves been immigrants with perhaps more anxieties of how far they should claim their place in this society. If young blacks, born and brought up here, felt this way, how was integration ever going to be achieved?

The Policy Studies Institute reports of 1984 and 1986 demonstrated that widespread discrimination persisted and that negative attitudes still prevailed towards non-white Britons.[31] The groups that were making progress (among them the Ugandan Asians with British passports) were those who had an economic base from which to start up their own businesses and buy their own homes, thus bypassing potential discrimination by white employers and landlords.

The raw and necessarily brief outline in the previous chapter and in this one of what happened to change the nature of this society to what it is today cannot give real meaning unless we can better understand the inner dynamics of the historical encounters. Who were the people who came over and what did they imagine this country to be? How did this then collide with or confirm what was actually happening in Britain at the time? The true and painful stories about high expectations and disappointment have been circulating for long enough without a befitting analysis of what was going on. It is beyond the scope of this book to go into each group which migrated but if we take three major flows, over three decades, it becomes clear that the political and cultural context played an enormous part in the narratives which developed in due course.

The *Empire Windrush* arrived here barely a year after the jewel in the imperial crown, India, had acquired independence and then disgraced itself with the bloody war of Partition. Anti-British sentiments were common around the colonized world. The beginning of the end was nigh for the Empire. The impact of this was immeasurable, as Paul Rich argues in *Race and Empire in British Politics*, particularly as the popular imperialism and jingoism of the late nineteenth century had become such an essential component of British national identity, which meant that 'opinion on both the right and the left took some time coming to terms with this new status'.[32] And if this was not enough to shake the confidence of this arrogant little island, the Second World War had altered the balance of power in the world as the US and USSR emerged as the only two superpowers.

If this vital backdrop is left out of the narrative you cannot possibly understand the mess which followed the *Empire Windrush* even as it berthed. In 1998 there were dozens of programmes, articles and books marking the fiftieth anniversary of the arrival of *Windrush*. Not one looked in detail at how Indian independence, the demise of Britain as a world power, seething ungrateful populations around the world who were not content to sit under the imperial umbrella for very much longer, and other events, marked the expectations of those who came and those who were expected to live with changed realities. Those first immigrants who came here must have had a much better sense of their complex relationship with this country than the myths and fables which have since been perpetuated about this historical period. Some may have been naïve enough to think nothing but the best of the motherland. But most must have had some knowledge of British hypocrisy (how could you live through British rule and not be aware of this defining feature of the rulers?) and of all the furious independence movements which had already gathered pace.

The internal context seems to be almost as important. When *Windrush* came, it started a process which not only disturbed a colonial relationship but also rattled class barriers which, in spite of the two wars, were still (and still are) an abiding characteristic of British society. Worship of the Royal Family was at its height, partly because it was felt that the King had proved his mettle during the war, and because the family provided a sense of continuity, affluence and victory during that war and its austere aftermath. This was a framework which gave this country stability in spite of the huge changes that were going on in the colonized areas and the postwar west. Brian Thomas, a Welshman who worked on the railways, explained how this was disturbed:

> It was a bit of a shock to us, you know, when these West Indians come and started demanding this and that. All this talk about equal this and that. We did the job, and asked for fair wages, then you went home, like, you know. These men wanted more respect, more rights. I thought, why should they ask for all this when we have been happy enough. These people who lived on trees came and started all this trouble. They couldn't see that we had won a hard war. That we

86

**wanted to feel proud to be English not upset by these complaints.
They were not grateful to be here.**

Over the years there has been much talk of a 'host' country. This is
possibly as inaccurate a description as you can get. The lack of hospitality experienced by black Britons is movingly laid out in *Windrush:
The Irresistible Rise of Multi-Racial Britain* by Mike Phillips and
Trevor Phillips. One of the people quoted is William Naltey, the
ex-RAF officer quoted above, who had joined up with enthusiasm. He
recalled:

> I suppose the racism crept up on me . . . Just after the war was over I
> was on a bus and there were these two service people in front of me,
> one a woman. And she was saying: 'Isn't it time they went back to
> their homes?', and it was the first time that it hit me that, you know,
> that people were putting up with us, that they really didn't want us,
> but we were a necessary evil.[33]

But even this needs to be looked at in more depth. It was mainly the
poorest white people who were expected to reach out, adjust to and
'tolerate' these immigrants. Those who had least to give were expected
to play the part of reluctant hosts. Life had not prepared them for
this role and their leaders had failed them miserably. Their minimal
education, the popular media and most politicians had told them they
were better than blacks but never to imagine that they could be better
than those above them in the class hierarchy. Their lives were hard
and most resented the obligations which were placed on them without
any politician bothering to consult them. On this and only this point,
Enoch Powell was right. Maybe politicians were right to judge that
asking people for permission for 'coloured' immigration would have
been unwise. But a narrative based on the pride and joy of the war
victory could have been developed and the people might have been
co-opted by skill and conviction.

But while people like Brian were clinging on to old certainties, the
entire infrastructure was being reconstructed. This further complicates
the story. It is indisputable that when the first wave of Afro-Caribbeans
came to this country, in spite of the raw racism they encountered, they
did also see the best of British courage, enterprise and statesmanship

as the welfare state was created by extraordinary idealists like William Beveridge and Aneurin Bevan. They were angry and humiliated much of the time. But even as their hopes and dreams were forced to crumble, their admiration for what the country was trying to achieve as a national project must have been overwhelming.

At least they could still bear witness to and participate in massive projects which made the country unique in this half of the century. The Attlee government which was in power from 1945 to 1951 mapped out a remarkable project. In 1946, the National Health Service Act established the principle of free health care for the nation. This was also the period which laid down the foundations for the welfare state. The wars had changed expectations and the cravings for a new beginning were rife. Black ex-soldiers and pilots still feel immensely important bonds with Britain, the Allies and what they stood for. Many of the immigrants who came in the fifties therefore felt anger but also, in almost equal measure, affection and pride. Some felt the anger because they resented the affection they did not want to feel. Serena Brown, whose husband was in the RAF and who came over from Jamaica, typifies this mass of conflicting emotions:

> We came at a time when things were not so clear as they are now. Our young speak too clearly about being Black British and being proud of their difference. We had fought in the war. That changes you. You think you have a common destiny when you have had a common enemy. And there was much to admire in this country then. Our children say we put up with too much racism without understanding this. But at the same time, too, you knew that people like Nkrumah and others thought very differently about the British. They felt a hate we could not feel because in spite of the terrible racism we wanted a stake in this new nation. It is probably too muddled what I am trying to explain, my dear.

Mrs Brenda Dole, midwife for forty years, felt similarly in the 1950s.

> How can I explain all those winds that were blowing through our hearts at the time? I was in love with this country and that love only grew when I came here and became attached to the National Health Service. I loved the clean hospitals, the efficiency and order. I hated

the disorder I had left behind. I was in love with this very nice white churchman, so all those feelings of pride and love were there. But they were beaten down, beaten down again and again by racism, ignorance, abuse, such unfairness to us, Christian people who had fought in the war with the best of them.

That this love could blossom in the fifties is astonishing in some ways because this decade saw an escalation in anti-imperial struggles. There was the Mau Mau rebellion and emergency in Kenya in 1952. Strong, uncompromising African nationalist leaders such as Nkrumah, Nyerere, Kenyatta created racist nightmares in white people across the world. Andrew Gibbs, who used to be a member of the old National Front Party, explained this:

We read about our women being raped and ritual murders and blood drinking by the Mau Mau. Thugs like Kenyatta stood up to us like we were nothing. So one night I went out into the streets with my friend Ken and beat up two black men, one so badly that one of them was blowing bubbles of blood out on the street. We did not want them here, not after the Mau Mau. They could do the same here, you know.

The relationship between the end of empire and the immigration of non-white people, the overlap, the confusion, the battle of loyalties and belonging cannot be overestimated nor oversimplified. Nor can any of this be disassociated from the other movements going on in this country for class equality and social democracy.

Most of Africa began to be liberated in the sixties. So did the children of Britain from the codes and social constraints of the past. Just as stony-faced diplomats and men in suits were supervising a semi-dignified exit from countries they had ruled for far too long, the new generation was indulging in one massive love-in, wearing unwashed kaftans and popping pills and travelling to India (not to Southall) to find eastern mysticism. Their love had natural limits. Remember, this was also the time of some of the worst racism in this country. The famous 'no coloured, no dogs, no Irish' notices stared out offensively in the coolest and most hip places. Immigrants were confronted both by the wildness of London and other places, but also by almost universal loathing. Maybe this is why those arriving or even those who had been settled for a while responded in the way they did. It was a response completely different from those of the people who had arrived in the *Windrush*. Manjit Singh Gill, a small shopkeeper in Birmingham, told me:

> We did not want to become English anyway. Not like the blacks who thought they were except for their skin colour. We had a better culture, better morality and we thought our children will be kept away from these bad habits. And we did feel very superior because all this mess was everywhere. The horrible short skirts, those young people having sex in Hyde Park like they are dogs. So all that admiration for that country disappeared and we just wanted to keep to ourselves because society was collapsing.

The diversity between different groups of immigrants, caused partly by particular experiences and expectations and partly by the history of that period, was already evident in the early years of arrival. This continued to be true when we, the East African Asians, came here from 1968 to 1972, as outlined in the previous chapter. We were probably even more naïve than the first immigrants. We were pushed to come. We then had to cope not only with ordinary Britons behaving badly, but with the governing classes – who we thought of as divinely able – collapsing when confronted by the chaos of that period. The relationship we had with Britain was deep, complex and contradictory. Arguably, we were more like the Caribbeans than those who came to Britain directly from the Indian subcontinent or black African immigrants and refugees. We thought of ourselves far too much as the children of the motherland, a notion which did not hamper the more sensible expectations of the other migrants, who might have been shocked by the lack of civility and fair play they had come to expect but who certainly never believed that they were the offspring of perfidious Albion.

East African Asians were oddly misplaced historical creatures, even before we came here. We had been in Uganda, Kenya and Tanzania for centuries. Early Indian traders had set up small shops and routes which the British then used for their own intrusions and ambitions. The end of slavery led directly to the indentured labour system, which one radical teacher of mine used to describe as 'slavery with pocket money' but which, unlike pocket money, was rarely paid. In time our ancestors turned themselves into entrepreneurs and we lived, traded and flourished in Uganda, Kenya and Tanzania but yet could never find it in ourselves to call ourselves African or to treat black people as equals. This too has historical roots. The British set us up as the middle class, the barrier between the black world which held unspoken Conradian terrors for them and their supremely privileged white world, high up on the hills where they could rule and drink gin, looking down on the rest of us. The social structure, which until 1963 was apartheid in all but name, meant that we Asians thought of ourselves as an arm of the empire not as resisters to it. We had emotional connections with the subcontinent but in time we saw ourselves as superior to Indians and Pakistanis too because we were a little more at home with western clothes and influences. I remember how we laughed at our Indian schoolteachers who were brought over to teach in the Asian schools because parents imagined the sap of Mother India could thereby continue to drip into our flimsy hearts. These teachers were good value. They worked long hours for low wages which most middle-class Asians were no longer prepared to do. So they came, Mr Kavi, Mr Gupta, Mrs Bose, Mr Amin. They pushed us, inspired and coaxed us to rise above our expectations but we still treated them like they were fools because they said 'wery' instead of 'very' and their convoluted grammar seemed to us so quaint, especially after we had seen the Pink Panther films. We foolishly gave our love not to Mother India but to capricious, indifferent yet flirtatious Great UK as we used to call it. Used to.

The early sixties had unsettled our beliefs about the upright British, but in a strange way the phenomenal popular cultural explosion which defined those times extended the colonial enterprise even as independence was spreading across the British Empire. Colonialism acquired its legitimacy not only through physical and political domination but by cultural hubris. This was made clear in the 1830s when we had the famous declaration of intent made by Lord Macaulay, who said: 'The great object of the British government ought to be the promotion of European literature and science among the natives of India.' In this they truly achieved their objectives and more, for we were not only taught about the tremendous creations and inventions of Europe, but were fed a racist interpretation of this excellence. Much of world civilization, we were taught, happened in Europe because only white

Europeans had the talents, 'natural' abilities and creativity to lead human progress. Such indoctrination was carried out with brutal self-belief. It turned into a self-evident truth impossible to resist.

Education, the arts, the rudimentary forms of media, all took for granted the superiority of British values and history and in one way or another built up the case for the ruling country and its manifest destiny. 'Like a Malaria mosquito bite, it is, this British way,' one of my teachers used to say: 'once bitten, always smitten, never to shake off.' The first cookery lessons I had in school taught me scones, Victoria sponges and sausage rolls. I came from a Muslim family but religious observance or even a lack of cash (a problem which lived with us like an unwanted member of the family) were no protection against a teacher's orders. We had to go to one of the two shops which sold European foods and buy imported pork sausages and learn to squeeze the sticky grey mass out of the skins. Some of us threw up and were allowed to stay away. But the rest carried on trying to roll pastry in the heat and struggling with the unpleasantness while our Anglo-Indian teacher bleated on and on about the theories of baking and when sausage rolls could be served, and how she had got her domestic science diploma in a place called Bournemouth. Caribbeans were even more culturally programmed, as many people testify. Ros Howells, community activist and counsellor, remembers:

> England was certainly the only place to come . . . It's like going to finishing school really . . . We didn't see England as a separate entity. For example, in my own convent school we spent a lot of time knitting little bits of wool for people during the war, you know the poor . . . We didn't see there was a difference between Grenada and England. 'There will always be an England and England shall be free' used to be one of our school songs . . . Empire Day was big in Grenada.[34]

And so it was throughout the pink world. This explains why independence fighters such as Gandhi, Nehru, Kenyatta, Nkrumah and others had to base their struggles on issues which went far beyond purely political power or economic freedom. All these leaders had the enormous task of deconstructing the cultural base which had so assiduously been built up by the British. The project was fraught with complexities because these leaders had themselves, from childhood, been nurtured on the values that they were now attempting to dethrone. Many were at home with the gentlemen of Eton. This is why Gandhi promoted with such passion his homespun India and why Kenyatta gave so much attention to reinstating tribal pride among the Kikuyu, something that he laid out in his book, *Facing Mount Kenya*. These men were pioneers in these earlier culture wars – not unlike those now happening in the nineties in the United States and, to a more limited extent, Britain – but theirs coincided with their emotionally ferocious political struggles for territorial sovereignty. It was exciting to go along with these ideas up to a point in the fifties. I did have a full week when I wore the white homespun shawl which a friend had brought back from India.

But then came the sixties and the reclamation foundered dramatically. For a while anyway. We became children of the sixties by proxy and through debasing envy. We wore diamond-patterned tights in the blistering tropical sun; op-art dresses were seen in mosques, and for the first time in their lives our parents had to learn to accept that the music we wanted to hear was not the same as theirs; that in fact we wanted to separate our lives from theirs at least some of the time, and that even if they watched us like hawks we would find a way to wet kiss and fondle and go steady. Not wild sex and drugs though. We were still too frightened to go all the way. So, even as we were freeing ourselves from one kind of British domination we had surrendered ourselves to another, perhaps more insidious, sort which was too attractive and exciting to reject.[35]

It was an affair with a distant lover which in turn had grown out of longings and foundations laid way back. It is a base so strong that for most of us the passion has managed to survive the pain of forced immigration, the horrors of racism and old age. While we were more than delighted to pretend that we were close to Britain, what many of us really wanted was to be here. Of course we would have preferred for it to have happened in a less ignominious way than it did in 1972. Since the beginning of a conscious me, pictures of this country had been floating in my head. With all the other longings young people have, I had ached for a place in this heart of greatness. I still do from time to time, usually when yet again I am spat at in the street for being an offensive Paki, or when I have to drag myself out of bed because I have forgotten to place a pail of water near the letterbox in case a burning rag is thrown in in the way it is night after night for so many people of colour, so that they never forget they will never belong. The middle-class white folk, equally determined to keep their ideas of Britain white, don't throw burning rags but ask you always where you come from. I had read the *Just William* stories and Noddy; I had tried when we could afford it (which was almost never) to drink cocoa at night before bedtime and to wear one pair of slippers only indoors in the evening. I yearned for a tie-up dressing gown, a strawberry, and little pink pixies.

It is crucial to understand the processes of colonial indoctrination which make subject people adore their masters, or how that adoration remains long after the masters have departed and surrendered to our indignant demands for independence. We know this but cannot help it. Anyway, even if it came out of an iniquitous system and racist world domination, how can one entirely despise something which gave in return, to someone like me, the wonderful possibilities of the English language and access to some of the greatest writers and dramatists in the world, not to mention endless ideas and inventions? What is important, though, is that the intimacy and complicated relationship we have with this country should have been understood when we came (what history did white Britons learn which left them so ignorant of their legacies?) and if it wasn't then, it should be by now.

But if white Britons have never understood our stories, perhaps we too have not given as much thought as we should have done to their disorientating experiences in the late twentieth century, of which the Ugandan Asians were a key part. We should have been better prepared and informed for the willed ignorance and hatred that greeted us. White and non-white Britons may resent the cards that were dealt out by history – slavery and colonialism for us, Black migration for them – but no one in this drama can put the clock back or deny that the same history which caused such pain has also been a creative encounter, making both sides not only different but better than we might have been if we had never met.

4
And So to Now

If the word integration means anything, this is what it means: that we, with love, shall force our brothers to see themselves as they are, to cease fleeing from reality and begin to change it. For this is your home, my friend. Do not be driven from it; great men have done great things here and will again.   James Baldwin, *The Fire Next Time*

        Take up the White Man's burden –
        Ye dare not stoop to less . . .
        The silent, sullen peoples
        Shall weigh your Gods and you.
               Rudyard Kipling, 'The White Man's Burden'

The minority communities are an integral part of British society and entitled to have a say in shaping its shared public culture. It is vital for them to be involved as full and conscious citizens in determining the kind of society Britain should become and their own place in it.   Professor Bhikhu Parekh, personal communication, November 1998

The historical account in the previous chapters reveals how the conventions for discussing and dealing with race relations and integration in Britain were laid down. They still underpin policies and discourse. Immigration policies are still linked to race relations with no real or demonstrable benefits to either area. A White Paper on new immigration regulations in 1998 says tough immigration policies are needed to ensure 'good race relations'. Nobody has ever proved to us, the

British public, Black and white, through proper research that the implausible equation invented by Roy Hattersley in 1968, which argued this race relations case for racist immigration laws, has worked to achieve this objective. Now even Hattersley has disabused himself of his own earlier position:

> **Good community relations are not encouraged by the promotion of the idea that the entry of one more black immigrant into this country will be so damaging to the national interest that husbands must be separated from their wives, children denied the chance to look after their aged parents and sisters prevented from attending their brothers' weddings. It is measures like the asylum and immigration bill – and the attendant speeches – which create the impression that we cannot 'afford to let them in'. And if we cannot afford to let them in, then those of them who are already here must . . . be doing harm.**[1]

Even worse than this, such rhetoric assumes that we are all stupid. If 'good race relations' depend on white Britons feeling that any more Blacks and their tolerance would snap, why have things got worse in terms of racial harassment since all primary immigration to this country (except for white South Africans, New Zealanders and Australians) has been stopped? Why is racism in white areas such as Cornwall and Somerset worse than in inner-city areas?[2] These white heartlands are reacting to the internal migration of Black Britons. And if we take this numbers theology to a logical next step we have to discuss reproduction. Birth rates in many ethnic groups are significantly higher than among white Britons. Are we going to castrate one in three Black Britons in order to keep their numbers in check for the sake of good race relations? This argument logically means that only zero will suffice. And if white Britons are still given these confusing messages – be nice to the Blacks here already but we'll keep the others out – it is little wonder that our nation remains lacking in cohesion or ease.

Not a single political leader in this country has the courage to change the policies we have or the assumptions on which these policies were laid down by xenophobes such as Powell. We are not free, as Sarah Spencer and others have said, to have either a rational immigration policy based on our needs or a policy which properly meets our human rights obligations to others.[3] Our dishonesty and/or capacity for national self-delusion is breathtaking. In 1995 twice as many US citizens entered this country as immigrants than did Nigerians.[4] Paranoia has rendered good sense dead. Writing in the *Spectator*, Anne Applebaum rightly points out:

> There is no evidence that illegal immigrants are 'stealing' jobs from natives; there is no evidence that they are 'stealing' from the state. There is no evidence even that they are a demographic burden . . . the best sorts of immigrants are precisely those who are illegal, at least to begin with. To get here, to live here, they have to be clever enough and entrepreneurial enough to evade the police. When they work, they do jobs the British don't want to do with unemployment benefit at current levels. They don't pay taxes – but neither do they use any services. By working as nannies and cleaners they enable thousands of British women to go to work.[5]

And these double standards still prevail. The term 'economic migrant' is used in Britain officially to abuse people and incite prejudice against those who are trying to enter this country for exactly the same reasons as unemployed white Britons are applying to go to Australia, Canada and South Africa. White Britons in the USA have for years obtained the green card through 'bogus' weddings with US citizens. In 1999 thousands of white South Africans fleeing the consequences of equal opportunity policies, have moved to Britain without any outcry. You never hear of police raids on unwanted white immigrants from the white Commonwealth. In a heated exchange after we had just finished being filmed in 1998 for the BBC's *Heart of the Matter*, the right-wing journalist Bruce Anderson told me that such people – unlike those with dark skins – were welcome because they were 'kith and kin'.

Even when ordinary white Britons indicate that they wish to break from these traditions, they are ignored by politicians and many opinion-makers. The surveys on attitudes to immigration I commissioned at the Institute for Public Policy Research showed that the majority of people interviewed thought refugees should be supported by the government and only 1 per cent thought the issue of illegal immigration was among the most serious problems facing the country.[6] Besides members of the family seeking to join those already here or those who marry spouses from abroad, the only group of people knocking at our doors in any numbers are those seeking refugee status – the country remains convinced that 'floods' of foreigners are still coming in because our asylum laws are so 'soft'. Evidence provided by the Medical Foundation, the Refugee Council and others makes no difference to those who should know better. What makes it all even worse is that vicious attitudes have been encouraged by some politicians and right-wing newspapers without any clear explanations that the 1951 Geneva Convention on refugees and asylum seekers, which arose out of the particular circumstances of the Second World War, only offers protection to those individuals who feel they are persecuted or in danger of being persecuted. It technically excludes all those millions of refugees who flee their countries for other reasons. A mother who tries to enter this country because her children are starving to death is in fact a 'bogus' applicant, an 'economic migrant' who is not entitled to refugee status unless we take mercy on her and offer her 'exceptional leave to remain'. This is the final stage of a prohibitive immigration theology which started in 1948 (following the good example of Queen Elizabeth I, whose proclamation against black immigration was issued way back in 1596). As this is being written, tough new immigration regulations have been established. They include forcing asylum seekers to move into 'whiter' areas and providing them only with essential needs in kind and not money. They are to be denied the basic human right to decide where they wish to live and are to be treated with less respect than a six-year-old with pocket money. They will be removed from others like themselves, will become easy targets for racists and will have to ask for their sanitary pads to be given to them.

As the unforgettable late Rabbi Hugo Grynn said to me one day:

> **First people were encouraged to fear the Jewish refugee. Then it was the turn of black and Asian immigrants who had every right to be here. Now we are told to turn our hearts against asylum seekers, for no other reason but that there are too many of them around the world.**

The damaging effects of contradictory messages about immigrants and ethnic minority Britons can be seen in a number of other areas too. Three generations on, there is still a belief that 'coloured immigrants' are not truly of this nation although they might be in it. The irony is that the British establishment prefers this view as much as traditional 'immigrant' leaders do. See, for example, how the Foreign Office has dealt with the issue of young Asian girls abducted and forced into marriage. It mostly abdicates responsibility on the grounds that these girls are still the responsibility of Pakistan, Bangladesh or India. Will they do the same if (say) they find abuse within a Scottish family living south of the border after devolution? Anisa, a young Muslim girl who has been a victim of this and is now in a refuge, quite rightly questions these attitudes:

> I was born here. My mother was born here. But I am still treated like I am a 'Paki' by the immigration people and my family. I was not even fifteen when they took me off to Pakistan and forced me to marry my thirty-year-old cousin. He raped me so many times I nearly bled to death and even my in-laws were afraid and took me to the hospital. A doctor helped me to escape and come home. My teachers complained to the Home Office and the Foreign Office after my sisters told them what was going on. They said they can do nothing. But they do so much when the nurses were arrested in Saudi Arabia for murder and those girls who are in prison for drugs in Thailand. They don't see me as British. My parents are sick in the head if they think this is right. But they also don't think I should be British.

If immigration and other areas of policy are in desperate need of modernization, so too is the education of public opinion. As before, mixed messages are given out by politicians and the tendency is to follow public prejudice rather than lead, change and inform public opinion. As Michael Ignatieff says:

> It is the invariable rule of European politics to think the worst of voters. Yet racial attitudes, since they are an unstable mixture of fears and fantasies, are especially susceptible to changes in the public culture. They are not a set of atavistic facts . . . before which all politicians must kneel. Racial attitudes can be changed. Witness how far British racial attitudes have changed since Powell's river of blood speech. Yet today few European politicians imagine they can lead or shape racial opinion, still less nail prejudice for what it is.[7]

Insufficient attention is still given to the need for coherent integration policies which would influence public attitudes and educate the population – black and white – on the realities of multicultural Britain and the changes that have taken place in the demographics, cultural and political life of this country. Myths have settled and are not challenged. This means that little is done to alter traditional practices and thinking.

But these are fresh new times. The election in May 1997 was a moment of liberation and so we might wish to ask: Are our political leaders enabling the British population to comprehend what has been happening to the country and to make this multiracial and complex democracy positively aware of itself? What have they done to answer the terrors in the national psyche? Have they helped people to move away from confused nostalgia or fitfully expressed pride in which both white and non-white Britons have been sheltering to avoid the winds of change?

There is some evidence that the ruling classes are now interested in creating something more relevant, exciting and fulfilling than we have had so far. In the summer of 1998, Gordon Brown was taking on the task of reconstructing the identity of Britain. He said:

> As the Tebbit 'cricket test' and the Stephen Lawrence case illustrate, there are those who would retreat from an expansive idea of Britishness into a constricted shell of right-wing nationalism. My vision of Britain comes not from uniformity but from celebrating diversity, in other words a multi-ethnic and multinational Britain . . . I understand Britishness as being outward-looking, open, internationalist with a commitment to democracy . . . [8]

At present, however, the project, exciting though it could be, is almost entirely theoretical.

'Re-describing the world,' once said Salmon Rushdie, 'is a necessary first step towards changing it.'[9] Thus far, I would argue, those with political power and influence have not only lacked the bold imagination for such descriptions, they have themselves sought safety in tradition and platitudes. Philip Dodd is spot on when he writes:

> So this is the crisis: the need to imagine a usable national identity for the next century. But there is also a further crisis: the failure of leading political and cultural elites to contribute to such an imagining. They are part of the problem.[10]

They are allowing themselves once more to be too inhibited and not open to the new realities, the new anxieties and, most importantly, to the new possibilities that are now before us. It is with despair that I see high-minded and quite deservedly respected thinkers such as Will Hutton falling into the same trap of assuming that the people of Britain are all white. On a stuffy plane ride to Glasgow, when I sat next to Hutton soon after his extraordinary book, *The State We're In*, came out, I asked him why race did not feature in his book. He was truly surprised by the question.

My inclination is to blame the politicians most of all for these absences of thought. With the increasing tendency of politicians to lay responsibility at the feet of parents when their children behave in anti-social ways, perhaps it is only fair for us then to ask why our politicians are failing in their role as parental custodians of the country and the people in the second half of this century. Politicians and most institutions – with one or two exceptions – have not done what they should have done and are still unable to see that a mature, much transformed, complex, multifarious, muddled democracy like ours needs more than new patches on frayed elbows to make it work and flourish. This is true as much for most of the black leadership and institutions as it is for the white. Wherever you look the new is repackaged (not even recycled) old ideas, and historical relationships and descriptions cling to everything like a musty smell in an old, airless house.

Plenty of room therefore for improvement. An urgent need too. As that challenging young writer (a heretic when it comes to cultural traditions of all sorts, though of Indian parentage herself), Bidisha Bandyobadhyay, who will be twenty-one in the year 2000, writes:

> The future does not look encouraging. Racially, socially, culturally we are all busy defining codes of behaviour, redefining attitudes and confronting modern dilemmas. Continual disappointment has led to politics being considered more of a national pantomime, part-comedy and part-tragedy, than a tool of the people.[11]

It is striking too that the narrative never changes even when this is the explicit purpose. MP and Cultural Heritage Minister, Chris Smith, a fair, modern, metropolitan chap, wrote a book, *Creative Britain*, in

1998. It was meant to be a celebratory tract on the new dynamism in this country after the 1997 election. Presumably. And in many ways it was indeed an unorthodox approach which tried to include the high and low arts and thereby avoid the fustiness we expect of politicians. But Smith singularly failed to see this country as other than mostly white (there are about eight Black names and four appear in a single sentence) and this exposes, perhaps, that when you look at New Labour, for all their talk about generating new ideas and ways of seeing, we Black Britons remain barely noticed and on the periphery.[12]

Black Britons, for all our protests that we are British by right (and such expressions in themselves are an embarrassing indication of how that right is still not taken for granted), are not at the heart of anywhere that matters at all. Yes, a few individuals are making their mark here and there. What would we do if Trevor McDonald, Meera Syal, Valerie Amos and Trevor Phillips were to be abducted by aliens? The numbers of black representatives on public bodies and in the media would fall by about 90 per cent. Reports by MP Keith Vaz on who sits on quangos and how the top end of the civil service is faring in terms of equal opportunities made for depressing reading. There are fewer than a handful of Asians[13] either sitting on the hundreds of public boards or in the top grades in Whitehall. Tony Blair himself accepted in 1997 that this country could not be 'a beacon unless the talents of all the people shine through. Not one black high court judge; not one black chief constable or permanent secretary; not one black army officer above the rank of colonel. Not one Asian either.'[14] He himself could change some of this without more ado. He could bring in black and Asian special advisers or consultants. To date there is only one such person.

The real influence that, say, the British Jewish community has managed to exert is not yet available to us. Will there be a time when a significant number of government ministers, European Commissioners, judges, BBC governors will be black or Asian? A time when they will be over-represented in terms of their numbers in the population? When there will not be a single area of life in which real power and influence is exerted, where the absence of Black Britons will be the lone exception rather than the rule? It is of course true that many Jews chose (because they had no choice) the line of least resistance and opted for assimilation, and that guilt over the Holocaust made some powerful people more conscientious when it came to this group. Assimilation is not an option for Black Britons, partly because they are more obviously identified and partly because most of us do not seek that any more. But we do have much to learn from the strategies which have been adopted by the British Jewish community on how to infiltrate places which really matter.

What all of us – Black and white Britons – should be wanting is to participate in the creation of a new nation for the next century; to work with the various tribes of white Britain and black Britain to create something as dynamic, to embark on a project as revolutionary, as the one taken up by idealists in South Africa. I am not only talking about entry, equal opportunities or representation. Those battles still need to be fought and others make better soldiers than I do. I am far more interested in a new society, a new country forged after melting down the best bits of the old. But how can we even begin the process when, as yet, all we have is exclusion and a dialogue of misunderstanding between the different parts that make up the body of this modern nation? This is a dialogue in which almost everyone secretly doubts the good faith of the other.

In order to carry out such a major project of dismantling and creativity, we need to foster trust and understanding and to understand ourselves better. Take issues such as immigration, politics, education, the media – almost any aspect of British life today – and it becomes clear how past failures persist. We must now put aside the various, largely useless templates that have been handed down by the establishment as tools. As Ian Grosvenor points out in his fine book on identities and the nation:

> The dynamics of the racialization process in post-1945 Britain have been mapped out in a variety of locations: in national and local political discourse, in media reporting; in the social policy 'solution' to educational 'problems'; in academic discourse and in pedagogical practice . . . minority groups have been, and continue to be, viewed as deviants from the norm which characterizes the national collectivity. 'Alien' cultures have infiltrated 'our' bounded nation, threatening 'our' culture, rejecting 'our' traditions, and undermining 'our' social

> cohesion . . . Racialized identities are a product of histories. Over a period of time they have been imagined, constructed, re-worked and developed in the English mind. Over time, there has been a process of sedimentation whereby they have become a constitutive part of the exclusionary ideology which underpins the idea of the 'British way of life'. Racial identities have become the cultural capital of British history. If 'race thinking' can be dismantled, the practices of exclusion and subordination which result from such thinking can be more effectively challenged.[15]

The concept of race (as opposed to the scientific truths of racial categories) is of course more than just 'cultural capital'. Racism is a brutal, live beast with teeth. It maims and kills our people as the black radical writer and artist Sivanandan says so powerfully. Or it destroys our hearts, souls, wills and aspirations by denying us a proper place in our country. Many friends and acquaintances have been victims. One is a lawyer, another a writer. They are both mentally ill today and on the sort of drugs which let you stay still in that awful space between life and death. Day in, day out, I hear stories of this sort. Tony's friend scooped his eyeballs out with a teaspoon while in a mental institution in 1991. Trevor still dreams about him and the eyeballs. Both are black men. Tony believes that these things happen because society does not will them not to happen:

> His whole life was about trying to tell whites that he was human like they were. Begging for respect. He never got it. Yes the eyes were tragic, but it was only the logical end to a long road where he learnt, every step of the way, that he was nothing. We can have laws against racism, training, punishment, big men making big speeches. None of that matters if the fundamental belief is that we should not be here. That this is not our land or our future. The boys who did Stephen Lawrence think they are patriots.

In the 1990s alone, besides Stephen we have seen the racial murders of Rohit Duggal (15), Rolan Adams (15), Navid Sadiq (15), Liam Harrison (14), Manish Patel (15), Rikki Reel (18), Imran Khan (15), Michael Menson (29), Ali Ibrahim (21), Ashiq Hussain (21), Ruhullah Aramesh (24), Panchadcharam Sathiharan (28), Donna O'Dwyer (26),

Richard Everitt (the 14-year-old white boy killed by a gang of young Bangladeshi men) and fourteen others. Thousands more have been maimed by racists – often young white malcontents who have never been taught right from wrong.[16]

What is barely accepted, though, is how that 'active' racism has been validated by the way public discourse on the nation (in which Black Britons are always interlopers) has been allowed to carry on, unchallenged. The two main parties still compete with each other on who can best keep us out of this country because that makes for better race relations – a claim which to this day has never been tested or proved by research or any other means. Black resistance and self-confidence has, miraculously, not been completely thwarted by this political dishonesty and thoroughly English trickery. Discrimination, racial hatreds, deliberate and unconscious exclusion are the reality. Tolerance is the empty word. Hardly anyone has had the foresight to see, as Bhikhu Parekh describes, that diverse immigrants 'bring in new sources of energy, break up the class system, and make [Britain] a culturally rich and lively society'.[17] This has led, perhaps inevitably, to a fundamentally unequal relationship between those who came and their descendants, and those who were here previously. English, Scots, Irish and Welsh people who moved to Australia and Canada did not expect to be 'tolerated' by those who were there before. They went to join them, as equals, to create new personal futures and to leave their imprints on the destiny of the country they were moving to. Sadly, madly, we, black and Asian Britons, became accustomed to this relationship too. Even when we were arguing for our fundamental rights, we had to make a case which was based on numbers, or we had to *plead* fairness and equality, or threaten street eruptions or remind white people that some of us had been invited over in the first place – all manifestations of our abject acceptance that we have little power or respect.

Some Black Britons have militantly (metaphorically speaking) avoided this route; they have assertively demanded not their small slice of cake but full citizenship rights and participation rights to determine what that cake is going to be – in other words, the politics of transformation not the politics of accommodation and appeal. Key people to mention here (and there are many more) would be intellectuals such as A. Sivanandan, Stuart Hall, Paul Gilroy, C. L. R. James and Bhikhu Parekh. These giants never parked themselves on the outskirts but have stopped the traffic by placing themselves at the major interchanges. They have seen race as part of the other battles for progress and it is for this reason that their controversial, conflicting, courageous ideas are even more relevant today.

For the rest of us, too many were co-opted, flattered, forced by desperate aspirations to take up that place that British society allocated to us. We had many plans to make these allotments habitable, exciting and vibrant. And in a limited way this did happen. But what did it achieve? As one ardent young Asian lawyer said to me at a Charter 88 conference:

> **What did you all do? Why haven't you had the impact that Martin Luther King made? Why does white society still not see what it is all about? How can it be right that at the LSE where I was, two of my tutors had never even heard of Sivanandan or Hall? Why have we always had to get our role models in America? Black Americans faced worse problems than you here – but they made an impact. You did nothing except complain about white racism.**

The point is that the tickets we had led to nowhere important. Neither black nor white Britons have benefited. Reading magazines such as *2nd Generation*, written for and by young Asians, is a salutary lesson. Past settlements are not good enough now. Black Britons have got to move out of that ghetto (or use it only for recreational purposes) and storm the centre and settle for nothing less. People with power will only take note if we don't hungrily scrabble round for that special deal, that scrap of Arts Council funding, yet another black slot on television or local authority handout. We must stop thinking of ourselves as marginal people at the edge and on edge all the time about whether we are being treated right or not. I don't want my children growing up in a country where they still have to make pathetic applications to keep a monitoring group or an Asian women's centre open.

Black and Asian people have made other mistakes and we must take responsibility for some of these. There was something terribly destructive in encouraging black children to think that they did not need to strive or shouldn't strive because of racism. That was surrendering to racism, which led then to the toppling of expectations and ambition for far too many of our children. The communities which took the opposite line – British Jews for example, who have chosen to over-achieve in order to defeat prejudice, even though this then becomes a further trigger for anti-Semitism – seem to me to have a better strategy than those who continue to feel that getting our children to do twice as well as white kids is worse than not getting them to try at all. It is important to remember too that, although all-pervasive, racism is not the only reason our children fall by the wayside. Other perfectly mundane causes take their toll too; not just poor teaching but laziness, bad learning habits, family breakdowns, the devaluing of education in some areas. All that is black is not gold underneath. The other major error was to use 'multicultural' as a euphemism for 'not-white'. Even today as devolution is upon us, we still cling to that term as if we own it. Mary Anne is a black school teacher and her views would be typical of this attitude: 'Why should the English want to learn about their culture? It's everywhere, anywhere. Multiculturalism should be about us and our history and culture which the whites have destroyed for centuries.'

And if we black Britons stopped dreaming in black, we could see that we have a magnificent alternative tradition to tap into. There was a time in this country when *ad hoc*, pathetic and small favours were all that disenfranchised working-class white people trapped in poverty had available to them. A system, the welfare state, was created where people became more aware and confident so that when they were claiming their rights to a half decent life it was not based on the idea of patronage or the notion that they should be content pecking at grains thrown out by the people who really mattered. That was the ideal and I know much of that has been destroyed by the politics of the eighties and nineties. But there is still something to learn about what happened at the time. The National Health Service and the welfare state were imagined and implemented as *national* regeneration, reconstruction ideas. The end result was not only to reduce inequality and improve access, but to make something which fitted into postwar Britain where class privilege and old ways were no longer desirable. It was something that the nation would be proud to own; it was a most worthy replacement for the pride that was beginning to dissolve as the Empire began to end.

Nothing of that magnitude was even envisaged to facilitate the post-imperial social and cultural developments which came upon the country. It must now happen. Lies and non-aspirational politics must surely be binned. The cost has been not only social fissures and political disenchantment, but also cultural backwardness, compared to what we could have been – not to mention a complete failure to know our attachments to this country and where these hail from. I cannot count the number of times I am asked why I speak such good English. A friend of mine, Nasreen Rehman, one of our most talented spokespeople on the arts and economics, fled the country and went to live in Pakistan because she could no longer bear this question. Seema is an artist. She is thirty and of mixed race and to her this deliberate desire not to know is unforgivable.

> I was born here. My parents came from Calcutta. They are among the most cultured people I know, who have a deep love of both India and Britain. For them culture is not a possession or a prison. They see their own culture like a vehicle which helps them travel into other worlds, arts and ways of thinking. They can recite chunks of Shakespeare *and* Tagore. Have you been to Calcutta? Even the bus drivers there will bore you with discussions on Margaret Drabble or Wordsworth. Over there we were intelligent enough – and our leaders were too – to embrace what was undoubtedly wonderful about British ideas and thoughts and words and we enriched our own long and wonderful traditions. Even though we hated the political domination. What have they done with what we brought here? Resented it. Wasted it. Why don't more white Brits understand ghazals? Or Bengali songs or Tagore? But the biggest mistake would be to become as ignorant as them in the name of our heritage. Can you imagine what a country this could be if white Britons genuinely grew to understand Indian music and dance or African sculpture?

Clinging to stupidity as an escape from complexity is one fairly common way of dealing with change. Simon, a young lawyer married to a Hindu girl, puts it like this:

My wife is an English graduate and she also speaks two Indian
languages and reads one of them. I look at her and marvel that she
has absorbed and learnt to love so much in her very complicated life.
Her parents though see this as a loss. As if there is something
dangerous and unwise in opening up your world too much. In that way
they are exactly the same as my working-class parents whose faces
turned to stone when I told them who I was going to marry. My mother
said she did not want to be bothered by all this strangeness in her life.
That she was too old.

Can you imagine where we would be if this country had been similarly
narrow-minded about food? When I arrived here in 1972, you could
not buy an aubergine in Oxford. I used to cry as I ate Birds Eye
hamburgers, which were what passed for food at my college. Today
the population has become so internationalist in its food habits, it
shames all the other countries in the European Union. New foods were
embraced with excitement and love by ordinary Britons and in almost
every area of this country – with the possible exception of the House
of Lords, and this too might change. Baroness Pola Uddin, the first
Muslim woman in the House of Lords, told me how her family chose
to eat at their favourite restaurant in Brick Lane on the day she was
due to be introduced to the House because South Asian food is not
served there. But with such rare exceptions, South Asian and other
'ethnic' foods have become an integral part of the British identity to
such an extent that even the *Telegraph* now describes Indian food as
'the national food of this country'. There are arguments one could
make that in many ways the lack of status afforded to oriental food
compared with even bad French and Italian food shows that Eurocentrism is still predominant among the elite who determine style
and status, even when the people have chosen otherwise.[18] But it is
nevertheless indisputable that this is possibly the only area of life where
the country has benefited enormously from its enthusiasm to receive
and learn from the 'other', to discard old ways. For every other area
of life it has been largely a story of loss, resentment, dutiful good
practice with the heart gone missing and general backwardness, which
at this point in our history is utterly and unnecessarily depressing. As
the theatre director and writer Jatinder Verma said on a BBC Radio

4 *Analysis* programme: 'I do not think that imaginatively we have become multicultural. I think in diet we have, absolutely, but I don't think that has translated from our stomachs to our brains yet.'[19]

Young Black and white Britons will not be able to live with this muddle for much longer and, unless we provide something clearer and more positive, tensions and confusion will lead to even greater social depression. I believe societies can show signs of depression just as individuals can. In the thirteenth British Social Attitudes Survey in November 1996, only 37 per cent of 18–34 year olds believed that this was a great country. It is perhaps no accident that across Britain young people are increasingly involved in inter-ethnic, inter-religious and inter-racial violence. A seminar I held at the Institute for Public Policy Research in 1998 to discuss this issue confirmed that, in the views of the Home Office Research Unit, community activists, the police and academics, these tensions and community flashpoints are a symptom of some deep sense of dislocation which we must take seriously.

Unmesh Desai, one-time fiery community activist, was one of the main speakers, and this is how he interpreted the problem:

> How are we to explain today the situation of 'gangs' of one communal origin attacking another communal origin? The way I see it is that the tensions are inevitable in dispossessed communities living side by side in conditions of urban deprivation. Partly it arises out of a desire to be in a gang, to feel powerful and to adjust to the brutal realities of the streets; partly it is because there is nothing else to do; partly it is a response to racism that goes overboard. But much more importantly it speaks of the failure of leadership, both at community and state levels to address these issues in a principled and courageous way.[20]

Alarm bells should ring. If the present is in danger of drowning our sense of well-being because it is so fluid, what hopes can we and our young have for the future? The interviews carried out with a number of 18 to 21-year-olds convinced me that the future looks as bleak even to the thrusting young like Bidisha quoted above (p. 101) because the past has been so disappointing. Rahim's comments are typical of the kinds of observations that were made. He has just finished his gap year after getting three A grades for his A levels. He is going to study medicine. He comes from an affluent middle-class family and his mates are of different racial backgrounds. They are all public school boys. He himself is a Muslim and feels this identity is important to him, though like his mother he hates the 'crap' that is thrown around by militant Muslims in this country. He feels no sense of a future for himself or his generation:

> My parents have made a lot of money but they have no understanding of what makes this country tick. They don't read the papers or watch current affairs programmes. They don't understand how Parliament works, how the civil service operates, nothing. Well it might have been fine for them then. But we cannot carry on in the way they did. So you start looking and you find out and what you feel is that there is no future for you here, because everything is fixed. You have one place because you are black. Or another because you are Asian. And somewhere else if you are white. Another if you are working class. Nothing has been shaken up here for centuries and they are not ashamed but proud of this. I went to the States for a year and things are not fixed in that way. You look around Clinton, around the generals, the top media chaps, the stars, and there are always people like us there. They are successful in the world because they are not set down in concrete like here. I am emigrating. There is nothing for us here.

We were talking in a group of six when Rahim produced this outburst. All his friends bar one completely agreed with him. Matthew, the white son of a solicitor, added:

> He is dead right. We are growing up with new ideas and the country is still stuck in the war or something. I hate it. Why shouldn't Rahim here become the Prime Minister of this country if he is any good? I don't want to be blamed for the empire and that but we will be unless we can show how we are changing as a country. I voted for Labour the first time I ever voted. But are they any different? I think I will probably leave too.

The exception was a young Jewish man who put up arguments which showed at least a trace of optimism and belief in the future. Now remember these are high-achieving upper-middle-class boys from the affluent suburbs. They are already better educated than many others, much older, are ever likely to be. They will go to good universities – two were destined for Oxbridge. Yet they do not feel the energy and optimism I felt at that age in Uganda where I was born. And though six even very articulate men do not a survey make, there is something going on here which social researchers confirm.[21] In March 1999 the Prime Minister and Jack Straw helped to launch my book, *True Colours: Public Attitudes to Multiculturalism and the Role of Government*. The event was at the House of Commons and we had forty teenagers from mixed schools in London come and ask questions of the government on this issue. The cynicism felt by these young people on the commitment of the government was a salutary lesson for us all.

To move forward, there is much to re-think and consider. As I have already said perhaps too many times, it is essential to shatter the usual patterns of thinking. One does not often hear of 'ethnic minority' Greeks or Italians in Britain. Nor do I see those who love opera entreating society for their space and right to be supported by public funds just because they are not part of the majority. They just demand the cash as if it is their right to have it. And they get it. But we, black and Asian Britons, it seems, are always to be described as too small to really matter, too far away from the centre of power for anyone to take note of what we know and what we can do. How it must reassure those who cannot sleep for fear that we will overrun this green and often for us unpleasant land. Nevertheless such configurations are enormously damaging to the reconstruction process. This pattern of thinking enables Charles Moore, the editor of the *Daily Telegraph*, to say in a powerful piece on what the Tories should do to pick themselves off the ground after the shattering 1997 election, that the minorities are insignificant because 'only seven per cent of the population comes from the ethnic minorities'. He advises William Hague to stop chasing their vote and instead concentrate on 'those people who are bringing up stable families, those who want to buy their first home or pay off the mortgage on their second one, those who are self-employed or entrepreneurs or devoted to public service or seeking secure retirement'.[22]

The fascinating aspect of this article is that in his head Moore does not see us as home owners or entrepreneurs. We are only 'seven per cent of the population', twiddling our unemployed thumbs possibly. This is not racism, but a view of the world where our incorporation cannot be imagined by the most politically influential people. The reality is much more complex than they would like, and is perhaps therefore studiously avoided. There are several other problems with the way we have taken such descriptions so much for granted. Under-pinning this motif is the assumption that this was and is a homogeneous, privileged (inevitably racist, according to some black thinkers) power-ful, harmonious white society which has been disturbed by the arrival of those aliens who would never understand the British way of life and would undo it for ever. Yet class divisions have ensured that this is anything but a wholesome, united, homogeneous country. What common British values unite the poacher, the gamekeeper and the lord of the manor beyond the belief that to stir up the *status quo* would destroy stability? While British men and women only partially share a world view and while cruelty and snobbery was always seen among white British women abroad, there were many more of them who, like the heroine of Ruth Jhabvala's *Heat and Dust*, resisted the demar-cations of empire and even attempted to subvert them. They married black men and had their children long before white men started along that path. There have been anti-racist whites in British society since the days of slavery. Blair Peach, killed by the police in 1979, was a white protester on the streets of Southall fighting against the National Front. Ordinary white Britons, even during the days of empire or the resentful period just before independence movements began to have an effect, were capable of electing the first Indian MPs to Parliament including one who was a Communist and another who was a Conserva-tive. They came out in their thousands to hear these men speak at public meetings; they honoured the Indian nationalist, intellectual and one of the brains behind Pelican Books, Krishna Menon. White people are as diverse as black people are and that right not to be seen as part of a herd has been denied to them for years. Many of them were and are as powerless as most black Britons and these days some black Britons have more power than whites, who see themselves as excluded minorities too.

When my daughter Leila was born at the fashionable Queen

Charlotte's Maternity Hospital in 1993, I, as a middle-class, articulate mother, could ask for anything I wanted. The staff were engaged and incredibly respectful. Next to me was an eighteen-year-old white mother from the neighbouring estate. She had no GCSEs and was both frightened and sullen. The nurses treated her with such contempt I had to intervene on her behalf. You saw this throughout the hospital and it is an observation I have made in many other hospitals across London. The young mother told me that she wished she was an 'ethnic minority', then she would be treated right.

Black people have also been failed by being described as minorities. It is a burden you can never shed. In a democracy, numbers become a crude way of asserting priorities and by giving us this label, we have been given our inconsequential place. It is not even factually always accurate, as Desai pointed out in his paper:

> It is my contention that in some areas of the country the demographic composition of communities is changing so rapidly as to make old policies outmoded. To talk of such communities as minorities is meaningless . . . Newham, my own area, shows that demographic estimates point to a borough where by the end of the century half the population will be of non-white origin and, by the year 2011, this figure will reach over 60 per cent. Rhetorical slogans from entrenched and vested community interests, usually based around giving of grants from the local councils, look increasingly out of date if not outright dangerous. For such rhetoric does not address the needs and aspirations of white communities who will after all be the minority, let alone the changed needs and aspirations of the majority communities of non-white colour.[23]

Increasingly in this fragmented society we are all ethnic tribes now, with diverse ancestral connections as well as several other identities (cross-referencing with each other), whether defined in terms of family relationships, locality and life chances, professional status etc. We are not and cannot all be diverse hybrid individuals living our lives as if we are bright new dishes in British fusion cooking, but neither are we merely members of a single hegemonic majority group or minority community. We must move away from the hopelessly outdated idea that only non-whites and maybe these days the Scots and Welsh have and need an identity; that the rest just are. And therein lie the most exciting conceptual and practical developments for the future. This may enable us to begin to include the English, who are in a state of inner uncertainty about what is going to happen after devolution.[24]

It might be useful, in thinking about the way ahead, to think European. That is our future whether we like it or not. If, over the next decade, we begin to get our collective mind around that reality, we will then have to accept that we are all minorities. No single ethnic group in the European Union is big enough to be a majority. There is something hugely reassuring about that fact. And this means that no nation or group can make grandiose claims or exert power the way perhaps that it was possible before. The end result of trying to hold in German nationalism is that all nations now have to be trimmer and more modest. We need to promote the idea and image of Europe not as some white Greco-Roman, Christian enclave, but as consisting of tribes (which sometimes go mad with blood lust, like the Serbs in the last decade and the Germans before them) which include the Romanies as well as the French and English or British Muslims and German Muslims. We may then stop seeking empty pride in senseless cultural competition (like Afro-centrists who simply reproduce the worst elements of Eurocentrism) and create an awareness of how diverse cultural and individual contributions have changed this nation, the continent and the world.

The real lives of British people reflect complicated attitudes and relationships with Europe. On the one hand they are a part of white Fortress Europe which sees itself connected through a common Greco-Roman history and Judaeo-Christian tradition. But there is also a huge chasm between Britons and other Europeans. Fear of assimilation into Europe is creating rejection of diversity on this island but that diversity is now so embedded in our lives that even the most xenophobic Britons are finding it hard to imagine this island white and homogeneous ever again. The elite can get all softly romantic about the Parthenon, but the reason white Britons mostly go to Greece is the sun and the sand. There is not much evidence of great European embraces taking place, unless one counts package holiday sex. Mr Patel and Mr Smith have much more in common with each other than the long-suffering residents of Corfu have with either of them. In fact Mr Smith and Mr Patel, fond, gay, twenty-something lovers told me so. Sam Patel, aspiring record producer just back from Corfu, was full of fury about those backward foreigners in Greece:

> It is so difficult for us English you know [*sic*]. They are not like us. When Jon and I were snogging quietly, nothing like we'd do in England, there was all this poison in the air around us. We are an island people; we are not like these peasants.

Jon, unemployed but wearing expensive sunglasses, agreed:

> Sam and me here, we share a history like. You know I love Indian food, clothes and Hanif Kureishi. When I go to Europe, especially as a gay bloke with my lover, it is one crazy foreign land. We are British. We have our own music, our ways. I can't ever imagine having a German lover. I mean we are enemies for ever. I went to Berlin and met a lot of nice blokes, but I am not comfortable with them. Not like with Sam.

Xenophobia is more democratically distributed, it seems, than we would expect but these observations may be pointing – in a very confused way – in the right direction. If defining Europe in this way takes away the notions of whiteness or of majority communities having to accommodate disparate aliens we can move forward. As yet there are no deep cultural bonds between the French, German, British, and other EU countries. What we have is an economic and political system which increasingly, we hope, will hold that diversity together and make various European countries work better.

In the latter half of the 1990s there are some optimistic indications that we are getting at least the domestic leadership we deserve. Gordon Brown is only one of the voices making the kind of statement the nation needs to hear, frequently and passionately, from all our leaders. It is important to note that between 1997 and 1998, three British Prime Ministers, three leaders of opposition parties, the Queen and Prince Charles, all made speeches which rejoiced in multicultural Britain. They made these speeches to white and Black Britons, something which had not happened previously to any significant extent. That must count for something. William Hague was mocked but he was the first ever political leader to appear at the Notting Hill carnival. Paddy Ashdown is possibly the first leader to have faced real physical danger from racist thugs in Yeovil, Somerset, in 1996 when he defended Asians and blacks living in the area who were being victimized by racists. The language used by key figures is at last moving on too from the demeaning catalogue of our contributions (as if we always have to show that we are over-achieving, paying our dues, making money for this country, to have the respect we crave) to something that lies at the heart of this book.

In 1997 both John Major[25] and Tony Blair,[26] his successor as Prime Minister, said that this country could learn much from the diverse people who now lived here. This is shockingly good stuff, although getting people to understand the implications will be enormously difficult. For centuries, we, the colonized peoples of the world and those who came to stay and lay their claim on the mother country, have been told that we have everything to learn from and nothing to teach our ex-masters. That your present is our future; that we have no option but to follow the path set down by our rulers and now their inheritors. That in spite of decolonization – maybe in revenge for it – that power relationship of cultural dominance can never be shed by either side. The alarming thing is that in the post-modern world, this cultural arrogance is in the process of reclaiming back the conviction which had to be shelved during the days of decolonization. As Ziauddin Sardar points out:

> 'Civilization as we know it' has always meant Western civilization. Civilized behaviour and products have been measured by the yardsticks of the West. Europe and now North America has always contemplated itself as the focus of the world, the axis of civilization, the goal of history, the end product of human destiny . . . Colonial history and colonial Christianity did their utmost to annihilate non-western cultures and obliterate their histories . . . Now secularism in its post-modernistic phase of desperate self-glorification has embarked on the same goal.[27]

A few knew better, of course, but even those confident folk were unable to imagine that some day wisdom might set in so that white Britons would see in us lessons to learn. Well, the time may be coming at last.

What is very important to note here, is that the sentiments expressed above by Sardar are those of a *British* person. The challenges he is posing could of course become dangerously self-justifying, although as a highly intelligent and erudite thinker Sardar does not fall into this trap. Usually. I am wary of people who believe that in spite of being of the west they are excused from the excesses of the west because they are from different cultural and religious traditions. We Black Britons are as greedy, consumerist, and as influenced by being part of the mighty west as the worst and the best of the rest.

Nadima, a young Muslim woman who is hell-bent on working in the City, with dreams of making her first million by the age of thirty, puts it like this:

> I may be Muslim and Pakistani by origin. But I am British. I want money, the good life, the works. I hate being seen as deprived. I hate the poverty in Pakistan. Why can't they get their fingers out of the till and do something right? I will not give to charity. Why should I? These people have nothing to do with my life here. I love the west, the freedoms and the lack of hypocrisy. We say we Asians we have such high values, it is a lie. We love money more than whites and we are so selfish that we have not developed anything like the welfare state to help the poor. We hate disabled people, poor people, gays.

The communities here who have historical and contemporary connections with the third world have as yet unexplored ambiguous feelings. It seems to me that even when Black Britons vehemently reject the label 'immigrant' they are announcing their acceptance of white perceptions which see third world immigrants as a blight upon this nice landscape. Many of them, for example, support our inhuman asylum laws and have strong anti-immigration views. The NOP survey I commissioned on this in 1997 revealed this clearly.[28] Their views of back home are increasingly coloured by the experience of living (even as underprivileged people) in the powerful half of the globe. Spencer, a retired Jamaican car worker, explained:

> It is very difficult to say this but you do change, become more English, even more intolerant. When I go back, in my heart I feel the place too dirty now, the people too sleepy. I get angry about this and I know

too that I should not be feeling such things. We are supposed to
pretend that the UK is all bad and the Caribbean is all good.

The responsibility that will need to be taken by us, the third world
people of the west, is to introduce a new perception which neither
idealizes the west and excuses the south and the east, nor its opposite.
Modesty and commitment is called for on all sides if we are to develop
a new sense of who we are, if we are to rebuild, renovate and rekindle
something richer than we have had out of mutual trust, synthesis,
respect and co-operation.

We will also have to stop banal utterings which have clouded the
way to such understanding. I want to spit out my teeth when I hear
people still saying that the problems we have are all due to 'ignorance'.
People from various tribes in this country have lived together now for
half a century. Our children have been in schools together and watched
the same television programmes, been ruled by the same politicians.
These three areas determine how we think about who we are and what
we want. If we are ignorant still, we should sack all the people running
these three key institutions. But we don't because too many have found
much comfort in the way they have not educated us. Marcela, who is
mixed-race, puts it like this:

> I was born here. My mother is English, my father Jamaican. We are
> not a species from another planet. When I talk about the racism my
> mother especially faces I am told by my teachers that people are
> ignorant. They are not. They are full of hate and violence for people
> like us. I do think that schools have done nothing to help respect
> between us, but that is another issue. No one in this country should
> claim that they are ignorant.

But, as Marcela says, schools have either chosen not to give, or been
prevented from giving, this central aspect of our lives due consideration.
Ten years ago the Thatcher government got rid of multicultural education and brought in one of the most retrogressive of curricula. As
the next chapter shows, the 1988 Education Act was one more gross
betrayal of black and white Britons. White children – like the sneering
thugs accused of the murder of Stephen Lawrence – have been through
the education system and some still obviously believe that this is their

country and that they are right to have racist fantasies about what they would like to do to Black people. I spoke to a group of extreme right-wing supporters for this book. Ian, carrying his sweet blonde baby (on whose arm he had drawn a swastika with a Biro), told me with true passion:

> Look, why don't you lot just understand that this is our country? We built it and made it. You were nothing, slaves and our servants for centuries. We don't want you here. And our politicians don't get rid of you, then a day will come when you will regret it. If I don't do it, this son will do it. You have no future with us. Your children are in danger – you saw what the Serbs did to those Muslims bastards. I have nothing against you. I just don't understand why you are here. Go and write this and tell your stupid people.

Exactly. Ian does not understand why I am here. Nobody has told him in ways in which he can understand. The tabloids and politicians have given him messages which have reassured him that his hatreds are, if wrong, nevertheless understandable. The schools have not done their job. But such negligence does not produce *ignorance*. It produces something much more potent and long-lasting. So Ian wants to kill me and my babies if I dare to stay on. Ian is not crazy. He is not stupid. He's got seven O levels and has read Martin Amis. A report published by the Association of Teachers and Lecturers found that four in ten children believe Britain is a racist country.[29] This should be taken together with new research carried out by the Home Office on the perpetrators of racial violence and abuse which showed that the abusers had the support of their families and communities.[30] For all the fine rhetoric, a multicultural, thrusting, proud Britain is mostly image-making of the most hollow and wishful kind. As Ada, a black mother of a mixed-race child, asks:

> Where is the sense in the way we are? We panic over whether the children can do maths – which is important, but it cannot be the only thing. The whole country is worrying about whether there will be blue rivers and green fields for their children or elephants in Africa or fish in the sea. I worry about all those things too. I want my child to inherit a clean, natural world. But what will be the use if our children inherit

our hatreds and cannot live together? What will be the point of the
blue seas and happy lambs? We have seen Northern Ireland and
Bosnia. Why is there no one in power at all interested in the ecology of
human relations?

Why indeed? Where are our fiery fighters who can move the hearts
and minds of this nation so they can be enlisted to create a country
which is not merely content with but truly stimulated by what Trevor
Phillips described memorably as the bio-diversity of its cultures and
which can give all its citizens a reason to belong?

The basis on which politicians on the left and right have worked
has been misguided. The way they have gone about generating impres-
sions and ideas about nationhood and national identity have been
limited. And they do not seem able even now, when the climate is so
favourable and right, to grasp and pull out these nettles and plant
something we can all be proud of. The Foreign Office remains a bastion
of (mostly) white Oxbridge men whose understanding of the world is
barely influenced by the world citizens who live here. To their credit,
Robin Cook and Baroness Symons have recognized this, but in terms
which are hopelessly out of date. They are still talking of changing the
culture and of equal opportunities. There is a greater prize available
to them. Getting Muslims into the FO, people with real insight into
the pan-Islamic developments which are a real force to be reckoned
with, would actually change the way we officially respond even within
the constraints of geo-political realities. Having a British Asian as an
ambassador to Pakistan might also help to solve the problem of the
young British Asian girls, like Anisa quoted above, who are whisked
off to marriages against their will. The government is paralysed at
present, not wishing to interfere and not wishing to lose the votes of
conservative Asians. Even more importantly, perhaps, having an Asian
as the ambassador not only to Pakistan but to the USA (why not? –
such things are taken for granted by the United States and Canada)
would finally put to rest the image of this country as still locked into
an imperial past and would show us at last catching up with a globalized
world. The possibilities of such an expansion of the national psyche
is too exciting even to contemplate. It is humiliating that we busily
encourage the idea of ourselves only as an old, royalist country, so

that tourists may visit us for our cute ways. The respect that we now need to build means developing something more worthy, more modern. Mark Leonard is so right when he says: 'Rituals are important. They are what bind a society together; they make sense of its hopes and fears. They allow it to be grounded and cope with change. But they must develop and change in tune with people's values . . . We need new causes to fight for and new things to celebrate.'[31]

This whole chapter is really one argument. It is an argument for a new culture of citizenship to which we can offer real allegiance. If we were to create another kind of society we would be able to heal many of the wounds that have been festering for decades. We might finally be able to destroy the pervasive class-consciousness which still exists.

Halima, a young science student at London University, must get the last word:

> I am twenty-two. I have talents, feelings, poetry in my heart which I wish to give to this nation, my nation. Will they let me? Can they let me or would it be like asking them to let the cleaner into their beds? What they will see is a young woman who has skin which is darker than it should be; a Muslim who can never be one of them. Well I am. But not on their terms nor on those imposed by my father. Whoever we are, Muslims in Britain have been profoundly changed in the years we have been living here. None of us would go to Saddam's country or to Iran or Algeria. I want to share my life and my dreams with this, my country. I want us to discuss, to fight and then make up. I want them to take me into their arms, with my difference, with all the light and shade I will bring with me. In exchange I am willing to do the same.

Distorted Mirrors

Identity has to do with a sense of sameness. That is what the
word means. A loose political identity can perhaps be built on
having the same nationality and the same rights. But a real
cultural identity means a cultural sameness, a cultural
coherence. Diversity is at odds with identity, by definition.

Minette Marrin, *Daily Telegraph*, 11 February 1999

All newspaper advertising and therefore the newspaper industry itself
is built on the premise that newspapers can influence the behaviour of
their readers. To argue that newspapers cannot influence their
readers' voting patterns but can influence their purchasing decisions
is irrational.

Martin Linton, 'Was it the Sun wot won it?', 1995

Three major strands of public life and the interplay between them
largely create, develop and change public attitudes in a working
democracy. The political leadership, the media and education between
them promote or confirm normative ideologies, manufacture assent,
hamper or encourage understanding. In addition, there is that large
space occupied by the arts, sports, music, literature, film and other
expressions of elitist and popular culture, which I believe have a more
limited – though very important – impact because in these areas choice
makes avoidance possible. I simplify. When Disney bombards the
public with a new product, the fragments fall on the entire population.
But nevertheless Disney has little direct control over what public
policies will be, or how we should think (based on what information
is made available to us) and what our children are taught in their

formative years. For this reason I will be concentrating more in this book on the first three although there is just as much to be said about the secondary influences on our lives, on which I have included a brief section in Chapter 7. One thing is clear too and increasingly so. The three giants who influence our thoughts and attitudes have mostly not fulfilled their role as arbiters in a multicultural society. In previous chapters I have examined the role of elected leaders. The next two chapters look at the role played by the media and educators in social engineering (which is what they do, even though they would deny it) and the social self-understanding of this, our multifarious country. Those who control sports or pop music have few hang-ups about this aspect of modern Britain. They have accommodated our contemporary urban society with exquisite facility – probably for devilish commercial reasons – and this has had an effect far beyond the offshore accounts. They have responded to talent and have understood the foolishness of not doing so in a way that most newspaper editors never have. Perhaps never will. No one needs to remind the pop industry or football chiefs how our mix of race and ethnicity has injected drama, excitement, new music, energy into the veins of this country. Black and now Asian kids feel that, hard though it will be, they *can* dream of being big names in football and cricket (even though here the old and the new world continue to wrestle for the upper hand), and most of all in the vibrant world of pop music. This is not a declaration of the end of racism in sports and pop music. Just an observation that in spite of this, black and Asian people have been able to gain entry, win adoration, and get promoted as *British* successes.

Of the four areas of the media – advertising, the press, radio and television – only one has managed to begin the transition in this direction and away from the cultural prisons they have built for themselves. Enormous influence lies with those who run and service the massive media operations in this country. They can make or break progress in all areas of public life. The impact of policies and politics on the changing nature of this once ethnically settled population is considerable but it is circumscribed. The ability of politicians to spin stories does make a difference but, like the emperor's new clothes, the importance of this tends to be overstated by all parties. The media likes to pretend that it wields no power and is only reflecting society, and the acolytes of politicians who are paid vast amounts of money to ensure control of what we are given to understand must exaggerate their influence.[1] In reality the media is playing such an important role today that editors are able to drive the political agenda even at a time when there is a government in power with an extraordinary majority and public support. That Murdoch is surviving and flourishing long after Thatcherism has ended reveals the extent of this power. We also have some of the finest newspapers, journalists and broadcasters in the world. So how has this powerful, highly professional and highly regarded British media done its job since it became an even more powerful fourth estate since the mid-eighties?

In 1990, the distinguished and passionate journalist John Pilger wrote a scathing attack on the British media in the *Guardian*. He denounced those who controlled various sectors of the media and reproached journalists who – with honourable exceptions – were pliant and simply maintaining the *status quo* by pandering to the establishment and to people's prejudices. They had, he claimed, failed to challenge untruth or seek the truth and (more seriously) had cynically perpetuated illusions about fairness and freedom to pacify the public. This failure of the fourth estate of the realm was in part the reason why, in his view, democracy had been devalued and often degraded in the country:

> **The narrowness of the British media is a national disgrace . . . The damage runs deep . . . Racism, for example, is all but acceptable . . . when will journalists and broadcasters break their supine silence and reaffirm surely the most vital and noble obligation of their craft: that of warning people that their rights are being taken away?[2]**

Pilger's criticisms have become even more acutely relevant, as the decade has progressed, for those concerned that the media is not just *reflecting* the depressing state of British society today but consciously or unconsciously undermining this diverse, mature, multiracial democracy and disabling the tribes of Britain by injecting or authenticating the prejudices which are bound to divide people and lock them in incomprehension.

The process by which this is happening, however, is complex and barely recognized by industry as it grapples with unforeseen levels of competition and commercial need or, more possibly, greed. There is a loop which goes round and round whenever the media is called to account and it goes something like this. The media is only reflecting the views of society, not creating them. And yet whenever their powers are threatened, the same people rise to claim that a free media is an essential part of democracy with a mission to explain and inform people so that they are not unduly influenced by vested interests. In a useful little study (quoted above, p. 125) carried out by the journalist Martin Linton, now a Labour MP, it was plausibly demonstrated that the outcome of the 1992 general election was affected by the pre-election coverage of the political parties by the *Sun* newspaper. And if this is true of something as precious as voting decisions, how can anyone claim with any seriousness that race, multiculturalism and other areas are not susceptible?

But the influence is less elemental and direct than was once thought. Until the late eighties, the influence of the media on race was discussed in relatively simple terms. Most commentators on the media were in broad agreement that the media *did* influence and reinforce public opinion, and even journalists were periodically willing to accept that, on race, the media had the potential to affect attitudes and behaviour. Harold Evans, when editor of the *Sunday Times*, made this the crux of a forceful speech he delivered in the Philippines:

> It is my submission . . . that newspapers have effects at two reciprocal levels on ethnic tension. By the information they select and display and opinions they present, they have effects at ground level on the creation of stereotypes and the stimulation to behaviour. Because of the volatility of the subject, they have also swift effect at ground level on the creation of policy . . . The Press must recognize that what it prints or broadcasts about ethnic groups can directly affect ethnic tension. Any organization not in league with the devil . . . must then recognize the commitment which follows. It must have a positive policy to avoid unnecessary damage. These are responsibilities which many in the press refuse to acknowledge. They do so basically . . . by insisting that they are mere mirrors and that news is neutral.[3]

Television is the most powerful of the three sectors of the media and it was easy, says the media critic Karen Ross, to take a deterministic view of it as 'an agent of social control feeding its audience with established propaganda'.[4] Stuart Hall in 1981, in his powerful essay 'The whites of their eyes: racist ideologies and the media', represented this line of thinking:

> How we 'see' ourselves and our social relations *matters* because it enters into and informs our actions and practices. Ideologies are therefore a site of a distinct type of social struggle. This site does not exist on its own, separate from other relations, since ideas are not free-floating in people's heads. The ideological construction of black people as a 'problem population' and the police practice of containment in the black communities mutually reinforce and support one another. Nevertheless ideology is a practice . . . It is generated, produced and reproduced in specific settings (sites) . . .[5]

Most critics also believed that television, radio and newspapers had and promoted a 'white' perspective mainly because ethnic minorities were largely excluded from key journalistic and technical jobs.

Their frustration was understandable. Until the early eighties, you mainly saw black and Asian people in broadcast institutions serving in cafeterias or dealing with the debris after journalists had finished. In the introduction to one of the first monitoring exercises carried out by the BBC in 1985, the author Cherry Erlich wrote that the Corporation gave the impression that the only black people who worked there were 'caterers or cleaners'.[6] It was the same story at TV AM and other commercial channels. Much of this information was for internal consumption and it did lead to the development of equal opportunity policies. Policies gave the right public image but changed little then. Thames Television, a company which has declared itself an 'equal opportunity employer' since 1977, had 40 black employees in its 2,000 plus workforce a decade later. It was simply not good enough, said the normally cautious Michael Day, the erstwhile Chairman of the Commission for Racial Equality:

> there is precious little information that we have about employment within the media as a whole. It needs to be monitored . . . it is no good saying we've got ten per cent ethnic minorities if all they are doing is sweeping the floor or if they are all acting in some modest

> support capacity . . . organisations are hardly going to change until
> ethnic minorities get into positions where the shots are called . . .
> many organisations have impressive equal opportunity policies but
> where does that take them? Not very far. The disparity between
> practice, activity and policy aspirations is grotesque.[7]

Those asking for changes argued strongly that an improvement in employment policies would change perceptions, inaccuracies and false stereotypes. The CRE made this direct link repeatedly: 'The portrayal of ethnic minorities in Drama, Light Entertainment and other programme areas depends to a large extent on the employment opportunities open to ethnic minority artists.'[8]

It was thus felt both inside and outside the world of television that if black people began to enter the industry and rise within it, not only would it be impossible to make offensive seventies' programmes such as *Love Thy Neighbour*, *Till Death Us Do Part* or *It Ain't Half Hot Mum*, but that we would see changes (long overdue) in the way factual programmes dealt with ethnic minorities and third world issues. Mark Wadsworth, one of the few black journalists to be employed in news and current affairs in the early eighties affirmed this eloquently in a paper he delivered to a meeting of black journalists in 1988:

> The white Euro-centric ethos of the British media is the nub of the
> problem. Black points of view whether from people here or abroad get
> virtually no coverage except . . . randomly through bitty television
> programmes where black people's concerns are normally identified in
> the white producers' terms.[9]

The highly experienced Channel Four newscaster, Zeinab Badawi, expressed her anxieties about the way Africa was represented on British television:

> Earlier TV coverage of Africa was born of a negative attitude towards
> Africans, and gave rise to negative effects. Africans were seen as
> colonised people. Their own culture, identity and history were not
> really recognised as being valid or important. So coverage of Africa
> was usually viewed from a position of overt imperial authority, racial
> superiority and cultural chauvinism. No attempt was made to cover
> this. With the end of the empire one might have hoped for change and

certainly there is evidence of a more enlightened and positive
approach . . . [However] cultural superiority is still presupposed, only
now it is much more subtle.[10]

In 1992, Samir Shah, then senior manager in News and Current Affairs, said: 'I believe very strongly that the programmes we get on screen reflect the kind of people who make them. By and large the BBC is run by white middle-class males and we get that kind of television.'[11] These were people on the inside who knew what they were describing and this was accepted by some key broadcast chiefs.

Compared to sections of the press, there was and is much less blatant racism in broadcasting. However, television in particular was guilty of imperceptibly excluding and marginalizing ethnic minorities. You rarely had the sense that Britain was a dynamic, diverse society. Ethnic minorities would only feature in numbers if they were held responsible for some crisis. More seriously, in news and current affairs, the set of assumptions which underpinned reporting often lacked any genuine understanding of black communities. This is how Tony Freeth, a freelance producer and director, described this process:

> When the safari hunters from the BBC or TV companies drive into Brixton or Brent, they've already decided what they want to say. Out come the cameras and anxious directors, looking over their shoulders for trouble; out come the long zoom lenses to capture the people, but not get too close; out come the bubbling production assistants, eager to please everyone and prove themselves by chatting up a Rastafarian to give an interview on camera. Safari tales in the bar afterwards – they bagged a real lion this time . . . the images and commentary, constantly reinforcing racist ideas isn't shoved in our faces, they are just woven seamlessly into the continuous flow of TV images. They're a powerful learning process for white audiences, who through lack of alternative information, have few critical ways of looking at television about black people. There's nothing 'neutral', 'balanced' or 'objective' about the way TV portrays black people.[12]

The BBC, much to its credit, even commissioned programmes to reveal the extent of unconscious racial prejudices in the most unexpected quarters. Two of these, *The Black and White Media Shows* I and II,[13] had Michael Grade, then controller of BBC1, acknowledging that there was a problem to be addressed and showed Robin Day and Sue Lawley making assumptions which created unconscious bias. It was this period of introspection that led London Weekend Television and subsequently the BBC actively to recruit black and Asian employees, to train their white staff on equal opportunity recruitment practices and to look at the way they catered for ethnic minority Britons.

When it came to drama and entertainment the picture was, until recently, similar, and here of course there was a direct correlation between the agent and the product you got to see. The Commission for Racial Equality carried out a study in 1986 and concluded:

> opportunities for and presentation of ethnic minority actors are still very limited and restrictive in both frequency and variety of roles. Most of the fiction roles given could be described as 'comic' or 'villainous' and it was doubtful whether the majority of roles could have been said to contribute towards racial harmony . . . there were very few ethnic minority appearances in comedy programmes or sit-coms. For the most part, where appearances were noted in this type of programme these were negative and stereotyped.[14]

There are now more black and Asian people working in the television industry than ever before and not just on the lowest rungs of the ladder. Ethnic minority presenters are no longer a rarity and a cursory look at the titles at the end of programmes shows that there has been important penetration of talent from these communities in all areas of employment on even the most highly regarded programmes such as *Panorama* and *Horizon*. We take it for granted that series such as *Black Bag, Black Britain, East, The Devil's Advocate*, all high-quality programmes, appear regularly on our screens and that black and Asian people are presenters and reporters on these shows. Trevor McDonald, Shahnaz Pakravan, Krishnan Guru-Murthy, Zeinab Badawi, Martin Bashir, Lisa Aziz, Nisha Pillai, George Aligaiah, Trevor Phillips and many others are highly respected presenters and newscasters now catering to mass white and black audiences. They do hard news, prestigious slots and some bring an understanding which comes out of who they are. When Aligaiah was covering the transition from apartheid in South Africa, he seemed to be speaking from his soul.

Trevor Phillips presenting the *London Programme* brings to bear not only his intelligence, but the experiences of being black and a Londoner. Of the few of these TV journalists who would speak to me on these issues none wanted to be identified and one said that it was very dangerous to suggest that their ethnicity counted:

> I know I am black and that in some way that must leak through. But I am a journalist and I would not want my bosses to think that I am any different in my news values or anything because of this identity. That would not help my career, to be honest.

Sometimes the process of change and advancement itself is revealing of persistent and entrenched problems. Popular programmes such as *Eastenders* and *Cracker* have integrated casting as a matter of course, but most of the characters are fixed stereotypes, as if anything else would demand too much of white audiences. *Coronation Street*, until the end of 1998, had remained resolutely almost all-white. Then came good news of the worst possible sort. A black character, a teenager played by the actor Joseph Jacobs, was introduced and promptly went and burgled the neighbourhood. In the same month Sayeed Jaffrey was brought in to play – yes – an Asian businessman in an arranged marriage.[15] He himself vehemently disagreed with this view when I spoke to him: 'I would never have taken the role if I felt it was a stereotype. I am very aware of the dangers of this. I am an international businessman, not a corner shop owner. Remember that.' Others' perceptions do not always tally with one's own self-perceptions but the very fact that Jaffrey had thought intensely about the dangers of typecasting shows how unresolved these issues still are and how much harder it is even for very talented black and Asian individuals – even those who have made it. Lenny Henry had to go through the same soul-searching times as Jaffrey and others if only to ensure that he was not allowing white people to laugh away their racism. It also remains true that stars such as Meera Syal and Sanjeev Bhaskar have not had the same massive exposure as their equivalents – Paul Merton or Jo Brand for example.

Over a two-week period in June 1996 the Glasgow Media Group looked at the main presenters of a whole raft of nationally transmitted programmes including gardening, cookery, quiz shows, game shows,

chat shows and comedy shows. Presenters of all the above, plus programmes on music, health, travel, consumer affairs, together with
weather forecasts, business news, current affairs and documentaries,
were all white. The BBC was as bad as the commercial sector. Children's
programmes had twelve non-white presenters out of ninety-three.
Sports did better than most. Curry may be the nation's food but not
a single Asian chef appears on our screens.[16] The report concludes:

> **Some areas of television have addressed the problem of under-
> representation by employing black or Asian presenters in areas such
> as news. Yet it is very surprising to see how unevenly this policy has
> been applied. Trevor McDonald from ITN is indeed black, but all the
> national weather forecasters are white; as are all the antique dealers,
> gardeners and game show hosts.[17]**

In 1996, Dr Guy Cumberbatch conducted a larger detailed survey
on race and television in Britain. His main findings were that the
representation of British Asians was the same as the representation of
African Americans on our screen – both at 2 per cent. If one compares
US output with British output, the representation of visible communities comes out at 13 per cent versus 6 per cent. Although serious factual
programming showed a high percentage of blacks and Asians, this was
accounted for by overseas stories and repeat appearances. Trevor
McDonald accounts for 3 per cent of all ethnic minority appearances
on the news. Afro-Caribbean Britons were well represented on sports
and music programmes and in fictional programmes. But others fared
much worse. There were only 40 Asian characters compared with 221
for Afro-Caribbeans. Britons from the visible communities are much
more likely to be seen as unemployed or working-class. Importantly,
though, a lower proportion of ethnic minorities are represented as
criminals when compared with whites.[18] With such uneven progress,
then, perhaps it is only understandable that immigration is discussed
only in terms of numbers and problems; black families are still patholog-
ized and Asians are *in general* only considered worthy of media interest
if they can be shown to be culturally 'backward', if they are victims
of racism, or (less frequently) if they have made good as hard-working
immigrants. Shami Ahmed, the millionaire Asian businessman, for
example, who started off with a market stall, is seen frequently on

television and has even presented *Dosh*, a series about making money, for Channel Four. Even when programmes appear to be doing the right thing, so much goes wrong. In 1999 the BBC ran a series on Southall and how the area had developed. There are hundreds of British Asian young people dying for a chance to present programmes. The BBC chose Melanie Sykes, a young woman previously famous for advertising lager who is a quarter Asian and who has no idea at all what the British Asian cultures are about. As she frothed over saris and showed cute ignorance about the food in the shops, most Asian people I know switched over in fury.

National radio has been even slower to change but here too producers and editors are becoming conscious that in order to raise audiences they need to expand their appeal to diverse groups. There is less educated awareness, though, that they need to do this in order to improve the way they inform and entertain the whole audience. In 1998 James Boyle, the controller of Radio 4, speaking on his own station, said that although he had cut all the 'ghetto' programmes aimed at black and Asian Britons, he was happy enough because Trevor Phillips was now presenting one of their key science programmes. Such attitudes are revealing and might explain why so little has been changed in the way the world is seen and understood even by the elite. Radio 4 is a pivotal station which exerts immeasurable influence on political thought and social opinion and some progress cannot be denied. Mainstream Radio 4 and now Radio 5 Live documentaries and features deal more than competently with issues of race and multiculturalism. Ethnic minority presenters are slowly beginning to appear on popular programmes and one or two people, such as Marina Salandy Brown, have become top executives. BBC Radio 1, Radio 4 and Radio 5 Live periodically take the issue of race as a theme and give over hours of high-quality broadcast time and resources. In 1996 the extraordinary Radio 5 Live series *Race Around Britain* showed what radio broadcasting was and ought to be capable of. Over fifty first-rate and challenging programmes were broadcast over a period of nine days, giving a real sense of the vibrancy of multicultural Britain, both white and Black. We heard the Scots and the English as well as the Chinese, Turks, Yemenis and others who people this island.

But although these are significant developments, BBC network radio does still on the whole remain overwhelmingly white and middle-class. In the highbrow programmes such as *Any Questions*, *File on Four*, *Start the Week* or *Analysis*, ethnic minorities hardly ever feature. White people are brought in to present programmes on multiculturalism (something that *Analysis* did with great effect in 1997), but black presenters are rarely asked to present equally heavyweight programmes about issues such as the National Health Service. As one young radio reporter said to me:

> If you are white you can do all the big stuff and now black stuff too. This leaves us with not even the crumbs. I work as a freelancer for Radio 4 and 5. I have two degrees. Yet when they are thinking about making programmes they will think of me if it is to do with curries or the *Windrush* but not genetics which is what I am really interested in.

The lack of imagination is staggering. When Hong Kong was handed over, not a single Chinese Briton was invited to go and report the event. We might then have been spared the endless requiems for the end of empire. The fiftieth anniversary of Indian independence had only two Indians presenting their views in over fifty programmes. Mark Tully, the ex-BBC correspondent, presented over a dozen programmes. Erudite writers such as the British Indian political philosopher Professor Bhikhu Parekh, or Sunil Khilnani who has written one of the best recent books on modern India, were simply left out of the orgy of imperial nostalgia. It was a moment of complete ignominy for BBC network radio.

And so the litany could go on. *Desert Island Discs*, for example, never got round to interviewing the distinguished Lord Pitt, or Norman Beaton, the talented veteran actor. Britt Ekland, though, got in because she had been married to not one but two famous men. Maybe also because she was blonde. A very good series about the ethnic press in Britain chooses not journalists working on those papers but a white presenter who then treats the whole journey as if he is somewhere in tourist-land, not here in New Britain.

But the position at the bottom of the class goes unquestionably to the press. Newspapers and weekly political magazines have never carried out any exercise of self-criticism. In the aftermath of the Stephen

Lawrence Inquiry some editors did have the decency to admit to this. The power of the press in determining the agenda, even for broadcasters, is beyond question. This dependency culture of broadcasters was the theme of a Fabian lecture delivered by Alistair Campbell, the Prime Minister's Press Secretary, in February 1999. What the press does makes an enormous difference. Their indifference, ignorance, prejudices are all amplified beyond their own pages. British society has almost got used to the rampant racism of the tabloid and mid-market papers such as the *Daily Mail*, which constantly peddle stereotypes. What has been less obvious is the extent to which what the *Mail* says is discussed on radio and television, often uncritically. The *Mail* shouts again about 'bogus' refugees. Rarely if ever do we get broadcasters questioning this definition of 'bogus'. Starving children from Somalia are not technically refugees under the terms of the Geneva Convention. Television and radio tends to follow rather than direct these debates. Politicians do too. Alistair Campbell's complaints about the power of the press would be more persuasive if his own government did not create policies (such as the 1999 asylum laws) to placate the *Daily Mail* and if his boss, the Prime Minister, had not enthused so generously about Sir David English, the late editor-in-chief of the *Mail* titles, whose stated mission in life was to preserve white old England.

Power has been knowingly used by these papers to put back the cause of multiculturalism and not always in the most obvious ways. The only other area where there has been a similar damaging consistency is the issue of political and economic integration into Europe. Both these subjects arouse deep xenophobic fantasies which are then translated into what passes for good writing.

In general there is more of a familiarity with the way the press functions. In that sense we at least know the beasts. We know that the tabloids tend to sensationalize news and to use racist language and promote xenophobia, and the broadsheets think they do not. The right-wing papers are unsympathetic to multiculturalism and anti-racism while the papers at the centre or left tend to be more supportive. And if some of the key events of the eighties are examined, these distinctions are clearly illustrated. You only have to look at the attacks in the right-wing tabloid press on 'loony' councils, the stories of 'race spies' banning the use of black binliners and 'Baa Baa Black Sheep', to see their predictable and rampant hostility. As Chris Searle wrote in *Your Daily Dose: Racism and the Sun*:

> The most recent butts of the *Sun* have undoubtedly been the local Labour councils which have moved towards the implementation of what they see as radical anti-racist policies . . . such policies and the details of their practice have been seized upon by Murdoch's journalists, ripped out of their contexts and made to appear absurd or in one of the most popular adjectives of the *Sun*, 'barmy' . . . This is a favourite device and almost every issue of the paper presents an example . . . usually employing crude and populist humour as well as distortion and inaccuracy.[19]

A report from Goldsmiths College London, published in May 1987, proved that many of these 'reports' were without foundation. What also began to emerge with some force at this time was the new racism of the right which no longer voiced views about racial or cultural inferiority but the more acceptable worries about the erosion of British values and a historical core identity as various communities with different cultures began to demand rights and space. Inspired by Margaret Thatcher (see Chapter 3) this bandwagon became increasingly powerful through the eighties, according to Nancy Murray, a researcher for the Campaign against Racism and Fascism:

> For the Thatcherite right to use 'race' as the focus of a cohering patriotism is simply to be true to its Powellian heritage – there is nothing particularly new in this. But what is new is the emphasis on rolling back the gains of anti-racism in the name of traditional freedoms, national pride and the liberation of the white majority . . . since the 'new right' began to consolidate itself in the early 1970s, the press has been a major platform for the propagation of its views. Considerable cross and vertical fertilisation has been provided by committed right-wing journalists and freelance writers whose natural haunts are the quality papers – *The Times* and *The Telegraph* – but who are willing to slum it for the sake of reaching the people.[20]

Immigration and inner-city disturbances in particular began to be discussed almost wholly in these terms from the end of the seventies. The *Sun*, for example, ran an editorial in June 1986 attacking Labour's position on immigration, claiming that this country could not afford any increase in immigration. Six days later an editorial was asserting the right of all white South Africans to settle in this country if they needed to because they were 'our' people, 'the children and grand-children of British settlers'.[21] Those who attacked multiculturalism were treated as heroic patriots. This was clearly evident with the resignation of the Brent school head Mrs McGoldrick who objected to the way the council was implementing multicultural education, and later of Ray Honeyford who had similar reservations when he was head of a school in Bradford. These events are described more fully in Chapter 6.

The employment profile of the newspapers was and is even more disgraceful. In most, even the tea-makers tended to be white (and male) since the orthodoxy was that you could move up from being a tea boy and into the editor's chair if you had it in you. The print sector has been the most resistant to change both in terms of recruitment and coverage. This is because jobs are not advertised. Instead, dinner parties and other informal methods operate, making the exclusion of black and Asian journalists inevitable. Until 1988, for example, when I joined the team, there wasn't a single black or Asian journalist employed by *New Society* although it was a magazine which regularly featured articles about equality and justice. Exactly ten years on, I started writing a regular weekly column for the *Independent*. With the single exception of the novelist and actress Meera Syal, this was the first time that a black or Asian woman had been given a column. The news is even more depressing than this. The *Guardian* carried out a survey in February 1999 and found I was then the only Black columnist in national newspapers. And yet the number of commentators and colum-nists is higher than it has ever been in the history of the press in this country. To date there are only twenty-four black and Asian journalists on the staff of national newspapers.[22] In 1995, out of approximately 5,000 staff journalists on national newspapers, not a single editor, regular critic or columnist was black or Asian.[23] Four years later section editors such as Kamal Ahmed who runs the *Guardian* media pages were only just beginning to emerge. The irony is that papers like the *Financial Times*, the *Telegraph* and the *Daily Mail* (which employs Baz Bamigboye, one of the highest paid showbiz journalists in Britain) have a number of black and Asian staff and their record is now better than liberal papers such as the *Observer*. Many newspapers continue to peddle the worst xenophobic and racist messages in ways which you would not get on radio and television which are more regulated.

We have also seen the rise and rise of the brutally 'honest' columnist in British newspapers. These voices are immune from responsibility or censure. They include not only the strange rants of Paul Johnson who wants the Empire back again because Africans cannot resist slicing each other up and eating the spoils,[24] and Richard Littlejohn (selected columnist of the year in the UK Press Awards in 1997) who produces thoughts like this for our consumption:

> **What I can live without are British women married to Iraqis arriving back at Heathrow and Gatwick . . . in full Arab garb and complaining about Mrs Thatcher's 'aggression' in the Middle East. They have chosen to turn their back on Britain, our values and beliefs. They should be left to rot in their adopted country with their hideous husbands and unattractive children.**[25]

In the wake of the Lawrence Inquiry Report Littlejohn attacked Tony Blair for accepting that racism was a problem in this country and in some ways more insidious than in the US. He wrote: 'one barking mad American feminist recently described Clinton as America's "first black president" on the grounds that he was sexually promiscuous, played the saxophone and like fried chicken.'[26] It was in fact Toni Morrison who said this when she was defending him against the Starr inquiry. For such wisdom, Littlejohn has ended up with his own television show and much personal power in the media. Littlejohn is by no means the worst – Gary Bushell makes him sound like a polite poodle – but he nevertheless exemplifies the way columnists have obtained licence to disparage black and Asian people and arouse racial antagonism. Carol Sarler is another voice of the people writing both in the tabloids and the *Observer*, who allows no temperance to get in the way of her deeply felt prejudices. Then there are well-regarded writers such as John Torode, Bruce Anderson, Janet Daley and a host of others who have made it their business never to endorse anything which is not old, tired, traditional, and riddled with inequality.

These days such views cross over from the popular to the broadsheet papers (it is common now for the same article to appear in both kinds of outlets) and this then gives the views *gravitas* and establishment legitimacy. And it is wise never to think that liberals are incapable of such xenophobia. In a brilliant exposé of these tendencies, Leon Wieseltier, literary editor of the American publication the *New Republic*, quoted two pieces from the *Spectator* which showed how this was happening.[27] One was a piece by the poet and anti-fascist Stephen Spender in which he wrote: 'Democracy is threatened in many countries now by immigration because immigration provokes the most reactionary forces in the countries now receiving immigrants (Le Pen in France, Nazis in Germany, neo-Fascists in Italy).' In another issue, the editor of the *Daily Telegraph* wrote this piece, already cited, in the *Spectator*:

> **Next door to me live a large family of Muslims from the Indian subcontinent. We are friendly enough to one another . . . During the gulf war, however, I heard their morning prayers coming through the wall and I felt a little uneasy. If such people had outnumbered whites in our square, I would have felt alarmed. Such feelings are not only natural surely – they are right. You ought to have a sense of your identity and part of that sense comes from your nation and your race. We want foreigners so long as their foreignness is not overwhelming.**

In the past three years I have monitored the coverage of so-called 'ethnic' and immigration issues in the press. Basically there are a number of set categories and frames which operate to keep us all in the dark. Black Britons can only really be muggers, under-achievers, rapists, part of some sordid underclass, anti-racist 'thugs and militants', drug dealers, sexual incontinents, good sports people and great singers. Asians are victims of their own culture, intolerant mullahs, fabulously rich, never-stop workers, and riddled with prejudices of their own. The fact of the matter is that all of the above are true and some are true enough often enough to be characteristic. But they are not the whole truth and the people swallowing this diet do so without knowing this.

It could be so different. One case which has rocked the nation illustrates the power of the media to do right rather than wrong. The

Stephen Lawrence case, until the report was published, was handled with unmatched integrity by all sections of the press. The *Mail* even published the pictures of the five suspects after they got away without a trial and the possibility of a trial. Stephen was seen as a young man who belonged to the nation which should have been better at protecting him and bringing his killers to justice. White people became involved in the fight against racism in a way not seen since 1959 when Kelso Cochrane, a black man, was murdered in Kensington. After the Lawrence Inquiry Report was published, however, the right-wing papers, afraid of this change in society, reverted to type by trying to discredit the inquiry team. The *Telegraph* called the Macpherson team a 'lynch mob'. The most telling part of this counterblast was this line: 'Middle England has been slow to wake up to what is happening . . . the report makes it intolerable for the defenders of bourgeois democracy.'[28]

But if there is one area in which the media has been almost criminally negligent, it is on reporting the issue of asylum and immigration. The journalist Paul Coleman carried out a survey for the race think-tank, the Runnymede Trust, in 1996. He found that the *Mail* had the largest number of articles on the subject, three times as many as the *Sun* and double those in other right-wing papers. None of the reports included information on the violations of human rights in the countries where asylum seekers come from, or explained that the Geneva Convention written after the war now provides intolerably little cover. None of the protagonists was interviewed.[29]

The *Standard*, another paper with this obsession to criminalize asylum seekers, wrote in December 1998 (just before Christmas as it happens) that we were in the middle of an 'invasion of immigrants'. The paper was describing a hundred Romanian gypsies with children. In February 1999, three pages in the *Mail* were devoted to what Somalis in west London are up to, claiming it was all no good. Jo-Anne Goodwin, who is billed as their top writer, wrote how these Somalis were chewing odd drugs and then without any respectable evidence claimed that they were unemployed (that being a crime in Britain in the nineties instead of being a shame for the country which disables refugees and asylum seekers from remaking their lives by denying many the right or ability to work) and furthermore that they were wasting public money or stealing private money.[30]

This kind of coverage is not only shameful for such a self-regarding profession, but is considered by groups monitoring racist violence to have incited violence against asylum seekers. Suresh Grover of the Southall Monitoring Group told me:

> We have started to get so many lies about refugees in the local and national papers, it is creating a backlash. We get many calls from asylum seekers, families, lone mothers with small children who cannot go out at all or take the children to school. They get worse in the days after such stories appear.

In 1999 Kosovans were similarly maligned incessantly by the press, and local populations in Kent attacked and abused these people as their applications were being processed. According to the London Borough of Hounslow, physical attacks on Somalis and other settled refugees in the area who had legitimate rights have gone up alarmingly since 1996.[31]

One reason the press has changed so much less than it needs to is that theirs is an enclosed, at times backward world. Huge structural changes may have transformed the sector, but the way they deal with news and features remains unchallenged. In 1998, for example, I wrote a cover story in the *Guardian* where I argued that the rise of the curry to the point at which even the *Telegraph* calls it the nation's food is no indication at all of profound cultural shifts. We are still disregarded by the food critics when it comes to status; it is European food – French and Italian – which gets all the accolades. Worse, it is only when white food writers appropriate the recipes that the food is given any place in the strangely mad world of the foodies. This is a drama about history, I wrote, and about making demands and amends. It is the Raj again, carrying with it lust without love, contempt and appropriation. It is also a drama about class.[32] The reactions to this were amazing. Media food pundits such as Fay Maschler and Drew Smith raged. Too many to mention were offended by the idea that what they called an 'Asian' (not British, you see) journalist had dared to question the way the food had been appropriated and then treated with disdain by this hideously snobbish society.

It is time we saw through this cracked mirror that reflects a distorted image of our society. But that's not all. We need to unpick the arguments

put forward by those who quite rightly are demanding change, and
test their assumptions too, because to take old solutions as still relevant
may be as foolish as keeping the *status quo* intact simply because it
exists.

For instance, it is doubtful if racist reporting would change dramatically if there were more Blacks and Asians working on the papers.
Personal ambition and a lack of real power would mean that they
could not challenge assumptions. I believe it is essential to have a
cross-section of people working in all positions in the media because
that is right and proper for a democratic nation, not because there is
an indisputable and symbiotic link between the producers and the
product. What we need is a complete change in our news values and
frames which does not just happen with a change of cast. If that is all
it took, we might have seen even more positive changes on television
where there are a number of black and Asian people in high-powered
positions. Trevor Phillips says this has not been allowed to happen
because 'on the executive floors where the real decisions are made
about scheduling, programme styling and tone – there are virtually no
black faces'.[33] I think this is simply pushing off the boat of responsibility.
Phillips himself and others such as the Channel Four commissioning
editor, Yasmin Anwar, have real power. They could, and do sometimes
(not often enough), break through the established values and produce
some interesting, important material. The BBC *Windrush* series, com-
memorating fifty years since the arrival after the war of black people
to this country, was indeed a monumental achievement and Phillips
was the key mover in this venture. Anwar's commissioning of a series
on Englishness for Channel Four, in which Darcus Howe and Peregrine
Worsthorne went on a journey of discovery in each other's landscapes,
was another brave and exciting idea, the purpose of which was not to
make black people happy-clappy but to inform us all of our affinities
and antagonisms.

More controversially perhaps, it has to be acknowledged that getting
ethnic minority staff into key journalistic and editorial positions has
not been an unmixed blessing. In too many instances it has helped to
validate racist and prejudiced reporting. Those in positions of power
have not, on the whole, made it their business to push for radical
changes. Perhaps understandably, they have instead absorbed the

underlying values of the white media to prove their worth. More dangerously we have examples now of black and Asian journalists and commissioning editors making racist programmes or writing inflammatory articles of the sort that white people tend these days to avoid. On TV, the highly respected *Panorama*, for example, made a programme on Muslims in Bradford titled 'Underclass in Purdah' (1994) which claimed most Muslims in that city were involved in illegal activities such as drug trafficking and pimping. Secret filming of innocent young schoolgirls was carried out without their knowledge and in situations which their parents were likely to find unacceptable. This sensationalist account – unworthy of such a department – was put out by an all-Asian team. All the main people involved in this programme have gone on to prestigious jobs within the Corporation. Ethnic minority editors defend themselves by referring to journalistic values. Samir Shah said in 1992: 'Some people argue that the distinction between propaganda and news value is a white establishment distinction . . . My own interest is not to make programmes that just propagandize or campaign for any particular community . . . I don't think that is journalism.'[34]

One also has to accept that white journalists can and do present 'black' issues very well. *Newsnight*, for instance, produces consistently sensitive and thought-provoking programmes on race and minorities. The *Guardian* and the *Independent* in the nineties have gained a well-deserved reputation for credible and well-informed reporting on multiculturalism, with insights that are rarely available in other papers. Black and Asian journalists on the paper are partly responsible for this proud record, although their numbers have been disappointingly small. But what is so heartening is that white journalists have shown themselves capable of understanding the deepest impulses of black and Asian communities and communicating these in a way that makes sense to all readers. They have also endeavoured not only to reflect the problems that multiculturalism has brought into a post-imperial society but do now, as a matter of course, celebrate these changes when appropriate. The *Sun* too is no longer easily categorized as a 'racist' paper. In the past five years the paper has carried highly responsible stories on racial violence, mixed marriages and high-achieving Asian children.

The opposite is also true. Just as we have women editors today who are as committed to naked women on the pages of the tabloids as men, we have black journalists who are co-opted to produce some of the most racist programmes and articles in the British media today. Or they are called upon to clear up the messy passions such programmes evoke. At the end of 1998 there was an appalling programme on Channel Four showing gang rape as a problem particular to young black men. Black people were incensed. Darcus Howe was brought in to chair a debate about whether such a programme should have been broadcast. He was then ostracized for his 'betrayal'.[35]

As the tabloidization of the broadcast media gathers momentum, we have also seen increasing evidence that black and white broadcasters are colluding in putting across crude and lurid manifestations of black and Asian life. As Dr Karen Ross says:

> There seems to be a definite and discernible trend in documentary programming, at least, whereby film makers invade and exploit particular communities for the sake of 'good television' rather than for the purposes of genuine understanding . . . for seven weeks during the summer of 1993, the newly formed Multicultural Programmes Department of the BBC exposed the soft underbelly of British Black life to the voyeuristic gaze of the television viewer.[36]

We had similar productions out of the Channel Four multicultural stable. A series on black–white sexual relations, *Doing it with You is Taboo* (1996), had black women speaking out on why white women were not sexually desirable, and also discussed the sexual prowess of black men. In 1996, the 'breakthrough' has been Badass Television, which celebrates blacks behaving badly.

There are those who believe that the price of getting to the top in the media in Britain is to surrender your community loyalties and regard yourself primarily as an individual. Others feel such victories are hollow and damaging. Such debates continue to rage among black media workers. A conference held by the National Union of Journalists on the subject in the summer of 1995 left matters still unresolved. It is not uncommon therefore these days to find black and Asian viewers who feel that both Channel Four and BBC ethnic programming have failed effectively to challenge the presumptions of white British society;

that the editors have played safe by reproducing stereotypes and only commissioned programmes that display the most negative aspects of black and Asian life for consumption by the rest.

Another big problem is that worthy people feel the media needs to change in the way it portrays people in order to make Black Britons feel good about themselves. By seeing better role models, so says this untested theory, Black Britons are both comforted and motivated to rise. Many an equal opportunity consultant expounds these virtues with religious zeal. The trouble is that such reasoning is demeaning and distracts attention from the central issue of how badly the whole society understands itself. And anyway, the role model theory itself is flawed and dangerous. The subtle but powerful message is given that determined individuals can always rise out of the stickiest swamp. Worse, for every role model the media fondly creates, there is in the shadows his/her nemesis. As the writer Kenan Malik puts it: 'To the same extent that society idolises certain black figures, it demonises others: for every Bruno there is a Mike Tyson; for every Barnes, there is an Ian Wright.'[37]

The point of having a Lenny Henry, or the hugely successful *Goodness Gracious Me* comedy series, which is now attracting even the resistant little Middle Englanders,[38] is that they serve to educate the white populations on the British nation as it is today. And in fact this is seen even by *The Times*, which actually ran a leader in 1999 approving of the comedy series as showing the face of integrated Britain.[39]

It is important to remember the context within which race in the media is now operating. We have had unprecedented structural changes throughout the industry and enormous political shifts which have impacted on the way the media and race interact. News International broke the power of trade unions in the eighties after the long-drawn-out strike at Wapping. It wasn't long before similar confrontations in the broadcast industry led to diminished influence for technical and journalistic staff in that sector. In the nineties the BBC has set about restructuring itself, mainly in order to cut costs. The consequences of these massive changes have been far-reaching as they have brought in intense competition, market forces, deregulation and a contract culture. There are no jobs for life, or even for a year, guaranteed any more and that volatility and insecurity is making it difficult to argue for equal opportunities or positive action initiatives, or even to compete fairly for work. And the outlook appears bleak, says Dr Karen Ross:

> without the gift of clairvoyance, it is fruitless to predict what a deregulated media might look like in the future, although it is not outside the realms of possibility to think that more will probably mean less . . . it will be a sad day if the precarious foothold that black media professionals have managed to obtain in the industry is blithely kicked away in the rush to embrace global EmpTV.[40]

The picture gets even more complicated. When you really examine the three sectors of the media closely, the differences between them in terms of how they have accommodated to New Britain begin to fade. For example, few, if any, custodians of high culture – book, film, theatre critics – are from the minority community. Ironically, even in popular culture – music, clothes, the club scenes where many of the leading purveyors are black – the writers are universally (and uniformly, some would say) white. When it comes to presenters and guests on the most highly regarded political or cultural programmes, black and Asian people are invisible. When the highbrow BBC2's *Late Review* started having black reviewers, shock waves of pleasure went through the intellectual community. As has already been pointed out, programmes that make things matter remain similarly almost exclusively white.

Black or Asian individuals never seem to chair mainstream programmes or write key editorials or comments, nor are they ever put in powerful enough positions to challenge all the central assumptions that still frame coverage of race and multiculturalism. The difference it has made to the Jewish community to have such voices is obvious. Columnists such as Bernard Levin and Melanie Phillips don't of course just deal with Jewish matters, but the way they feel about most issues is informed by their historical roots and their personal backgrounds. But when the Middle East erupts, such access is not forthcoming to Muslim intellectuals, or when South Africa was transformed, it would have been riveting to read the responses of a black columnist, had there been one. VE day had unprecedented amounts of air time and newsprint devoted to it in 1995 because it was the fiftieth anniversary. But although we had such overwhelming coverage, the media totally ignored the enormous contribution of the 3.5 million black and Asian soldiers who volunteered to fight with the Allies, at a time when many were struggling for independence from British rule.

Other problems have been emerging in the past five years in the way that race is dealt with in the media and (more worryingly) about how white people now feel about multiculturalism and British society. Highly intelligent liberal thinkers have started expressing views which would once have been unthinkable. Unexpected voices such as those of Fay Weldon, Melanie Phillips and others have been raised against what they perceive as threats to values they hold dear.[41] These are genuinely felt responses. Many began to feel those misgivings when the Rushdie affair blew up. Although there has never been any evidence to show that the majority of British Muslims supported the *fatwa*, because no survey was ever carried out, this is what commentators with influence assumed and still assume. There were hotheads and fanatical leaders who of course did declare their support, but their significance was overplayed because it served the purposes of the media better. The late Kalim Siddique, infamous for his extremist views, is the only British Asian to have had eight full-length newspaper profiles published of his life and views. His Muslim parliament had the backing of a few hundred people out of 1.5 million British Muslims. The burning of *The Satanic Verses* by Muslims triggered off memories of Nazism and totalitarianism. It was a false, if understandable, comparison. This was a gesture by a group of people who felt frustrated by their sense of powerlessness, and not an action taken by those bent on absolute power. It was indeed misguided and foolish, especially as the organizers had not considered the deep echoes it could arouse in this country. As Tariq Modood wrote in the *Guardian* in May 1989:

> Even when the Muslims began to take to the streets, as in Bolton's 8,000-strong march, on December 2, they were determined to be orderly and thereby doomed themselves to continuing invisibility. They found themselves silenced by the racially discriminatory judgements that lie at the heart of how race is reported and theorised

about. Faced with this powerlessness, the unfortunate but true
conclusion the organisers reached was that they would remain
unheeded till something shocking was done. This led to the
book-burning publicity stunt. That started a reaction with the
libertarian-left, which, when such stunts were interpreted through a
prism lent by the Ayatollah, culminated in hysterical denunciations
of the demonstrators as Nazis.[42]

Actually what the Rushdie affair demonstrated was a real crisis of
identity in the media and the larger cultural arena. Many of the people
who have gained control of our institutions were children of the sixties
who are no longer able to relate either to the empire or to the war in
the way previous generations could. A new cultural protectionism has
emerged out of this loss, and nowhere is this being played out more
clearly than in the media.

Four separate and inter-connected threads have emerged out of the
crisis of identity. The first is the label 'Political Correctness' which has
been used as a shelter by the politically troubled, says the critic Patrick
Wright:

[PC] provides the present-day realist with a neat way of mocking every
political and ethical challenge back into the obscurity of its corner
while avoiding even the remotest engagement with its claims . . . it
has become the reflex sneer of the Right that is no longer prepared to
argue its case. However it also has attractions for refugees from the
collapsing Left, stepping out from behind all that ideological baggage
to catch up with the opportunities of a world where everything seems
to hang free.[43]

One only needs to examine the writings of Ann Leslie, Simon Hoggart
and Melanie Phillips on Political Correctness, to prove this astute
observation.

The second point arises out of the PC defence strategy. Long,
unbroken Conservative rule followed by New Labour has ensured the
arrival of a neo-conservatism which is regarded as 'common sense'
across the political spectrum and the media, ensuring that any left-wing
radicalism is generally viewed with suspicion. What the perspicacious
American editor, Walt Lipmann, described as the 'manufacture of

consent' is these days more likely to be located on the right than the left. Examples are not hard to find even at the BBC, which is regularly attacked by Conservative politicians for having a left-wing bias. The highly respected programme *The Moral Maze*, for example, features regular panellists such as Janet Daley and David Starkey who come not only with impeccable right-wing credentials but express their views with a ferocity which would previously have been unacceptable on this station.

Third, we have seen a growing trend among journalists and media experts towards triumphalism and self-glorification, typified by these two examples.

> It only requires the most superficial stroll through the National Gallery, the Louvre or the Vatican to see the evidence before your eyes that western art is indeed an extraordinary phenomenon which has never been matched by any other culture. (Mary Kenny)[44]

> Britain in world terms is a society relatively free of racist tension and historically it was the British rather than the equally implicated Arabs and Africans who abolished the slave trade, so we might reasonably congratulate ourselves on being the most anti-racist culture on earth. (Bryan Appleyard)[45]

If you believe that the traditional west is the best, you say so, in your columns, in your programmes, many times over. Which is what we have been seeing. Carol Sarlar objects to the suggestion made by the Commission for Racial Equality that children eating food with their fingers was as acceptable as children eating with knives and forks, so she writes:

> [The CRE says] they are merely '. . . different ways of eating' and no one way is better or more 'proper' than another . . . There are also some cultures where they don't use loos; they just squat wherever they happen to be when the urge comes. So what should we do about that? Ban potty training?[46]

This assertion of superior values is playing itself out most starkly when it confronts Islam. The Rushdie affair gave permission for those who had never quite felt at ease with Islam in their midst to lay down

149

caution. Bhikhu Parekh, describing the contempt with which the British press treated Muslims at the time of the furore, writes:

> Neither the quality nor popular papers published the offending passages or invited Muslim spokespeople to state their case, or themselves made an attempt to read the books with their eyes. Instead they mocked the Muslims, accused them of 'intolerance' . . . Muslims were called 'barbarians', 'uncivilized' 'fanatics' . . . Many a writer of impeccable liberal credentials openly wondered how Britain would 'civilize' them and protect their innocent progeny against their parents' 'medieval' fundamentalism. Even Roy Jenkins, the architect of our race relations laws and believer in cultural diversity, lamented the 'creation of a substantial Muslim community'.[47]

Once liberated, this distaste has simply snowballed. Conor Cruise O'Brien writes with impunity: 'Muslim society looks profoundly repulsive, because it is repulsive from the point of view of Western post-enlightenment values.'[48] When the bomb exploded in Oklahoma, Bernard Levin fulminated against Muslims, accusing them of wanting to create 'Khartoum on the Mississippi'.[49]

What is disappointing is the way black and Asian people in the media have not managed to challenge any of these trends. In fact the anti-Muslim clamour was orchestrated in the ethnic programmes as much as it was elsewhere. People such as Farrukh Dhondy and Tariq Ali, in their rush to support Rushdie – their friend – behaved no differently from the way mainstream media was acting. They too assumed all Muslims supported the *fatwa*, that they were ignorant. They did not open up space for the counter-arguments, even if these were contemptible to them. They failed themselves and democracy. If they had had the imagination, they might have examined how the terms of the debate were moved. Freedom of speech stopped being a sacred cow. When we had the stand-off over the Orange Order parades in Northern Ireland, the philosopher Mary Midgley wrote:

> The freedom to insult other people when one feels like it merely corresponds to a freedom to discharge noxious fumes over their dwellings. This kind of freedom is not seriously defensible. It follows, however sadly, that we cannot always have the freedom to go on doing

exactly the things that our forefathers did. But if we can do something better instead, perhaps this need not be a disaster.[50]

A Muslim could not have put it better.

Finally, then, to the fourth thread, the underlying anxiety which is increasingly also reflected in the media. There is a reassertion of Englishness, or a Britishness which reveals the extent to which people are feeling insecure about their historical identity. To see how that is infecting the media we only have to look at the ongoing cricket controversy. A few years ago, Norman Tebbit pronounced that the true test of identity for a British person was which cricket team they supported. In July 1995, the Wisden Cricket Monthly published an article expanding this theory to the players, claiming that the desire to play for England was 'instinctive, a matter of biology' and that 'outsiders' were unlikely to put their hearts and souls into fighting for Britain. What was deeply disappointing was the fact that Matthew Engels, an experienced *Guardian* journalist with impeccable liberal credentials, did in part agree with this thesis. He argued that in team sports those with a strong and unequivocal 'national identity' performed better than those without.[51] What these writers are grappling with is a British identity which takes them back into some glorious past, and in some ways away from the complicated world of multi-culturalism. They are simply examples of what Philip Dodd describes as 'the national psyche which in most of its variants is a tale of backward looking insularity, melancholy, decline and loss'.[52]

Finally, a word about advertising which itself is both slave and master of much of the media today. Except for public service broadcasting, that is. There is no doubt that advertising influences society. Sir Michael Perry of Unilever has spoken of 'interpreting aspirations'. In a report on advertising and race the Glasgow Media Group argued that advertising permeates our social relations and perceptions.[53] In 1996 the *Sunday Telegraph* ran this headline: 'Are Black Faces Good For Business?' Leaving aside the offending headline, the article was a depressingly honest account of what was going on in this sector. The advertising agency Ogilvy and Mather stood accused of racism when it was shown to have superimposed white faces on what had originally been a happy picture of the team of black and white workers at the Ford car factory.

The change was made for a new brochure. Ford said workers had been whited up because the brochure was going to Poland where the population was 99.9 per cent white. There was no evidence to show that brochures produced for the South African market, say, were similarly blacked up. In 1995, British Airways had been caught up in a similar scandal because their commercials director claimed that the company had insisted on images of 'cheery white' faces. As the writer Dominic Mills asserts (in the *Sunday Telegraph*, remember):

> Despite the assimilation of ethnic minorities into this country, the vast majority of advertisements do not feature blacks, Asians, Chinese, Greeks, Muslims or, indeed, any of the 5.5% of the British adult population who describe themselves as belonging to an ethnic minority group. Not a beer ad, not a car ad, not a bank or building society and certainly not an Oxo ad or anything for a household cleaning product.[54]

This is even more remarkable considering that the advertising industry likes to think of itself as modern, at the cutting edge of social change and promoting binding and 'warm' values. Some stars such as Ian Wright and boxer Prince Naseem are increasingly beginning to appear, as are brightly coloured Indians advertising spices and the like. Children too are now seen more and more but even here a cool and calculated selection process is well established and understood by all those links in the chain from product to advert. In 1997 when I interviewed casting agents on the use of children in advertisements and commercials, most told me that white children were still preferred, with mixed-race children coming second, especially those not too obviously 'coloured', as one of the agents put it. In 1996 an advertisement for Vauxhall Astra featured 2,000 babies. Only one black baby was seen, right at the back.

It is bad enough that these attitudes still prevail, but it makes it even more unacceptable that they are based on so little good business sense. As Yvonne Thompson, managing director of ASAP, Britain's largest specialist advertising agency for black people, says repeatedly, black families have more children on average than white families, and therefore buy more food, nappies, clothes. There are more black and Asian people than before in higher education and entering the middle classes.

Things are changing, but so slowly that you always note the adverts which are breaking the mould and you remember them. A report commissioned by the Race for Opportunity (a conglomerate of British businesses committed to promoting equality of opportunity for black and Asian Britons) revealed that these communities – who spend £10 billion a year – feel they are ignored and at times insulted by the advertising industry. Examples were given, such as the Persil advert in which a Dalmatian was shown shaking off his 'dirty' black spots, and the almost deliberately offensive series of Benetton adverts. What was most interesting about this survey was how ethnic groups were still drawn to big name brands which were perceived to be truly 'British', and the report concluded that this showed a 'fervent desire to be accepted, understood, and integrated' into British life.[55] This would indeed be true of all the sectors described in this chapter. Many, many of my interviewees felt more outraged by the way the British media, rather than any other sector, had responded to multiculturalism. I include a small selection of these comments.

> The British media is racist, and wants us out of here. I have stopped buying white newspapers and only listen to Sunrise, the Asian radio station. (Sunita, aged 20, a council worker)

> I don't trust any journalists, white or black. Not even you. You have sold out and sold us without any respect. Not even the BBC is trustworthy. You have done such damage to race relations, I hope you pay for this one day. (Ringo, 25, a black musician)

> I now have a daughter-in-law who is Chinese. So I have had to rethink how I have been taught about my country. Now I look at television and the papers and I can see how blind they have kept us. I knew nothing about the British Chinese. Why not?
> (Edward, 65, ex-bank employee from Scotland)

6
Learning Not to Know

In 1999 the much admired BBC special correspondent Fergal Keane
(who describes himself as a liberal) wrote: 'I don't have many black
or Asian friends here: I don't meet a great many in my daily rounds
but by and large I have been impressed by the way that people of all
races seem to get on with one another.'[2] This was an uncomfortable
account of himself, prompted, says Keane, by the case of five young
British men – all Muslims, most born here – who were incarcerated in
a Yemeni prison accused of acts of terrorism against westerners in that
country. He looked at himself and realized that these men, because
they were called Shahid, Malek, Ghulam, Mohsin and Sirmad, did not
arouse in most indigenous British people the same sense of national
brotherhood as they would have done if they were white. This little
confession unsettled me for days. This is a man I have admired for
years because he has truly had a mission to explain the world in ways

154

which are essential. He showed us the humanity behind the inhumanity in Rwanda, and the truth of third world and global iniquities, by breaking away from numbers and giving us real lives. Yet he says he has hardly any black or Asian friends in this country. If this is true, then is not all our multiculturalism completely meaningless?

Other alarm bells ring too around this particular story of the five Muslim men. If there is any truth in the allegations that these British Muslim men were involved in anti-western activities how did this come about? How can British people so readily turn on their own compatriots in spite of growing up here? The men have probably been set up in Yemen by a government embarrassed about the rising number of kidnappings. But some of these perfectly ordinary young men, like many others, have indeed had some kind of contact with raging anti-British Islamic fanatics in this country. Remember too that these British Muslim men are the children of those who were prepared to give up their lives fighting for the Allies. Their fathers don't understand them any better than the rest of us can. Abdul Reza, a butcher in a small town in the north, is the father of a young Muslim man who is disenchanted:

> My father fought in the British army in Burma. We have framed
> photos of him in medal. Sajjid, my son, he doesn't want that photo in
> the house. He has joined some Muslim group. I am afraid of his
> anger. All this talk about Muslims will rule the world and learning
> about bombs. I tell you, the children are learning nothing in the
> schools and then all that space in the brain is filled with anger and
> stupid hatred.

This hatred is even more dangerous sweltering and sheltering in the heads of young white people. The Stephen Lawrence Report, commissioned by the Labour government, was published in 1999. Stephen was murdered by five young white racists who will never now be brought to justice. They grew up in Greenwich which has been a solidly multi-ethnic area for fifty years. It has also been a den for young fascists and British National Party supporters. One such boy, aged fifteen, told me:

> I hate niggers, Jews, Pakis and those bastard half-castes – they are
> the worst. They are dirty like. No pure blood. Sure I beat them up

**when I can. Even in school. I hate school. It's full of Jew teachers.
This is a white country. We ruled these monkeys before they came
here with their horrible smells. The whole school smells with them.
My mother is Christian like. She thinks I am mad.**

In 1997, the pop broadcasters MTV conducted a survey among 16–
24 year olds across the European Union. In Britain these young people
were more sexually active and promiscuous than in the other countries
and were also the most racist. While 12 per cent of other Europeans
disagreed with the statement, 'All races are equal', in Britain the figure
was 29 per cent, with the same proportion saying that they themselves
had committed 'acts of racism'.[3] One year before the end of the
twentieth century and some 500 years after a number of Black people
arrived on this island, this is at least part of the story of our country.
In January 1999, two teenagers, Christopher Furlong, 14, and Mark
Horrocks, 13, were sentenced to three years' imprisonment for tortur-
ing, sexually abusing and then beating up with a metal bar and spiked
planks some young Asian children, one only 11. They bragged about
this, saying: 'We've beaten up two Paki lads – they are all the same
aren't they? They'll probably be in hospital now or dead.'[4] The crimes
were committed when the white boys were barely into their teens.
There was no national panic at this, as there rightly was when James
Bulger was killed. Another dreadful case was that of a black teacher
in Catford who was racially harassed for a year by National Front
supporters and then kicked unconscious in her school playground, an
attack which seriously damaged her spine.[5] Parents can and should be
blamed, but in our culture today parental power over children is
diminishing. If politicians and the media have to take some of the
responsibility for these attitudes, so do the people charged with imparting education to those who will make or break our dreams for the
future.

But here we have more of a muddle and a mess than in any other
sphere of public life. Nicholas Tate, the special advisor to the new
Labour government, accepts this:

**We don't really debate education and its fundamental purposes in this
country. Nor do we relate educational policy to the social arena. How
we educate young people relates to our social vision, how we see the**

**world and ourselves. When we started the reforms in the late eighties,
we did not discuss these issues adequately . . . we cannot make
educational decisions unless we debate these issues.**[6]

Unfortunately Tate is a man of many shades and of some confused
thinking. For he is also one of the people most adored by the *Daily
Mail* for advocating that education should be imparting old British
values, history and culture. In 1995, speaking to head teachers in
Shropshire, Tate said that it was multicultural education which had
created most of our problems and that what was needed was an
indoctrination of another kind – by which all children had a British
identity instilled in them through the teaching of English history,
Christianity and European values.[7] Maybe the two positions are com-
patible and one has to be grateful to Tate in some ways because he
does not pretend that education is neutral. His is an important public
declaration that education has a wider purpose which can be organized
for in a society.

We know this but cannot name this purpose, perhaps because that
would make us much too much like dreaded communist regimes of
yore. But education has long been a tool for social engineering, albeit
in subtle and selected ways. Yet in this country it seems not to have
done the job that has long been needed: the eradication of class prejudice
and the development of a positive multicultural identity. Privilege
continues to breed privilege, generation after generation, and although
some black and Asian Britons are part of this expanding group of
affluent and powerful people, they have no more sense than do white
people that there is a task to be done to change the way this country
is working against its own self-interest by not adapting to new global
and domestic realities. None of our masters in education, neither the
government, nor the inspectors, nor the head teachers or unions, have
taken it upon themselves to deal with this terrifying failure. There is
much talk of standards, grades, exclusions, league tables, but I have
yet to hear one public statement on the responsibility of educators
to create a forward-looking, integrated, mutually respectful young
population. A black mother, whose child was racially so bullied that
he tried to commit suicide, said this to me on the day the boy came
out of hospital:

157

Tell me what good is this education which is doing nothing to stop
white children to hate black children with such impunity? Or the other
way around or black and white kids hating the 'Pakis'? What good
will the world be, even if we save the elephants and have our rivers
running blue again if our children are hurting each other like this just
because of the fact that they look different? So many years have been
wasted. So many lives left in ignorance and full of hate or pain. Who
is to teach our children the correct way?

Soon after this she left the country and emigrated to Canada. The boy
is flourishing out there in a community-based school where citizenship
education lies at the centre of the curriculum. More subtle failures
become visible when you look at the private sector where good education is also unacceptably limited in terms of what the country needs
and what the pupils themselves must learn.

The teachers we have are barely qualified or ready to take on
these massive tasks – some because they feel burdened enough by the
increasing pressures placed on them by the culture of inspections;
others, sadly, because they don't know any better and don't want to.
Some weeks after the Lawrence Report was published, I met a teacher
at the Oratory School (where Tony Blair sends his son), who not only
knew nothing about racism but vociferously argued that what he did
not know was not worth knowing because it was 'probably biased
and part of government propaganda'. Talking at a conference held by
a major teaching union at around the same time, my suggestions that
there needed to be an overhaul of the national curriculum were greeted
with polite noises of protest. With a few exceptions (most of them
were Black people), among the hundreds assembled there, it was just
more work, more uncertainty, which was the last thing they needed.

My son went to a top London public school. For me, as a socialist,
this was a decision based entirely on the view that gaining power in
this country means buying into education. At least a fifth of pupils of
the school were either British Asians or Chinese. Two of them had
won international science awards. The top scholarship boy and the
music scholarship boy were from this group. But this had not made
any difference to the way the world was seen and it did not seem to
have injected a sense of mission in the pupils – not even those who

were non-white – to use their position to challenge the system. One of them, the son of a multi-millionaire family from India, said:

> This is England and I am happy to get a top-class English education. I don't want all this crap about Diwali and that like in those state schools. All the men in my family have had this kind of education. We are Hindus at home. But here, we do as the English do. This opens so many doors for me. That is all it is about.

If the children of the cream of society are this easily pleased by the *status quo*, where can the impetus come for change?

When writing this book I interviewed many children and young people, white and black and Asian, and from these interviews some clear common themes emerged. Until the age of around thirteen, on the whole, the children were idealistic, interested in changing society to make it fairer, in the environment and in the future. There were many cases of terrible racial bullying but also many natural friendships across the racial and religious boundaries which seemed to flourish within the world of the school, although often these seemed very vulnerable indeed. Indeed, the words of the wonderful black poet Jackie Kay were lived out again and again as I spoke to these young people:

> Today my best pal, *my number one*,
> called me a *dirty darkie*,
> when I wouldn't give her a sweetie.[8]

The relationships were also fragile because they were entirely school-based. There was little evidence that the children visited the families of these friends or stayed overnight, the natural extensions of school relationships. Ayisha who is twelve and a Muslim, and her friend Lizzie, a middle-class white child, have been close friends since they started school in Enfield. Ayisha explains what the limits of that friendship have to be:

> She has never been to my house. Why? I don't know. I have not asked her. It would be so strange for my parents. They are from Pakistan and we are very religious so they would feel a bit ashamed I think. Like what happens in the home is a secret, you know? If people knew they would start calling me Paki and that. I don't want Lizzie to hear me

talking Urdu, and see how we live. My parents eat with their hands and speak English with an accent and she wouldn't treat me like she does if she saw all this. But I have never been invited there so maybe they feel the same.

Lizzie's reasons are not the same.

I have talked to my mum about asking Ayisha to stay over but she says that her parents would not like it because Muslims are very strict and they might get angry if she asked. But I think she herself feels uncomfortable. Like with my other friends the other mothers get on and they chat and know one another, have coffee, you know. She has only now started saying hello to Ayisha's parents but it is like she doesn't really try any harder. I don't think they are racist or anything. It is just that they don't know how to act. They really really like Ayisha and think she is a good influence on me because she works hard and isn't always talking about boys.

Research done by Adrienne Katz shows how as children get older divisions begin to appear and, by the time they are in their mid-teens, in many schools tribal allegiances begin to make demands and break up long-term friendships.[9] I have been to secondary schools in leafy outer London suburbs where Hindus, Muslims, Sikhs, Jews, whites and blacks operate entirely separately one from the other, and although some resort to gang violence, most don't, but they are still disturbingly committed to living, breathing and thinking within their own ghettos.

A long, rocky and uncharted road has led us to this alienating dead end. And one key reason is the fact that historically educators and politicians themselves were barely literate in the new realities they had to plan and provide for, so caught up were they in their own mad terror over black immigration. Professor Eggleston of Warwick University, who has been researching and writing on education policy for forty years, believes the seeds for this management were put down in the fifties.[10] Instead of beginning a process to recast education for the nation to make it appropriate for fast-changing times, an obsession grew that the way forward was to assimilate the black and Asian children by treating them like trainee whites – in other words, to pretend that these organic changes were not happening in society.

Modern-day Luddites. These children were expected, often forced, to leave behind their home lives, values, dialects outside the school gate, like they were dirty wellies. What white working-class children had been obliged to do at great cost, as Professor Halsey's research showed, was replicated for black children only in a much more cruel way.[11] Parents were not only treated as interlopers, but the children were deliberately taught to reject the values of their parents. Lemos, a black man who came here with his parents in 1959, remembers this well when he was growing up:

> It was awful. I went to a school in Birmingham where my teachers used to ask me to tell them if my parents were being too strict. My father was treated like he was nothing when he came in to complain that I was not getting any homework. The head teacher said to him that he should remember he was in the greatest country in the world and not in some village in Jamaica. Finally they gave up coming to the parents' evening or anything. And what was worse was that I started to despise them until I realized what was going on. We were told we were going to be English but it was your black skin that the kids saw. I am now a doctor and middle-class with a white wife. But I can tell you if our children have problems I ask her to go in because I know the effect will be different if I go in.

And so it continued throughout the sixties. As the academic Ali Rattansi writes:

> Just as in a previous era, an official 'gentling of the masses' by way of induction into a culture of civilization had accompanied the educational and political entry of the working classes into citizenship within the nation, so now assimilation into an imagined British national culture and way of life became the preoccupation of the educational establishment.[12]

Teaching English (including to Caribbeans to get them out of what was referred to as 'plantation English') to new Commonwealth immigrants became the one overriding policy. Money and all imaginative work was devoted to this enterprise. In 1966, a special budget – Section 11 – was made available by the government to help those schools which had to cope with large numbers of pupils from the new Commonwealth, especially those 'whose language and customs differ from those in the community'. Vast numbers of head teachers and others felt this was their vocation, and it was at this time that you came across dozens of teachers who once might have gone on worthy civilizing missions to Africa and India who were now able to nurture little coloured natives of their very own. They were devoted and professionally competent individuals, but they were doing the wrong thing at the wrong time in the wrong place and in entirely inappropriate ways. This was what I too had grown up with in Africa. In my schools, you were punished by *Asian* teachers if you were heard speaking 'vernacular languages'.

This is not to argue against the idea that the language of the country is an indispensable tool without which no individual progress is possible. A common language well spoken and understood with all its deeper nuances is an absolute requirement for binding the nation together and creating a collective sense of who we are. But it is important to question why this was the only policy response and why other languages had to die in order to make English live. We are also entitled to ask why no education policies were envisaged for white children to enable them to understand their changing society and relationships. This was not even on the minds of those in charge. There were grave problems too with the theoretical framework.

This assimilationism was, as Rattansi points out, essentialist, and it was based on a set of questionable assumptions of 'an obvious, definable, homogeneous essence (British culture) into which the hapless immigrant might be inducted, given a suitable dose of English and an undiluted diet of the official school curriculum'.[13] It was getting people to mix into the stew of Britishness, adding a little spice maybe. This philosophy was allowed such unscrutinized ascendancy that the Labour Education Secretary in the mid-sixties, the otherwise liberal Anthony Crosland, gave his backing to, for example, the bussing out of children from schools in Southall which was initiated by the LEA.[14] That such questionable policies and theories were sprouting at the time when child-centred education was being promoted by modern child psychologists is even more astounding.

The first official signal that the leadership was beginning to grow up came in 1966 when Roy Jenkins made his famous speech putting forward the incredibly enlightened view (even for now) that assimi-

lation was wrong and that society should aim for integration, which
he then proceeded to describe:

> **I do not regard [integration] as the loss, by immigrants, of their own
> national characteristics and culture. I do not think we need in this
> country a 'melting pot', which will turn everybody out in a common
> mould, as one of a series of carbon copies of someone's misplaced
> vision of the stereotyped Englishman . . . It would deprive us of most
> of the positive advantages of immigration which . . . I believe to be
> very great indeed.**[15]

Sadly, what followed in the next decade was not an examination of
what this credo might mean in education. This was, as has already
been said, the same year in which the Section 11 money was announced.
Instead of looking to how the vision put forward by Jenkins could
become the inspiration for educators, the under-achievement of black
and Asian children in schools became the focus of both the black and
white experts, the first blaming racism, the second blaming culture. This
wilful ignorance and self-limitation carried on through the following
decades in spite of vital information and advice which became available
then.

I refer here to five years of intense work carried out by many of the
great and the good who were given the task to look into the education
of black and Asian children in 1981. Lord Rampton was appointed
to lead the first of these task forces, and an interim report was published
in 1981. There were many unpleasantnesses and disagreements in this
first committee and eventually (thankfully) Rampton was replaced and
a new group was set up which included unique thinkers such as
Professor Bhiku Parekh, who has long rejected the views of those who
espoused and advocated ethnic absorption rather than pluralism. This
is what made the 800-page tome produced in 1985 under the chairman-
ship of Lord Swann completely different from anything which had
been done before. It was a radical departure from what the Rampton
report would have been. It is illuminating to note that Rampton
produced an interim report in 1981 which was called 'West Indian
Children in *our* Schools' (my italics).[16] It was concerned about the
'dysfunctional' black family, under-achievement and, strangely, how
'West Indian' parents did not know how to interact with schools and

did not understand how education worked in Britain. That these parents came from a colony seemed to have bypassed those writing the report and there was an astonishing ignorance about the fact that Afro-Caribbean parents had made enormous sacrifices in order to get their children an education in Britain. Looking at it all these years on, what is striking is both the dated tone and presumptions, but also how we have recently gone back to this way of thinking. Like then, once again we are locked in the battles about the dysfunctional 'West Indian' family, one-parent households, school exclusions, and so on. Bangladeshi parents, we are told, cannot help their children with their education. This may well be true. Many Bangladeshi and Mirpur Pakistani parents come from a rural background with literacy problems of their own, and black children may indeed be suffering as a result of family problems. But so alienated are black and Asian people from the politics of education, that such vital discussions are not yet possible. In any case these reasons are incomplete explanations for what is going on. The more important cause of failure may be the fact that there is so little investment in the idea that schools should be sites of social progress for all children.

Today a number of black parents prefer to make the journey back home in search of a good education for their children, or to take other more radical decisions. Trevor Phillips, the broadcaster, was sent back by his parents to study in Guyana. His brother, the novelist Mike, has decided to keep his young son at home. He explained why:

> [M]y own experience had imbued me with a high degree of cynicism about school and schooling. I had been through school and university myself and had been taught in secondary and higher education. As a schoolboy in London I had felt isolated and alien, threatened by racist harassment in the playground and deskilled by the expectations of the teachers in the classroom. As an undergraduate and postgraduate I had continually confronted the assumptions behind most of the texts I had read. As a teacher I had been depressed by the prejudiced attitudes of my colleagues and angered by the widespread assumption that education failure was an inevitable part of black man's cultural destiny.[17]

We would not be in this position, perhaps, if more attention had been paid to the Swann Report which – albeit in a limited way – took an altogether more sophisticated approach to education. Instead of looking at 'problem' black children, the team chose to consider what kind of education was appropriate for a multi-ethnic society, for all our children. The focus had moved to the damaging effects on Black *and* white children of racial prejudice and also to the urgent need to promote cultural pluralism in all schools, including or especially white schools. A fundamentally important change was signalled by this report: a move away from the idea that our schools were failing because of the very presence of black and Asian people. There was a recognition that education had not prepared either Black or white people for the new circumstances in which they found themselves, living as equals on this island. Unfortunately the Education Secretary at the time was the right-winger Keith Joseph, who through a clever strategy of equivocation killed off the impact of the Swann Report. In spite of this, the report did have an effect in that the hard-line assimilationism of the earlier periods was laid to rest and did not reappear with any significance until the nineties.

Had some of the fundamental recommendations of the Swann Report been implemented with vigour, perhaps with the same level of vigour as was put into the abolition of the 11-plus and the creation of comprehensive education (even though this in the end brought in a different set of problems), we would have gone a long way forwards in terms of postwar structural and ideological adjustment. But to have a real effect, an even broader analysis was needed than that which was provided by the Swann team. Many forces combine to make education effective in the life of a child so that he or she actually benefits or loses out.

There is no denying the influence of a stable family home and regular income on educational attainment. An article in *New Economy* in 1997 concluded that three factors made the real difference to educational achievement: parents, well-resourced schools and peer group attitudes towards education – the last being the most important. Class also has an enormous impact on achievement. There is much talk and action around education, education, education, but no real discussion either about a national curriculum to which all children can relate without standards being compromised, or about the damaging attitudes to education which prevail in the working classes and the underclass. The wood is not seen because people have been so involved in particular species of trees. There has been an alarming disregard for the obvious key connections between how the white working classes regarded education in this country and how this affected the many bright and eager children of immigrants who found themselves both in competition with, and in need of approval from, these white children. Martha, now a grandmother, remembers just how long-lasting was the damage done to children like hers:

> Unlike anywhere else in the world, in this country, the poor see education as frightening, as an interference, as something to be ashamed of because it removes you from your family. We see education and the improvement of the next generation as vital for our very existence. But the children from our home, how could they deal with the terrible atmosphere in the schools where white parents would want to beat up the teachers and where some children I know were kept away from exams so that they wouldn't get above themselves? I myself saw a hysterical mother slapping a young teacher who had punished her daughter for swearing. I was shocked. Back home, we revere our teachers and teach our children to respect learning. It is so sad so many of us travelled over to give the kids a better education. They learnt nothing but hostility with the white kids.

Like many black and Asian parents, Martha is of course passing up the blame for what happened to her two children, George and Lisa. Peer group values were of immense importance but so, according to her own children, was the fact that their mother was out working for so long when they were young, and general racism and poverty which created in their lives a terrible hopelessness. Lisa, now 23, describes this:

> School was hard, but home was tough too. Mum was on her own, she had two jobs. She was often too tired to help us. I am not blaming her but I used to see that and wonder what the point was. And she doesn't understand how angry she had become over the racism. So as a black child I thought there was no way out. If you worked or you didn't racism would block you.

They both left school without any qualifications and went back into training only years later when they realized they were destroying their own life chances. The causes of black under-achievement are therefore many and complex but there can be little doubt that Martha here has highlighted a crucial flaw in this area of public life, that all talk and action on education in Britain has been item-based and too particular. And fashion dictates which group and cause gets to be in the public eye at any given moment. This serial concern is easily validated but almost as easily invalidated. Black boys and school exclusions are the major panic of the moment, as is the under-achievement of working-class boys. That the two are intimately related does not seem to have occurred to most people. Racism, of course, is a major factor in what is happening to black boys, but an overdeveloped awareness of racism is denying them the insight to go beyond simple cause-and-effect explanations. Those who never see the common problems of behaviour found in Afro-Caribbean boys and white boys from underprivileged backgrounds are guilty of senseless oversimplification. Herman Ouseley made this point in 1998 when he accused the Qualifications and Curriculums Authority (led by Nick Tate, quoted above, pp. 156–7) of being not only Eurocentric but oppressively middle class. But if all this is true, why is it that so many Asian and Chinese Britons are doing stunningly well? Well first, because most are from the middle classes. Bradford head teacher Alan Hall is very clear that other factors are important too and these may actually help children to cope with the debilitating effects of racism:

> The biggest single advantage they gain from their family background is that they are seldom cynical about school, teachers and education in the way that white teenagers can be. They are hard-working and polite partly because of their culture at home and partly because they know the value of getting on at school.[18]

Many black boys display the same attitudes as white boys. These are then the kids who often set upon Asian children in schools, a story of violence and abuse one is still not allowed to tell because it might 'encourage racism'. As if racism has ever needed help. I have yet to understand how not talking about inter-ethnic prejudices and racisms helps the cause of anti-racism. People are not stupid. Black and white

Britons know all too well that although white upon black racism is by far the bigger and more devastating problem, relationships between Sikhs and Muslims, black and Asian youngsters have also deteriorated dangerously in many areas. Hamid, 16, and a 'strong Muslim', says:

> I hate all these devil worshippers. We have nothing to do with people who worship monkeys and don't wash their hair. Our gang is Muslim and we just hate the others in this area. Yeah sometimes there are fights. But our religion tells us you can force people to go on the right path.

His schoolmate Harbans is a quietly spoken Sikh boy:

> These Muslim gangs they are just junglies. Look at them. They are uneducated bastards who think Allah will give them everything. They are so stupid, always the bottom of the class. We are the warriors of the East. If they try anything with us, they learn that.

In education there are many taboos on how you might discuss the school effect on the lives of British children. Black and white children from working-class backgrounds, as well as Asians at the bottom of the educational pile (who are picking up the cool habits of their white and black peers), would benefit immeasurably if they learnt some lessons from other successful ethnic groups where there is a much more positive and hard-headed attitude towards education and qualifications and where racism has not been allowed to become the refuge for all failure. It was interesting that, in the self-flagellating weeks which followed the Lawrence Inquiry and the declaration soon after by a schools inspector that British schools were 'institutionally racist', one of the most sensible responses came from William Atkinson, the black head of a school which he turned round from being the worst to almost the most desirable in the neighbourhood. No, he said, racism was too simplistic an explanation for what was going on in education and that solutions needed to go beyond this kind of labelling.

Navnit Patel, a doctor in an inner-city area and father of three children at top universities, is very clear about the need for this:

> All my children went to state schools in Ealing where there was awful racist abuse tolerated by teachers because they believed that bullying

168

was part of life. The great British education system we heard of back home in Gujarat amounts to one-third violence, one-third indifference and one-third lazy, bad teaching. But at home the message we had to give them – and they are grateful for this now – is that if you want an education, you can learn under a lamp-post and that without it we are doomed especially in this country with so much racism. So instead of telling them racism is an obstacle they have to conquer, we told them that racism leaves them no option but to get on top of the tree to escape the beasts barking underneath. And they just knew from day one that this family will expect nothing but their best effort in education.

Allowing racism to be the only real explanation for failures increasingly makes less and less sense. Asian girls, or so it is said, are kept down and often out by stereotypical expectations of teachers. This is indeed partly true but then how do you explain the fact that some Asian girls are doing brilliantly well? And how does racism on its own explain family interventions by which many Asian girls are removed from schools and colleges, thereby denying them qualifications? It is not racist to suggest that black boys and Asian girls who are doing badly are the victims of several forces and that racism is only one of these. Peer group pressure to be cool and not work, the quite rational conclusion that many young people – white and Black – have reached that there is little sense in working to make good if your colour or accent will still be what you are judged by, must have made an impact on the aspirations of these people. None of this seems to be openly discussed at the moment. And even when it is, it is hemmed in by orthodoxies. For example, Dr Tony Sewell, a black academic with an impressive background, offers up his theories that black boys are seriously misunderstood in schools and punished too readily by teachers. Writing in the *Sunday Mirror*, he concludes:

The reality is that there is not a sudden increase in bad behaviour in schools. But we have a change in the values of schools which speak less and less to the needs of black boys and white working-class boys.[19]

In his book *Black Masculinities and Schooling*,[20] Sewell says that teachers are failing to understand the behaviour of black boys, which often manifests itself in an exaggerated form of masculinity. He also argues that teachers are not able to relate to the importance of ethnicity and identity for these boys. His research shows too that white boys are more likely to play truant than black and Asian boys and that, although overall achievements are low, black boys are doing better than white boys. In spite of this, exclusion rates of black boys are higher than those for white boys.[21] What other research has indicated is that many black children are sent home because they have lost control after being racially abused. The racism is not dealt with but the reaction against it is. In one report by the Institute of Race Relations there is a litany of such incidents, including that of a child of three who went into a mostly all-white nursery and was driven wild by children prodding him and asking him about this skin colour. He was thrown out for being 'impossibly violent'.[22]

An extremely valuable research review conducted by David Gillborn and Caroline Gipps at the Institute of Education concluded that at a policy level silence had set in on race issues and that the education system was still scarred by racism and inequality and that things were getting worse.[23] Important messages emerge from these various sources: that racism is a problem in our schools and while black people keep having to point this out (perhaps ignoring all those other factors which contribute to failure) white authorities choose to shut out the implications of the realities around race and will seize on almost any other more palatable reality. The subject is still seen in isolation from white pupils.

So what should be done about it? Do we, as Sewell himself has suggested, make provision for separate schools for black children because they need a new curriculum to make sense of their experiences? Or is this actually condemning them to an even worse future? Is the answer simply to ignore cultural difference and process all children through the same machine with top-quality control inspections? Or do we make the school more open to the diverse values of these children and all others while maintaining a common curriculum which has been imaginatively expanded or changed? What is the point of teaching a particularly rosy version of black history to black boys? Why not teach a much more honest, integrated history to all children?[24]

Tony Blair at the beginning of 1998 made a widely publicized speech about wanting to expand the middle classes and about the role of highly qualified human capital.[25] Remaining within a class or an ethnic ghetto is not the way to compete in the world today which is itself changing and homogenizing (even as we hate the fact that this is happening) and this is why I have argued against separate schooling for Muslims or black children. The schools, however, can be brilliant. In 1999 the John Loughborough school, a black Seventh Day Adventist school, doubled in size because it was finally granted state funding. Pupils I have talked to at the school speak of feeling safe and encouraged in a way they never were before in their comprehensives. Muslim girls will tell you similar things.[26] But I still think opting out of multi-culturalism in this way is wrong. I hold this view in spite of the evidence that children thus separated out can do much better academically. In the secondary school league tables in 1998, a Muslim school in Bradford did better than Eton. I wonder, though, how the pupils' qualifications will be regarded by the outside world and whether the bright children will have the skills to negotiate their rights and status in a difficult and prejudiced country. And nothing will be achieved until we think the unthinkable and stop state funding for all religious schools. I had my young daughter (who is half Muslim) baptized so she could get into the local Church school. This is one of the academically best schools in the area and I wanted my daughter to acquire a sense of faith in God. It is also mixed in terms of race and ethnicity. The other schools in the area are so weak academically that there really was no other choice. But I still believe we should look again at state-funded religious schools. I don't feel my personal choices should form my wider opinions. Without a radical restructuring of education, simple justice will demand that our children be fenced off in small and perfect enclosures. They are official ghettos which will prevent integration. Separation is not the answer, but the vacuum in education cannot be allowed to go on.

The irony is that in the eighties some radical thinking did begin to penetrate the mind-sets of those in charge of running education. Not only were pro-active employment policies to get black and Asian teachers into the system taken up with some energy, but the curriculum was challenged and where possible transformed. History was one area where a major shift began to occur. The radical Institute of Race

Relations produced cartoon books to explain the history of slavery and colonialism to children so that they might understand what really happened and learn about the bond between the folk who came to stay and those who were already here. The search for black heroes took off. I learnt for the first time about Walter Tull, Britain's first black professional footballer who was born in Kent in 1888. He played for Tottenham but left after suffering racial abuse, and joined Northampton Town. When the First World War broke out, he joined up, became a commissioned officer and died fighting in France during the last appalling months of the war. Mary Seacole was discovered at this time as were other stories of Indians in Britain and of the deep relationships which had existed between this country and its ruled people. There was not as much support for these excavations as there might have been. The book on Mary Seacole written by Ziggi Alexander and Audrey Dewjee had to be published by a local authority on a tiny budget.[27] Kusoom Vadgama, an Asian optician, paid to publish her book on the relationship between India and Britain.[28] Two other invaluable works, already much quoted in this book, *Staying Power* by Peter Fryer and *Ayahs, Lascars and Princes* by Rozina Visram, were also published. Not that any of this had much impact on the mainstream elite. To this day most of the information contained in these books is unknown to all except a few intellectuals and anti-racists. The best-read people in this country haven't a clue who C. L. R. James was or that Edward Braithwaite was a British writer, but for a while it seemed that the world and its arbiters would change.

Other initiatives were more problematic. White teachers were obliged to go through tough racism awareness training which forced them to examine their own assumptions. It was an idea imported from the United States, where the de-segregated army had brought in this kind of training to wash the sins of slavery out of the system. Judy Katz, an American writer, was the guru of the time and her book – which I used myself when training professionals – was a rag-bag of superficial analysis and unworthy mind games. There is little doubt that far too many inept and furious people got into racism awareness and anti-racism training in this period. They did more damage than if they had left the issue untouched. They upset black people on the left partly because of this and partly also because there was a fear that racism was being helped to dress better so that people would stop objecting to it, leaving structural inequality firmly in place. A. Sivanandan of the Institute of Race Relations[29] and the black educationalist Ahmed Gurnah were the most vocal critics of this training.[30] But there were also some very good trainers too whose work was sullied by the reputation such training had soon acquired. But like everything to do with race, the attacks which were orchestrated against all such training were not only unfair but unwise.[31] I myself watched trainers working with teachers in Birmingham and Essex and I could see that even within a short period, if trainers were sensitive and not dogmatic, teachers were helped to educate themselves to break through the narrowness of their own formal and informal education. Sylvia Brown was one of the ILEA teachers who went through a number of anti-racism courses:

> There were some terrible courses when we white teachers were more or less abused just for being white. I think it is one thing to be told about how slavery has affected future relationships between white and black people but another to be told that I was still responsible for what white slave owners did all those centuries back. Anyway I come from a family of Welsh miners, something that seemed of no importance. But two of the courses were run by really thoughtful people who did help me to question my own assumptions. One case study we were asked to think about, for example, was of a young very bright Asian girl who wanted to go to college but whose family were very frightened that they would lose her if she went to university. I used to condemn these families before but I began to understand better and then when such a case did actually come up when I was teaching at a secondary school in Walsall I was able to communicate with the family and help the girl to get to college.

Some of this criticism was part of a concerted campaign by papers such as the *Sun* and the *Mail*. In this period, when right-wing nationalism had such a grip on the nation through the powerful Margaret Thatcher and her cabinet, it was inevitable that there was going to be a massive clash of civilizations. But it was the fact that such training was offensive to the left as well that gave added ammunition to the right.[32]

Other alliances were also to prove to be lethal, and here the role of teachers was crucial. The right-wing *Salisbury Review*, with retrograde academics such as Roger Scruton and others expressing ideas about ancient and vulnerable identities, influenced unhappy and marginalized head teachers who found anti-racism and multiculturalism an infringement of their status and a threat to their comfortably limited knowledge. A number of highly publicized cases illustrated this potent rage. Two of these are now deeply embedded in the national psyche. In Dewsbury in 1986, an assimilationist headmaster Ray Honeyford had attacked multicultural education which, he claimed, was being imposed on schools by the 'race relations industry' and by those whom he described as 'half-educated' Asian and Afro-Caribbean parents. The mainly Pakistani parents in his school protested for weeks, refusing to send their children to a school run by a man with such views about their lifestyles and culture. In the end Honeyford was forced out of his job and he remains to this day an embittered opponent of all forms of multiculturalism. Another head, Maureen McGoldrick in Brent, had become embroiled in a similar battle with parents and the local authority, although in her case it was less clear whether it was the risible antics of the LEA which were more to blame than a jingoistic head. Brent had acquired a reputation for hard-line policies enforced in neo-Stalinist ways, something which anti-racist intellectuals still have to address with a degree of honesty.[33] Then in the summer of 1988, a group of white parents in Dewsbury went to court and won the right not to send their children to school because there were too many Asians there. The parents had been teaching them in a room in a pub. Meanwhile the papers were full of daily stories about what the loony left councils were doing in the name of multiculturalism. Columnists fulminated that 'our' children were increasing their knowledge of other cultures and were not being left in white ignorance about Diwali. All this was going on, possibly not coincidentally, as the 1988 Education Act was going through Parliament and laying down the immovable stones of the core curriculum which enclose us all today. Education was firmly established as something which was not anti-racism.

Looking back at this period, it is impossibly difficult to pin down absolute lines of blame and responsibility. Good and essential work was being done by the most innovative boroughs who had taken on board the ideas in the Swann Report. The most striking work was being done in primary and nursery schools after research indicated that children as young as three already knew the negative impact of skin colour and the cultural hierarchy which prevailed in society. Social psychologist Dr David Milner had carried out a longitudinal study[34] to show this, and the possibilities of interventions at an early enough stage became something to strive for, to believe in. There were nurseries across the country, including working-class areas such as Camberwell, where I watched workers transform the environment and take parents with them. I saw children able to break away from an inheritance of racial prejudice.

The sad reality is that, for years, the ideological battles in this country have been fought on the playing fields of our schools not, as in the USA, on campuses. I interviewed a retired black teacher, a truly pioneering spirit in his time, in an inner-city school in Birmingham:

> There was a brief period during the seventies and early eighties when we were providing a genuinely relevant education for black and white kids. We weren't doing all the stupid things the *Sun* and others said about us. We were simply undoing past relationships and making new ones. The most interested kids in my school were white boys, I remember. They thought I looked like Marley, so they used to follow me like puppies, come to my house and ask all about our lives back home, the imperial masters, how they hated toffs too. We were trying to get there. Then down came the hand of Thatcher. I left the profession soon after. There was no point in bringing up another generation of whites who were ignorant about us and blacks who were getting angrier. You want to know why so many more black boys are not in school today, look at the Thatcher period and the 1988 Education Act.

For this book I interviewed several white teachers to see if they were aware of their responsibility to educate our children to feel at ease about their own society (and even perhaps proud of it) and a globalized world for the future. I wanted to know if they had a vision. The teachers were all in their thirties and came from mixed and all-white schools. Only one teacher had given this any thought. The rest were consumed with tests, the league tables, and big bad inspectors. It felt like I was interviewing a passport official about our immigration policies. Their worlds were so officiated that they could not see beyond them at all.

What is so disheartening is that we have known what to do for a very long time. In 1989, an excellent research report, *The School Effect*, by the independent and scholarly Policy Studies Institute, said:

> There is much to be done in secondary schools to make secondary education reflect the broader outlook that is needed in a multicultural society. This would be invaluable in itself and especially because of the benefits it would bring to the majority of children whose families originate from Britain. Multi-cultural education should not be seen as methods of improving the performance of racial minority groups, but an aspect of good education for all pupils.[35]

Many of the teachers I interviewed did not know of such research. Perhaps as a result they fly from even the idea of an education which has such ideals underpinning it. The Tory backlash against multicultural education and bad multicultural teaching which made white kids feel personally guilty for historic crimes and which excluded them as an act of historical retribution, did serious damage and people do not wish to tread out into the area in case another land-mine explodes in their faces. Jackie, a Scottish science teacher, says quite simply: 'I am not interested. I am not a loony left-winger, not a zealot, not a guilt-making machine. I just want to do a job and get these kids through their exams.'

And in some ways her caution is entirely understandable. Much else is in serious need of reappraisal. We see the results of partly digested theories applied with more zest than intelligence today in our social services with the adoption issue. Black and mixed-race children in care are, in a number of cases, denied adoption because of fundamentalist beliefs that they should only be placed with black families.

Far too much of anti-racist education was doctrinaire and attempted to create a new hierarchy of culture. To be black and Asian meant to have a culture and to be blameless because racism could always be held responsible for whatever a black or Asian child did. White children, on the other hand, were assumed to have no 'culture' which was worthy of celebrating and they would be punished for doing exactly the same sorts of things that black and Asian children did. Bad black and Asian teachers were recruited and then made excuses for, instead of being trained. I was the head of department in a college of further education run by the Inner London Education Authority and had the misfortune to have two such tutors to manage. One was an Afro-Caribbean woman who took terrible pride in her ignorance because she had had no formal education. She had convinced herself that this meant she was uncontaminated and therefore deserved to control the rest of us with our pathetic, educated, middle-class ways. Another woman on my staff was a born-again Lesbian whose obvious skills and intelligence got drowned out by an overwhelmingly charged atmosphere in which her sexuality and blackness mattered far more than it should have done. What was even more frustrating was that the previous head, a white, gay, middle-class Englishman, had simply allowed these unprofessional people to take over the department. It would have been a very funny sitcom, if only it had not been all too real. There were others, much worse. One department in a college in the Midlands had its white tutors agreeing to wear badges announcing that they were racist because they were white, and during staff meetings (as in an AA meeting) they would confess to acts of racism that week. Or invent them. What is unforgivable is that enough of this was going on for the very good work to be drowned out. It took the already hostile media no time at all to sniff out the bad practice and make a meal of it.

The most important thing to remember, though, is that what opponents of multicultural education wanted to destroy was not the work of the deranged, but those institutions where at long last education was beginning to have an effect in getting people to understand their society for what it was. It was the block they had to get rid of because it diverted people away from the new fixed agenda for education in this country. The market was the dominant factor in the formulation of educational policy. As John Rex says: 'The state is no longer seen as a potential agent for engineering greater social equality.' Instead of humanist liberal goals of social justice and personal achievement, vocationally job-ready people were to be the unchallenged outcome for the purposes of a Thatcherized economy.[36] If this is true, anti-racism was seen not only as undesirable in itself but also as an unwelcome interference in these big battles over Britain.

But in both the attacks and counter-attacks, there was a lack of awareness of these deeper meanings of the confrontations. As I wrote in the *New Statesman* in 1988:

> The fallacy is that education and anti-racist education are mutually exclusive and that there was a golden age when good or real education happened. One reason why this belief has been easy to float is because many anti-racists themselves have interpreted anti-racist education in superficial ways, looking at it as some kind of substitution exercise. Anti-racist education challenges the ideology of open enterprise. It begins with a presumption of operational inequality in this society and struggles against it, by making proactive demands, holding up mirrors transforming core perceptions.[37]

In 1989, it all came to a head and it took a murder to get there. A 13-year-old boy, Ahmed Ullah, was murdered in the school playground by a white boy. It happened in Burnage in Manchester. A report on what happened was written by a group of people with excellent anti-racist credentials.[38] Ian Macdonald QC had a reputation for fighting against injustice throughout his career. Gus John was a highly respected black professional in education, as were Reena Bhavnani and Lily Khan. Their findings shocked everyone, used by now to drawing the battle lines between anti-racists and racists. The authors condemned the school not for failing to have anti-racist policies and practices, but for having anti-racist policies which were pushed through so vigorously and thoughtlessly that they had created division and suspicion between children of different backgrounds:

> One gets the sense of white working-class parents who have little basis on which to root their own identity and whose education has given them little or no value of their own experience as English working class and who, therefore, react angrily and resentfully to a school which, in sharp contrast to their own experience, caters directly for the needs and preferences of Asian students, thus indicating the extent to which they and their culture are valued.[39]

The report also noted that there was much resentment on the part of white parents in Manchester prior to the murder. Some of them had set up PEER (Parents' English Education Rights) which was campaigning for 'good Christian English education'. In a 1992 study of relationships between black and white primary school children, the authors quoted many examples of conversations like this:

> Interviewer: **Why do you think Miss G** [the teacher] **was so annoyed at people calling racist names? Was she more annoyed at that than other names that people call?**
>
> M: **She was. They've got rights in this country haven't they as well. She is always saying things about racist name calling . . .**
>
> Int: **I wonder why.**
>
> M: **I don't know why.**
>
> Int: **Do you think that calling people names about their colour is worse than calling other names or not worse? Like calling you things to do with fleas?**
>
> M: **I don't know because Miss G seems to think so. Miss G never says why.**
>
> Int: **Do you think that somebody who calls a name like 'Paki' or 'chocolate' . . . should get into more trouble than somebody who calls you things about 'fleas'?**
>
> M: **I don't know. I think it should be the same because I mean they should have equal rights if they get called things by them, and we get called things . . . they call me 'fleas' and stuff. Rajvinder he calls me fleas and Miss G don't do anything about it, but she really told me off for calling him a racist name.**

Another white child felt that 'both should be treated the same way'.[40]

The Burnage Report, of course, was exactly what the right-wing press needed. A martyr to their particular cause. Even the usually supportive *Independent* concluded that the misguided anti-racist policies had led to the killing. The white head-teacher, Mr Gough, had apparently created an ethos where little account was taken of the deprivation suffered by the white children as the poor and disenfranchised. Class was pitted against race instead of being used to make connections. All this meant that by the time of the 1988 Education Act, which established not a national but nationalist curriculum, the fragile liberal consensus of the Swann Report and the slight moves towards an inclusive multiculturalism had been undermined and put aside.

None of the subsequent changes in education has even attempted to revisit this legislation or the Swann Report, to take up lessons which were broken off. It all seems several histories away now and even white parents these days are to be found showing some nostalgia for the good old days when education was more than a militant campaign for the three Rs. Recently there have been three new developments in this area which need to be taken extremely seriously, but which I can only touch upon in this book.

The first of these is the PC panic. In the first half of the nineties, both the left and right have become powerful allies in this in a way which makes the battles of the eighties seem like fairground skirmishes. Their common enemy was something they called Political Correctness, a notion imported from the United States, where for over a decade this same issue has created the most unseemly mess in the media, academia and elsewhere. In 1991, the *New York Magazine* carried a warning article with a photomontage of Nazis, Red Guards, burning books and other images.[41] It was a piece about how 'Political Correctness' was 'the new fundamentalism' led by 'multiculturalists, feminists, radical homosexuals, Marxists, New Historicists'. The article claimed that what held these various dissatisfied groups together was their belief that western culture is irredeemably racist, exclusive and oppressive. This was a gross misrepresentation of what many were actually trying to do, which was to make university education move forward from the static, Eurocentric, assimilationist, genteel and settled terrain it had become. This scenario in the US was played out mainly on the campus and in the media and, it being America, it was often hysterical on both sides.[42] But if one ignored the volume of noise being made, it was interesting to see how the drama unfolded along the same lines as we had seen in this country with anti-racist education. Those against change were driven to blind protectionism, and of those involved in the campaigns to promote change many were careless and misguided enough to make them all vulnerable. The next step was even more riveting. And depressing. The insane conflicts in the United States were imported to this country. They were carried over here as warnings, possibilities, nightmares. And in no time at all PC became our issue and was used by the left in this country as a way of extricating itself from multicultural education in schools and much more besides.

There was a strong reluctance, as Lisa Jardine explains, to accept that PC in education is not something coercive but progressive:

> [it] aerates the debates, it widens the mesh which defines the shape of our critical attention and allows alternative points of view. Instead of locating itself in the position of the dominant culture and consigning those who do not recognise themselves there to the position of passive spectators, it operates inclusively . . . PC in the classroom addresses just this muted (and often unrecognised) sense of exclusion.[43]

This set the scene for what New Labour then proceeded to do. Tony Blair and Harriet Harman decided not to send their children to their local state schools. School inspections and league tables scarcely took into account whether or not the schools were preparing children to live with confidence in an atmosphere of diversity. Increasing numbers of nearly all-black and Asian sink schools emerged. The very words 'multicultural education' have been banished from the replanted garden of New Eden. People at dinner parties feel they can say to me that they would not send their children to schools with too many Asian children. Subjected to similar remarks by trendy London parents after he decided to send his children to just such schools, Peter Aylmer wrote in the *Observer* about this retreat:

> [These parents] fear corruption of culture, they fear mingling of race, they fear the Babel of languages . . . Perhaps for some the real fear is that their homes and values may not be strong enough to stand exposure to the multicultural light.[44]

We now know that white working-class boys perform worse than boys from other groups (even the *Sun* calls them 'The Great White Dopes'[45]) and that Asian and Chinese children are more serious about education than white children. So why do so many white parents choose to keep their children out of multiracial schools? Some make the decision in order to preserve their privileged position and particular view of the world which they do not want challenged. Others do this because they are prejudiced. Still others base their actions on their own ignorance. Again and again I come across people whose teenagers have a much deeper awareness of different religions and cultures than they themselves do. Some at least of this reluctance to participate in the creation of a new multiculturally literate nation comes from the fact that so many mistakes were made in the past.

This is what is feeding the second issue which is gaining attention at present. In spite of the shock waves of the Burnage Report, there has been a singular lack of attention paid to gathering evidence to show the effect of multicultural education, good, bad or indifferent. Ideology has hampered research but small significant pieces of work have crept through nevertheless, and one of the most important of these is work carried out by Roger Hewitt in the borough of Greenwich, the area where racist young white men killed not only Stephen Lawrence, but Rolan Adams (another black teenager), and Rohit Duggal, who like Stephen was a young, bright student. In his book *Routes of Racism: The Social Basis of Racist Action*, Roger Hewitt found:

> In examining what *has* changed in the way white people, both young and old, talk about race issues, we find a radical new theme: the theme of 'unfairness'. By this we mean that, although there is greater awareness of racism and of the agendas of multiculturalism, there exists also a contrary bundle of related opinions and beliefs. These stem from the view that ethnic minority concerns are given 'too much attention' and that the problems, grievances and perspectives of the white community are ignored by the press, the local authority, the schools, the police, the government and so on. We find this theme to be widespread in all age groups and all social classes in Greenwich.[46]

Hewitt's qualitative research among racist thugs was denounced by some black and white people. But his findings and conclusions merit careful attention. The young white people he interviewed and their families were convinced that black and Asian Britons got special treatment from state institutions. This was in spite of having been through some kind of multicultural education when they were young. More alarmingly their anger against non-whites had actually been made worse by their education.

> White pupils, to some extent, seem like cultural ghosts, haunting as mere absences the richly decorated corridors of multicultural society. And when they attempt to turn to the symbols and emblems of 'their'

cultural identity, they find either very little that fits their needs or, in the case of the Union Jack, that that emblem itself is already a contested battle-ground.[47]

This kind of miseducation must never again be allowed to happen. English, Scottish, Welsh and Irish children, as well as those myriads of mixed-race children in this country, must be enabled to feel pride in their ancestries while belonging to a whole and binding state. The people who argue for multicultural education for reasons almost entirely to do with the needs of black and Asian children are seriously misguided. The education this country should be designing would aim to equip *all* children better for the cosmopolitan world. It must help children to get out of their conventional ways of thinking.

It should be obvious to anyone reading this that I am not primarily concerned with the achievement levels of black and Asian Britons in schools, or about the much discussed problems of school exclusions and league tables. The facts, however, are crucial for any future policy work. Briefly, the picture here is now much more complex than it has ever been. East African Asians, Chinese and some Indian pupils are out-performing their white peers. One Birmingham study in 1998 of GCSE science results showed Indians at the very top with 45 per cent getting A–C grades and Afro-Caribbeans at the bottom with 14 per cent. The figure for whites was 36.9 per cent.[48] Afro-Caribbean boys and white boys from non-middle classes are causing new worries and Bangladeshi and Pakistani pupils are also seriously under-performing. What further complicates this picture is the gender divide which is showing itself in the black and Asian communities as much as in the white. There is no sustainable argument any more to suggest that black and Asian women *en bloc* suffer from a double or triple jeopardy or that ethnicity provides the only explanations. Professor John Benyon of Leicester University says: 'it is probably the case that Afro-Caribbean girls are doing better than whites and a growing number are going into university.'[49] These girls, it appears, are able to do well at school while retaining their street credibility.[50] Higher education establishments are full of bright black and Asian students who, nevertheless, do not get the same opportunities as white graduates when they have finished. Asian and Chinese children are also to be found in large

numbers at private schools. At Dulwich College, Asians have been one
of the largest ethnic groups. And yet Oxbridge was found to have
discriminated against such students in their admissions interviews in
1996.[51]

All this brings me to the final development. As late as 1996, the
government finally showed some awareness that colour-blind education had failed. The Chief Inspector of Schools, Chris Woodhead,
said: 'Schools must address ethnic diversity, as failure to do so has
proved counter-productive.'[52] Woodhead and others were concerned
about specific issues to do with black and Asian pupils. He failed to
ask a bigger question. But do any of our young people – black, Asian
or white – emerge from a dozen years in our schools with a sense of
how they must relate to one another, how their stories brought them
to this point and how they are children of a new nation? I would argue
not – not even in the most highly resourced of our schools. We don't
yet have the teachers to do this and the whole system is loaded against
this growth.

Linda Plath is a teacher in a girls' school in Hertfordshire. She is
one of the teachers picked off for big things in the future, and at least
one neighbouring school has approached her to see if she would be
interested in applying to become a deputy head. Both schools are white
and in 'good' neighbourhoods. She, however, has decided to quit the
profession and set up her own business. She knows exactly why she
feels she has to leave:

> I am an idealist and when I began teaching I thought that I was to be
> one of the instruments of real change. My father was mixed race and
> although I pass for white, I am in fact a right racial mix. So many of
> us are now and the whole of this country is a testimony to that
> remarkable history. But we don't teach our children any of this. We
> have not given them a sense of how this country of immigration is
> what has made it so great. I don't want to process children so that
> they can read and write and count but they have no idea that
> Shakespeare was already dealing with some of the dilemmas of a
> culturally changing population. I felt like a factory worker who is not
> allowed to share in an enterprise. I used to watch the racial bullying of
> Asian children not only by white but by many black children and I

know that we are unable to tackle this kind of bullying except in a
fire-fighting situation. If the government does not sit back and take
stock, our young people are going to be more antagonistic and
ignorant than even the children of the seventies.

The ethos in schools is central to this disenchantment. In the schools
I knew in Africa there was no assumption that bullying or vile and
violent behaviour was an inevitable expectation. In this country this
is an expectation, and within a culture of bullying racial fissures thrive.
But you cannot deal with the problem only by concentrating your
efforts on racist behaviour. Such a solution would only add to the
problem. A holistic approach would engage the whole school community in setting targets to remove all bullying and, by influencing the
attitudes of the young, to make it unacceptable. This is what has been
achieved by the remarkable black head William Atkinson (see above,
p. 168). He has turned the school around not by banning racist
behaviour but by tackling truancy, lying, generic bullying and general
anti-social activities. Racism and prejudice has gone out of fashion in
the Phoenix school as a result of this approach. Both white and black
pupils tell me they feel valued in this school and that the teachers are
fair to everyone.

We have serious problems before this can be replicated nationwide.
The 1988 Education Act took away the scope for an inclusive, mould-
breaking, expansive curriculum and replaced it with the idea of a
strictly controlled regime. Time and resource constraints mean that
there is little that head-teachers can do beyond the core work. Multicultural education was wiped out by one clean, legal instrument and
the only place it now survives is in the margins. In the nineties we
had a further process of sterilization where league tables, endless
assessments and bureaucratic demands have also taken their toll on
all those bright and idealistic white and black teachers who wanted
so much to make it better for the next generation. Higher education
is more promising, with the new universities attracting many able black
and Asian students, but the main problem of our time remains: there
is no multicultural education envisaged for all our children which will
enable them to see each other as proper citizens of a new nation. There
are worries too that 'New Labour have adopted the de-racialized

language (and policy-making tendencies) of the Conservatives ... There is an opportunity, finally, for genuine progress ... To make the goal a reality, however, will take a break with the past.'[53] This is the view of David Gillborn and it is one that I share.

There will be much to sort out before this can happen. It will mean looking at history so clearly that both white and black eyes will probably hurt. For example, the moves to set up a museum in Bristol to describe and explain the empire should not be discouraged but actively supported by all Britons. The glory as well as the shame, the multiple effects and responsibilities, need to be excavated. Only then can we create a sense of who we are collectively. People such as Nicholas Tate who have such unassailable power should be forced to confront the extraordinary limitations of their views. When he says that the culture of this country is rooted in Greece and Rome and Christianity (something the Prime Minister has also been heard to say), he is simply wrong. No one has the right to exclude us and our children from the treasures of world knowledge and historical links. And that is the most serious task that faces us in education.

Hopes are high, though, that the teaching of citizenship values which has been proposed will begin this in a way that we have not seen before. If it worked we might finally get the development of core values which are not tied to the idea of colonial dominance and victimization. Professor Bernard Crick has carefully built up an argument for the creation of an educated, caring society with different perspectives and collective responsibilities.[54] If this initiative ignores the powerful presence of ethnic, racial and religious diversity, it too will fail. And it will deserve to. And more generations will then be lost.

Ain't I a Woman?

I no longer care, keeping close my silence
has been a weight,
a lever pressing out my mind
I want it told, and said and printed down
the dry gullies,
circled through the muddy pools
outside my door.

And you must know this now
I, me, I am a free black woman
My grandmothers and their mothers
knew this and kept their silence
to compost up their strength,
kept it hidden
and played the game of deference
and agreement and pliant will.

Christine Craig,
a Jamaican poet,
The Chain, 1984

My own search over the years has certainly been based on an effort to
reveal suppressed possibilities – those understandings that time
rushes past but which can also be a means of releasing aspiration.

Sheila Rowbotham, *A Century of Women*, 1997

This chapter examines the way feminism, loosely defined and in all its
forms, and other women's movements have described the lives of
British women and chosen the locations for struggle in recent years.

What have been the issues? How have they been tackled and explained? How has awareness been increased? How have the leading voices chosen to interpret the lives of women? Why have almost all of them been white and what does that say about their theories, methods and approach? Why have black women allowed themselves to be relegated to the margins? Why do they not see their own lives in mainstream terms? And finally, and most importantly, what are the key areas where race and gender both need to be applied in any analysis if we are to make sense of what is happening and what the possibilities of progress are?

Women in Britain – white, black and Asian – have been at the front line of the mammoth social changes in the demographics and identity of Britain which escalated after the Second World War. This was happening at the same time as further tremors of the women's movement in the west began to be felt. People began to fear and understand that getting the vote was only the beginning not the end. Just like the end of empire was never going to be the end. But instead of gathering up our collective forces, we remained (and remain still) largely apart. I became most acutely aware of this in 1988 when I was asked to contribute a chapter in a book to be published by Virago on motherhood and feminism. After moving beyond the point of feeling flattered and enormously enthusiastic, I fell into weeks of gloom and mental paralysis. The problem was that I could not find the language, the concepts, the pictures, the images, a commonly understood history which could communicate even to the editor of this book – a very bright and empathetic white feminist – what it felt like to be me. I was the daughter of a woman who lived out the most extraordinary feminist life before such a thing existed.[1] I was born and brought up in Uganda. My father was a brilliant man but a bohemian, unattached to notions of family obligations, with self-convincing explanations for why this was right and all right. My mother had to take on the burden of working (at one time doing three jobs) and bringing up the family in the forties and fifties. In exchange he gave her the freedom to do as she pleased (except never to use any make-up and wear western clothes, or cut and style her hair the way many of her friends had by then started to do). She accepted both conditions because there was no real choice, and in due course she found her own way of dealing with the burdens my father had bequeathed to her. I remember all too well her going to films alone, making her own friends, using them when she needed to, not allowing herself the luxury of pride, and surviving the pernicious looks of disapproval, until people grew to love and respect her for what she was. She was one of three such women in our community who had feminism thrust upon them by circumstance. One became the first Asian woman MP in Uganda after independence and the other a star teacher and sportswoman. The courage and individuality of these three women was something I had grown up to marvel at, but it was hard not to have mixed feelings about whether it was all worth it. My mother was always ill, worried and tired. Her friends in more traditional marriages were not. They wore imported pearls and silk saris; their husbands fleetingly touched them in public, possessively and with love. These women had softer lives, said my mother, scorched with envy, although I dare say there was much hidden pain behind the public façade and the expensive pearls.

There were other complexities which of necessity had to be explained in a preamble to my chapter. I was Asian, had been born and lived in East Africa. I was a twice-removed involuntary migrant with at least three cultural cross-currents within me. I had a son who was growing up in this country where he would forever have to fight for his place and where he would be seen as a threat and an object of hatred, especially when he hit adulthood, leaving me, like many black and Asian mothers, living in constant terror that one night racists would kill or maim him. I was coping with the intolerable burden of being a lone mother abandoned by her partner in a community where such things are rare and always the fault of the woman who cannot not keep her man happy. I was an activist and was beginning to get furiously political. There was obviously much to say and yet I felt it was not possible to have real discourse with women across the racial divide because we, Black women and white women, had not evolved that equality of status which is a prerequisite to genuine communication. I wrote then, speaking to white British women because I felt they were the only ones who would bother to read such a book. (I was wrong in this at least.)

Your ancestors and mine have had a relationship for generations now. And yet you do not know me or mine with any depth at all. Many of us interested in this subject will, I suspect, be women of the same

generation. Women who through shattering world changes have created and coped with unique opportunities and responsibilities. We have had to live too, with the frustration of finding out that when we thought we were running and well away, we were only running on the spot. But these common experiences have not linked us in the way they might have done because they have been embedded in global power relationships and assumptions of white supremacy, which have informed the Women's Movement as much as anything else . . . things have been so one-sided. Even though I can never belong to it, [your world] has vibrated in the background of my entire life. Yet you hardly know my world.[2]

It remains a mystery to me as to why this should be so. Long before large-scale immigration from the New Commonwealth, many white women had established bonds with black people on these shores. In earlier centuries – and some of this is touched on in Chapter 3 – there were extraordinary historical accounts of how in the sixteenth and seventeenth centuries white prostitutes and ordinary women in London and the slave ports harboured and took up with escaped slaves. In 1578, one George Best was already fretting about this as he recorded his thoughts:

I myselfe have seene an Ethiopian as blacke as a cole, broughte into Englande, who taking a fair Englishe woman to wife, begatte a sonne in all respectes as blacke as the father was.[3]

Through the years which followed, a number of white women carried on this tradition of crossing the menacing and strictly demarcated racial boundaries on this island. Their men were none too pleased. Sexism mingled with racism to create a potent, explosive mix which, between 1911 and 1958, erupted in skirmishes and even riots on the streets. The American writer Beth Day described such attitudes (which were even more dramatically on display in the US) in a passionate, polemical book. She wrote:

One of the sad features . . . is that the white women never did ask to be protected from those black men. It was their fathers', husbands' and brothers' idea. White women were as much victims of the system as black men.[4]

In many other ways too, women in all the communities of Britain have always been significantly over-represented among those who challenge social codes, historical and political relationships, and martyr themselves if necessary to make their case. The rules which define their lives were never of their making and most women to this day still have little respect for systems and beliefs which have been set down by male prophets, politicians, fathers, husbands and brothers.

This means that racism and sexism, feminism and anti-racism, not to mention class, have been tangled up for as far back as the historical eye can read – except that most of us seem to be able only to keep our eyes on one of the threads. I am simply making the obvious but still barely understood point E. M. Forster made a century ago when he said: 'Only connect.' These two words captured my soul when I was a young teenager at school and I have spent my whole life trying to do just this. I am not talking here of the simplistic way race and gender have often been described previously. These are not additional effects along the same continuum of disadvantage – nor merely more stones added to the burden carried by the oppressed which leads to hierarchies of victims and to an unsustainable set of beliefs about the way the world works. This is what is often meant by those who propagate double or triple jeopardy arguments, an approach which achieves little and ends up instead dividing and alienating people even from the complexities of their own lived experiences. It also denies the complicated configurations, subtle identity and identification changes which take place in the course of a single conversation, so that black and white women can have intensely similar reactions to one situation and vastly different ones to another.

Here is but one example. As this was being written, a particularly furious public debate was raging in the British media. It was a skirmish over whether the new victims of society are men. Fay Weldon, considered an apostate and scourge of British feminists, brandished this provocative opinion, and the guardian of good, old fashioned, middle-class feminism, Polly Toynbee, assertively disagreed with her. As this was playing out, one magazine reader from Henley-on-Thames wrote this letter in frustration after reading yet another furious encounter between these two women of substance:

> I wonder how many women are as socially snobbish as Fay Weldon
> and Polly Toynbee reveal themselves to be. Their argument implies
> that any woman who stays at home – whether to look after children or
> to 'run the house' – is a dull creature, lacking in initiative or
> intellectual capacity. They write about women as if we are all the
> same, and as if they have the right to speak for all women.[5]

Many of the black and Asian women I talked to during the course of
writing this book had identical objections to the way Weldon and
Toynbee claim to represent all women. Others spoke in similar, critical
terms when they were discussing feminism in general, a word the
majority of black women I interviewed reject, and with some venom.
They thought (wrongly) that their irritation came from the fact that
they were not white. In distancing themselves in this way they were
displaying their own narrow focus and shallow grasp of what was
being discussed. It is, I feel, one thing to say that you don't agree with
ideas and quite another to say that the ideas are not worth listening
to because they come from the heads of white feminists. Life, thank
God, is more messy than this.

Gender or race perspectives on their own, or the idea of multiple
add-on disadvantages, simply do not make sense any more. What, for
example, would be the frame for the growing number of white women
with black or Asian partners attempting to bring up mixed-race
children? Sandra, a mother of teenagers, is one such woman:

> I started women's studies as an access student. I learnt about power
> and men and women. My man was African and very macho and I knew
> that often the reason he was abusive was because he found it so hard
> to get the respect he deserved. But he was beating me up. I couldn't
> ever discuss this in even my own mind because it seemed so racist to
> attack somebody from the poorest country in the world. Then he just
> disappeared after giving me a right pasting which left my eye
> damaged. My children were watching and my son, who was 14, was
> crying like a baby. I felt so confused and would have liked to talk to
> black women about this. And you know, I still think about him and
> would have him back. It wasn't this male control thing with him. It
> was racism which killed his kindness. I understand that now. Am I
> just making it easy for him?

Six out of ten 'Caribbean' children have either a white mother or a white father, each bringing a batch of such issues to confront. There are step-families where white men are learning to parent black children. Asian women might proclaim very loudly that they are not feminists, but the influence of feminism is seeping into the thinking of young Asian women who are choosing to marry white men instead of Asian men in order – they think – to have more autonomous lives. Black women and Asian women were and are having to bring up their children in a racist country. Rearing children in this atmosphere is so tough I sometimes wonder how we have had the courage to reproduce at all. Do white mothers – except for those who are in a situation similar to Sandra's – understand what it is like when, added to all the moods and furies of teenage life, your child hates you for bringing him or her into this country, or regards you as inferior, or worst of all turns to self-destructive acts because he/she expected to be embraced and was instead rejected, and there is no place to go? What is more, it is a thankless task, one that our men have mostly left to us. That of course is the same for the majority of white women. So why is it almost impossible to conceive that black, white and Asian women can talk about these problems with one another? I recently looked at a manuscript sent to me by a black woman writer and trainer, Rosemary Crawley. The book is based on workshops with black women and is full of honesty and invaluable insights into the relationship between black men and women, which she explains:

> Black political thought is dominated by males and promotes the male perspective. Sexism experienced by black women at the hands of black men and the role of black families and black communities in the subordination of women are topics which are rarely discussed or acknowledged.[6]

There are many reasons why there is so little discussion of these issues and these need to be confronted before the barriers can begin to be pulled down. They also need to be tackled because, as the next chapter reveals, they are affecting the most intimate, personal aspects of all our lives. So why is this essential discourse not taking place? At times it is that white women are uninterested – and I do consider this to be one of the most serious obstacles to dialogue and allied action. Others are too ready to stereotype and exploit the information or turn themselves into unwanted social workers with a mission in life to enlighten or rescue those of us from other communities who don't conform and don't wish to conform to their norms. But there are also some benign reasons for this distancing. Sometimes, perhaps, white women – especially those who feel deeply about racism, exclusion and justice – are scared of treading in places where they are not wanted or where they don't know how to behave. (This anxiety is much more present among white urban professional white women than in white women from more deprived backgrounds. During the course of doing interviews for this book, I was struck by how many deep, natural and open friendships there were between white and black women living on estates, many of whom were locked into a life of benefits, under-education and little hope of escape.) On the other side, many educated black women do not wish to make the links between their lives and those of white women because they feel that there is nothing there to connect them except a racist relationship, or that they will encourage further hatred against their men, or that it is and should be only their business. One woman, Cherry, an ex-GLC worker and now a child-minder (only of black children, out of choice) typifies this position.

> I would never join up with white women. How can you fight on gender issues when their racism is always in the way and they are leading everything? And I can't be bothered about who is doing the cooking or whether I can sleep with another woman. My priorities are different. They are about the police, about jobs and about abuse, domestic too. They can't understand that.

Others go even further than this. I go along to some meetings and I still hear that all the male oppression suffered by black and Asian women is the work of the white imperialist devil.[7] Still others deny any common humanity between white women and themselves and cling on to the idea of identity as if it is pure, historically fixed, homogeneous.

None of these reasons – although understandable – is really sustainable any more in the multifarious, mixed, hybrid society we now live in. This book has repeatedly argued that we are all getting more tribal and separate, which does not bode well. This is not to deny the genuine dilemmas and obvious tensions between cultural autonomy and gender equality; between racism and sexism; between the priorities of powerful white women and powerless white and Black women; between the achievements of the women's movement in three decades and the new problems brought about by those achievements. But if we never talk about common aspirations and our all too real differences, how are we likely to resolve any of these? Let me say it once again – it is that important. More bonds should have been established between black and white women. But they weren't. Sadly. Individually, many friendships do of course exist – and (dare I say it?) two of my best friends are white – but that deep understanding of values and ideas cannot be presumed, even in these friendships.

There is nothing new in what I am saying here. The only reason for reasserting such pessimistic thoughts is that nobody seems to have listened for far too long. All the concerns, disappointments have just been swept into nothingness, like sighs in a storm, as we gather for comfort among our own in our own back rooms. What I was saying, particularly about the neglectful behaviour of professional white feminists, has been said for years, decades even, by black women in the United States. In a moving lecture delivered at Spellman College in June 1987, Angela Davies said:

> During this decade we have witnessed an exciting resurgence of the women's movement. If the first wave of the women's movement began in the 1940s and the second wave in the 1960s then we are approaching the crest of the third wave in the final days of the 1980s. When feminist historians of the twenty-first century attempt to recapitulate the third wave will they ignore the momentous contributions of Afro-American women who have been leaders and activists in movements often confined to women of colour but whose accomplishments have invariably advanced the cause of white women as well? . . . If this question is answered in the affirmative, it will mean that the women's quest for equality will continue to be gravely deficient.[8]

In 1999 I would say quite categorically that that quest for women's equality continues to be 'gravely deficient' in Britain because most white spokeswomen, thinkers and activists have walked past the lives of women of colour and because in many ways that difference and indifference has been institutionalized most damagingly by powerful, white middle-class women. Post-feminists – that scary band of women who claim grand political power because they wear strappy sandals, skimpy tops and hot red lipstick – sound intolerably presumptuous to many black and Asian women. Most of us have never felt the need not to paint our lips or adorn and perfume ourselves in order to be serious about equality. They, the PFs, have little interest in us and feel no guilt about this. Perhaps this is because we might muddy the sparkly Perrier enthusiasm for their own positions by asking dark questions – for instance, it is all very well to adore Margaret Thatcher as a role model, but does it not matter that she supported some of the cruellest anti-family immigration laws in this country and was responsible for destroying anti-racism for a good many years? Or that the alluring charm about being really really really bad girls like that Prozac lass, Elizabeth Wurzel, and others, is that they do not ever mention racial injustice?

In fact, most writers on this issue in Britain in recent years have failed to include properly the lives and thoughts of black and Asian women. Do we not bleed and breed, that so many key current writers simply leave us out? Look at this very incomplete list taken within a single year. When that brilliant *Observer* writer (and a friend, still, I hope) Nicci Gerard wrote a scathing essay on the sisterhood, she forgot to mention that she was really only describing the white female experience, both here and in the United States.[9] Ditto Decca Aitkenhead, Angela Phillips, Maureen Freely, Charlotte Raven.[10] Sixteen women are profiled in Charlotte Raven's piece looking at the future of feminism. All are white, all part of the middle class, inherited or acquired. Even Alice Walker is left out. What about the radical film-maker Pratibha Parmar, or the academic writers Parminder Bacchu, Amina Mama or Kum Kum Bhavnani? I wonder how many of these names are even known by the journalists I have mentioned. The unstoppable feminist's feminist, Joan Smith, is incensed that a flagship Radio 3 series on the hundred most influential people this century includes only ten women. She provides some further suggestions. They are all women of European backgrounds except for Nawal

El Saadawi, an Egyptian who has, understandably, little to say about our lives here. Again and again, in the very act of making their protests about exclusion, white feminists, reproduce the worst examples of that exclusion. Even more ironic is the way in which those who then attack these feminists of small worlds, themselves carry on the white tradition. John Pilger laid into Bea Campbell, Julie Burchill and Natasha Walter for not being concerned or informed about global politics and the feisty women fighters in the third world. Having slaughtered these writers (he thinks), Pilger gives us *his* perfectly formed feminists – both white, both British, both middle class. Has he ever bothered to find out anything about British black and Asian feminists?[11] The *Guardian* and the *Observer*, where such writers write, are *the* papers of informed black people. What's more, media feminism has a greater impact on the general understanding of feminism than the best book in the world. They, we, might not deserve this power but what is said in the liberal section of the media is what people think is real. So when these journalists see the world as blindingly white, feminism becomes white. Ignorance may be bliss but not if it stems from a wilful desire not to know so you can stamp your ideas and theories over those who would beg (literally) to differ, a tendency increasingly common especially among 'feminist media babes', as Heidi Mirza describes them. And once they sweep through the media, *their* version of truth is established and *their* star burns out other truths in the galaxy, killing their light, causing them to fade out of sight. Mirza is apopleptic about such arrogance:

> **New feminism is not just the voices of Natasha Walter, Melissa Benn, and Kate Figes . . . there are other new voices out there who never get a look in as they are not part of the powerful and privileged media brat pack; the hidden voices of black women who live in another world.**[12]

At least traditional feminists sometimes showed traces of genuine inclusion and some, such as Germaine Greer, Gloria Steinem and Andrea Dworkin, were concerned to educate themselves with humility and have, throughout their lives, made links with different forms of oppression.

As one of the handful of white feminists who does not ignore our lives or those of others increasingly relegated to the margins, Bea

Campbell echoes and widens the scope of Mirza's valid and timely criticisms. She feels that:

> contemporary debates are fascinating. But what is being aired is fixed, paranoid, white hetero laments. I don't hear this stuff among black women, young or old; I don't hear it among women with disabilities . . . it isn't even an argument among men.[13]

There are other exceptions. When I interviewed black feminists, the one name which kept coming up was that of Sheila Rowbotham. She is instinctively, intuitively, an internationalist. Nothing she writes ever gives the impression that we are an afterthought or that she needs to make a gesture in the direction of black and Asian women or indeed to wipe them clean off the agenda in order to claim a universality which did not, could not and indeed should not exist. Her last book, *A Century of Women*,[14] surely one of the most outstanding books to be published in recent times, should be compulsory reading for all our big-time, big-voice feminists – and for black and Asian feminists who say that all white feminists are Eurocentric. Rowbotham does not know how not to be inclusive. On the third page of her introduction, she pays tribute to two African-American sisters, Bessie and Sadie Delaney (at the time she wrote her book they were aged 106 and 104), daughters of a slave who lived through and fought against 'Jim Crow' segregation. Their struggles against institutionalized racism make them heroines in the narrative of women's equality. And so it is in the rest of the book. That white feminists did not discover feminism is the message here, nor are they now the only or most interesting fighters in the struggle for equality (this is my conclusion; Sheila Rowbotham would never be so unkind). If women such as Gloria Steinem have inspired black women and been inspired by them, surely it should not be beneath white British feminists to pay some homage to non-white feminists around the world, not excluding many more of us here in Europe who have played as big a part in the reconstruction of womanhood as have white women.

It has to be said that, on the whole, women's editors on the liberal papers have also been open to our influence, and three in particular – Hilly Janes on the *Independent* and Claire Longrigg and Sally Weale on the *Guardian* – have appeared almost revolutionary in the way they have refused to exclude or simplify our lives and ideas. The same is true for *Woman's Hour* on Radio 4, though not for any other section of the BBC. In their articles, individuals such as Suzanne Moore, Yvonne Roberts, Katherine Viner, Melissa Benn and Libby Brookes do manage, without patronizing, to incorporate and include us through trying to understand the profound beliefs of our lives. They do this by depicting us neither as aliens nor as honorary whites. And that, it seems to me, is the key. Far too few, however, are concerned to find it. In academia, especially in Women's Studies, a much healthier approach has been adopted and in some of the best courses there is an unselfconscious incorporation of culture and race within gender considerations.[15] Exceptional work, such as the book by Morwena Griffiths, *Feminisms and the Self*, are also distinguished by the commitment with which they make connections.

> In the past feminists have had a dream of sisterhood and a common language. Recognition of hybridity and multilingualism shows that, far from this being desirable, differences between women and their different languages combined with the points of overlap between them, actually improve the possibilities of political change.[16]

But this is still rare. There are dozens of other feminists who assume a colourless position and believe that to be unproblematic. To name but two random examples: the fiery *Of Her Sex* by Kate Figes (which has a black woman and a white woman on the cover) or Patricia Hewitt's *About Time: The Revolution in Work and Family Life*, make no attempts to expand the world they are describing.[17]

We – Black British women – would carry on regardless if the only problems we faced were at the level of theory, ideology and cultural understanding. What is unacceptable is that these attitudes affect our daily lives, our rights and struggles to survive and grow. White women, especially middle-class white women, now occupy more powerful positions in British society than ever before. They still have their battles, of course, to reach the parts that men often get to those positions without effort or talent. But many of these women who have climbed nearly to the top do not seem to display much need or desire to carry us with them. Sometimes the will, you feel, might be awakened if only the awareness was there. Take Women in Journalism, an excellent club of highly talented and high-achieving journalists, editors and columnists who are making an important impact on the media. They have, thus far, not taken up the cause of excluded black and Asian women journalists. Amongst thousands of women working in the print sector, there are at present about eight of us in proper jobs on newspapers and about as many again having to make do with freelance careers in which all that we are expected to know or care about are black issues. I mentioned this at one meeting (why should it always fall upon our shoulders to bring this issue up? Do people understand how demeaning it feels always to have to do this?) and I have to say that the powerful sisters on the platform *were* very interested. But they had not thought about it and it is not clear to me what is going to happen as a result of one voice making a noise about this. How are we then supposed to respond to bubbly enthusiasms like those displayed by Natasha Walter (a fine writer it has to be said) when she observes:

> In journalism, the profession I know best, there is certainly a 'girls'' club that runs alongside and inside the traditional boys' club . . .
> working both as a commissioning editor and a freelance journalist, I
> have found that most women journalists like most men are locked into
> a dense network that brings them lunches, commissions, jobs . . . [18]

Should not Walter and others who have an extraordinary degree of influence in public discourse on women's issues be a little more humble in their claims and (in order to show consideration if nothing else for those of us not in the magic circle) try to avoid presenting their own privileged lives as the 'norm' in a society as varied, complicated and unequal as we have in Britain today? Most of all, should they not be more aware of realities which could further change if they put their minds to it? As Heidi Mirza says:

> Black British feminists reveal other ways of knowing . . . In our
> particular world shaped by processes of migration, nationalism,
> racism, popular culture and the media, black British women reveal
> the distorted ways in which the dominant groups construct their
> assumptions. [19]

I am only using Walter to illustrate a point, not to join in the unfair, vicious attacks on her by many other feminists. And I use her because she does have such an impact at present and because, as she herself says, she represents the *new* feminism which should be capable of greater insight and inclusivity.

Although by no means enough, there are books around which would enlighten anyone who was interested. Besides academic work based on sociological or anthropological studies, there have been a few exceptional publications which deserve mention. Among these are classics such as Amrit Wilson's *Finding a Voice: Asian Women in Britain*; *The Heart of the Race – Black Women's Lives in Britain*, edited by Beverley Bryan, Stella Dadzie and Suzanne Scafe; *Telling it Like it is*, edited by Nadya Kassam; *Charting the Journey*, edited by Shabnam Grewal and others; *Flaming Spirits*, edited by Ruksana Ahmed and Rahila Gupta; and *The Hidden Struggle* by Amina Mama.[20] Newer books include excellent edited volumes by Delia Jarrett-Macauley and Heidi Mirza.[21] *Feminist Review* has always been a trail blazer in this area. Add to this the work of academics and others such as Haleh Afshar, Avthar Brah, Women against Fundamentalism, Anne Phoenix, Pragna Patel, and you get a body of work which is no bad starter pack. What is clear, however, is that so far you would still be hard-pressed to fill a single medium-sized shelf with books of this sort, and that almost all the non-academic books have been published by small publishing houses. The irony is that if you are African-American and a woman you are likely to get an embarrassment of riches and unconditional devotion from white British feminists. Here is a conversation which took place between a young, female, sassy, black British songwriter and a white, female novelist at a party – it was a conversation I first listened to and then joined and it took place at a media party in 1998.

> W f n: **Did you go to listen to Maya Angelou in Brighton? I think she is a goddess. You must be so proud as a black woman to watch the way she rises (sic). It was just incredible to watch that power and the style.**

> Y, f, s, b, B, s: **No I didn't go. I don't much care for her. There is nothing real about her, lady. It is all one big expensive act and I find it makes me angry. She thinks she is a queen now. She isn't. She is good, was good, but now it is all this royalty stuff which she**

loves and white folk lap up. And you like her because she is
American. Why don't you all go and listen to Linton [Kwesi
Johnson] or Merle [Collins] or Benjamin [Zefaniah] when they do
readings?

W f n: Oh I don't know. I saw a number of black people in Brighton.
She is great and not because she is American. Excuse me . . .

The lack of status given to *British* (and it is different if you are Indian
too, as I discuss in Chapter 9) black and Asian writers – really the core
of the argument above – is indisputable. The consequent lack of
interest damages us all as we attempt to live together on this small and
fast-changing island.

The involvement of white women is required in crucial areas – if
only they knew and accepted this responsibility. There are many
examples where this engagement could make a significant difference
to the way politicians and policy-makers carry on. Immigration and
asylum laws have a particularly harrowing effect on women, on whom
even positive changes can impact negatively – something which is
unknown to policy-makers because black women are not usually
consulted. For instance, the Labour government (rightly and honourably keeping their manifesto promises) abolished the primary purpose
rule which discriminated against black and Asian people by assuming
that if they chose marriage partners abroad these were not genuine
marriages because they were arranged by families and not entered into
'freely' by two people in love. The previous law was racist and was
implemented by officials often in discriminatory ways. What the
government did not know was that many Asian girls used the rule to
avoid forced marriages. They would either tell immigration officials
that this was a marriage they did not want, or warn their families that
they would tell officials they were being coerced. This stopped a number
of forced marriages. This was highlighted by me in an article and it
caused serious consternation within the Home Office. Another key
area which affects black or Asian women from abroad is the one-year
rule. A wife without British citizenship can be deported if she is
widowed, or if her marriage fails, in the early months. Husbands use
this rule to imprison women in marriages, using violence and other
threats to keep the women docile. Female asylum seekers looking for

refuge are often not admitted into this country as *bona fide* refugees because officials will not accept that they are targets by association, and because often their experiences involve rape which leaves no physical scars. The treatment of Bangladeshi mothers in ante-natal care wards is a national disgrace, especially when one considers how much progress there has been in this one area of health care. They are deliberately left ignorant about painkillers and modern medical technology, and are thereby denied real choice. I myself have witnessed how medical professionals in the East End of London often fail to inform women about their choices, and I have met young mothers who knew nothing about epidurals and other pain relief. Black women are among the most active and highly educated people in the labour force and yet they are denied access to top jobs – even in areas where they form a central part of the workforce, such as the nursing profession. And though some Indian, African and Afro-Caribbean women are doing well in the labour market, most of the rest are still having to fight each step of the way for their basic rights.[22] Are such fights not at the heart of feminism? And if they are not, why should black and Asian women give a toss about how many white women are on the board of News International or Marks and Spencers? What is also frequently missed out are the incredible success stories – against massive odds – of visible women. A report by Dr Spinder Dhaliwal in 1998 showed that 7,000 Asian women own and run businesses with employees.[23]

There is another difficult area to be explored (and it would be good to get some social research commissioned on this one) which has a bearing on the relationship between white feminists and women of colour. What are we to make of the real (sometimes surely deliberate) discrimination that we are now seeing perpetrated by white women against black and Asian women? I interviewed a group of Asian women cleaners at a hotel in west London. Their supervisors, the human resources manager and one other manager in charge are all white women. They have done nothing between them to promote the Asian women – some of whom have been in the job for over a decade – to supervisory positions. Meena (not her real name) describes the treatment they have to put up with:

> I have worked with a male manager. He respected me more than
> these three women. These ones here, they treat you like you are a
> cockroach. They do not understand that we are mothers so sometimes
> children are ill and we need time off. They tell us to get child care –
> on £3.15 per hour. You know you think a woman can maybe
> understand these things better. But no. Exactly the opposite. They
> have no children, no *maya* (maternal feelings, empathy) you know.

As the keynote speaker at three conferences (UNISON Black Women
in the Workplace, NUT Black Teachers Conference and London Voluntary Organizations Network) in the year 1997–8 I heard incredible
tales of cruelty, racism and discrimination directed at black nurses,
teachers, local authority workers (including within Equalities teams)
and voluntary sector workers. The perpetrators were all white women.
One black health visitor said quite simply:

> The racism we face from our white female colleagues and managers
> is the untold story. This is why when racist complaints are lodged by
> patients we have nowhere to run for comfort. Women managers
> understand sexism, but have little interest in dealing with their racial
> prejudice. The inconsistency hurts. They think that they know it all
> and that as women they could not be unfair. This is a delusion they
> love.

In politics our neglect is reflected most strikingly in New Labour
politics. When people have faith and extraordinary changes happen,
expectations grow and frustration is that much more acute. As a
woman I was elated (and still am) to see the influx of women into
Parliament in the 1997 election. But dragging down that elation were
the questions about why in this year of all years, we black and Asian
women failed to get a single seat. Labour has over 100 new women
MPs. Not one of them is black or Asian. Oona King is half African-
American and half Jewish. That means that at present over 2.5 million
of us have one and a half Members of Parliament to represent and
explain our lives. How could this be right? How could one not feel an
enormous sense of betrayal at the same time as the joy? Did the
influential women in the Labour Party expect us to feel the second and
not the first? Did they not care what we felt? If so, why not? Diane

Abbott, one of our most intelligent MPs whose performances at the Select Committee meetings on finance were legendary, has been relegated to the margins. She has the same straight-speaking and brave qualities of Clare Short. How many white feminists have ever spoken up for Abbott the way they do whenever Short or Harman are being treated with contempt by the Party or by the media? Black and Asian women are not doing any better in the other two parties either. Nor in the higher echelons of any of the professions. White women in power has not been a panacea for us or indeed for most other white women.

For a project for the Institute for Public Policy Research I interviewed fifty black and Asian women just before and after the election. There were two main sets of responses, represented by the following two women:

> I never felt disappointment like now in all the past eighteen years. Our future and past I thought should be put on ice while the Tories ruled. The only thing to do then was to survive; to stop them – the police, the state – killing too many of us and not to let them win by taking our hopes and aspirations. Like those slaves in Mississippi I waited for the day to come when we would inherit our place. Now? There is no hope. I have started thinking for the first time that Nation of Islam and other separatists are right. I shall never vote again. And when I look at Blair's babes, I feel taunted. Sisters you care nothing for us.

(Marcia, 29, married, social worker)

> I am a member of the Labour Party. I worked very hard knocking from door to door with others in the area. And I know that we are not in their heads any more, but I have great hopes. I admire Joan Ruddock, Cherie Blair, people like Oona King, and I know these women will not let us down. I hope I am not being stupid. At the moment though I feel I am out in the cold while the rest are at the party.

(Sunita, unemployed, 25, living in Manchester with her family)

I confess, even as I write this book, that I am inexplicably afraid that white feminists will react with anger instead of understanding, when (if) they read any of it. But silence on my part would be contemptible at this point in our joint histories. And so the show must go on.

But could it be that the reasons for this split between politicized black and white women has less to do with cultural and political arrogance or myopia and more to do with the fact that many white feminists and women in general feel there are real and often insurmountable barriers between us? In the summer of 1997, the *Guardian* columnist Linda Grant wrote a deeply felt piece on the racial divide which has for so long infected the women's movement and feminism in general. She asked: 'Can white and black women talk to each other again?' And then she explained why not – not yet anyway.

> It began, I remember, when black women asked white women to listen to what they had to say, to hear their experience. This led to the dutiful asking of questions, followed by a new assertion – 'it isn't up to black women to educate you. Go and educate yourself' . . . If it is impossible to hold an opinion about another person's experience unless you have shared it, how can you have an opinion about anything at all except what has happened to you? White people in general seem to be in retreat from friendships with black people because they are terrified of saying the wrong thing, of giving offence.[24]

Is this then why I can count on one hand the number of events, parties, receptions and meetings to mark women's achievements, publications and events I have been to this year where there are more than two or three non-white people present? And here I am describing events in London, mostly in 'metropolitan', liberal circles. Why is this, I wonder? Are we on the must-have lists and do we merely refuse to attend, or are we, most of us, still invisible to those responsible? Linda Grant is right when she says that fear and mistrust sometimes preclude genuine interactions and these days, in some black groups, whites can do no right. But Grant must know that there is a history of failure, misjudgement and anger to get through before such things can realistically happen. Men could make exactly the same complaint about their fear of offending feminist battleaxes. It is also an incomplete analysis, which lets white women off the hook a little too easily. I am unconvinced that in some situations it is fear of offence and not smugness that makes white feminists treat us with so much caution (to the point that they would rather we weren't there at all) that it feels remarkably like disrespect. But more seriously I wonder how much someone even with Grant's sensitivity and obvious anti-racist credentials understands what exclusion – ongoing, constant, unreasonable, never explained – feels like.

If you dare to speak out you are treated like you have fouled up the very air. Picture this scene which took place at the ICA at a gathering of legendary feminist luminaries. A book had been written on feminism in the 1990s. I was asked, among others, to comment upon it. I was honest in both my praise and my reservations in succession. I said that I found myself unable to relate to some of the sweeping statements, and that I was unhappy that implicit in the book was the assumption that if you criticized any manifestations of British feminism you were considered part of the backlash within and outside the 'movement'. The chairwoman at this meeting, a name in British feminism, thereafter physically turned her chair away from me so I was left facing an audience on my own while the three of them faced each other and carried on talking even when I was answering questions from the floor. Were they afraid of upsetting me? Or are they now utterly convinced that their world view is so inviolable that even mild questions are seen as effrontery?

I would like to see in our public spaces the kinds of important debates that are taking place in the United States about cultural group rights and gender equality. Women such as Susan Moller Okin[25] and Leila Ahmed[26] speak out with a freedom on these thorny issues in ways which would be unthinkable here. The Council of Europe has been organizing seminars on cultural diversity and women's rights since 1995. British feminists, black or white, are rarely part of these.

But I have digressed from my own original question, as to whether we, black women, are being narrow-minded when we object to our exclusion? Is our own inclusion not implicit and is that not better than forced token entries? Are we not women in the end? Should we at least try to be more loyal to the mainstream women's movement? In some ways this is like asking Cinders to stop whingeing and to have generosity enough to take pleasure in her sisters' good fortune. Moreover, it does not address the massive difference between what Linda Grant is complaining about and the thoughtless, automatic neglect of women of colour from any grand narrative on feminism or womanhood. It is as if we have never been there, never done anything, or that our fights have been irrelevant except as footnotes.

But we turn a corner at this point, for this is most emphatically not merely a book about our continuing exclusion by villainous whites or about fixed histories. I couldn't write exactly what I wrote a decade ago in my essay in *Balancing Acts* because so much has changed in our own lives. In spite of the obstacles put in our way, many of us are emerging as incredibly successful women, particularly in areas where we can make our own way – in business for example. Pola Uddin, the first Muslim woman to enter the House of Lords, spent most of her life on a Tower Hamlets housing estate – with the usual disheartening problems of urine and syringes in every corner – bringing up five children, including one suffering from cerebral palsy. Valerie Amos and Patricia Scotland, who are also now in the Lords, came up from being on the margins to the heartbeat of this country through their own resilience and obvious abilities. Usha Prashar is the head of the Parole Board. Meena Pathak and Parween Warsi are top businesswomen. Wasfi Kani is the founder of the Pimlico Opera. Shobhana Jeyasingh runs her own phenomenally successful dance company. Zaha Hadid is one of our most exciting architects. The list is too long to go on with, and that is the real indication of how far we have come.

This is enormously liberating. As a black woman I now feel free to be more honest about where *we* might be culpable and to discuss it openly. I think that, increasingly, many of us share these feelings of relative security and want now to take these debates out into the public arena. Indeed it is essential that we do. This may entail examining whether (maybe) there are some credible reasons why white feminists in particular and white women in general avoid dealing with us. There is in place a set of pervasive beliefs, perpetuated most perhaps by political black women, that black and Asian women are homogeneous, all at the bottom of the pile, utterly virtuous because suffering makes you so, and living in their own specially demarcated worlds which are so special and separate that others could never understand them or have anything relevant to say about their lives. These are in part senseless battles between the victims of domination and injustice. Such enclosures lead to empty spaces. Over the years these orthodoxies have lain comfortable and unchallenged at least partly because many of them were invented by Black women and therefore by definition were assumed to be correct, universal and forever true. Again, black American women led the way and far too many of us subserviently followed. Just to give a single example to represent these theorists, look at the writings of Filomena Chioma Steady and read such gems as these:

> true feminism springs from an actual experience of oppression, a lack of the socially prescribed means of ensuring one's well-being, and a true lack of access to resources for survival. True feminism is the reaction which leads to the development of greater resourcefulness for survival and greater self-reliance. Above all, true feminism is impossible without intensive involvement in production. All over the African Diaspora but particularly on the Continent the black woman's role in this regard is paramount. It can therefore be stated with much justification that the black woman is to a large extent the original feminist.[27]

It is important to challenge such competitive and ultimately separatist notions of womanhood. None of these convictions bears up under even the most superficial scrutiny. They insult the experiences of white women trapped in poverty, or violent relationships and powerlessness. To be white is not to be right, and neither should it mean than you are by definition all right. These notions also divide sisters of colour from one another. It is foolish to state that Africa is the towering continent where the 'intensive involvement in production' of women is unique.

Even more importantly such theories do not any longer make any sense strategically. During the course of researching this book, I found myself invited to a black women's group meeting in London. It was only for black Caribbean and African women. I promised not to disclose what the group is, why it exists, and where they meet. As the meeting progressed, I found myself gasping for breath as it became more and more vociferously intolerant. I was told that white women could never have any of the experiences of black women; that they were a 'breed apart'; that they smelt because they did not wash (this opinion was also peddled with obscene merriment by other black sisters on a Channel Four series on mixed relationships, presented by the black journalist Donnu Kogbara), that any integration with them led to the death of black autonomy and the black community. Finally one of them (a fiery, thirty-something woman newly renamed Africa) asked to see what I might say about them and then demanded that I go back to 'those shits and those bastards at the *Guardian* and tell them to give us more access'.

We want it every which way. Like the woman known as Africa, some wish to live as a nation apart and yet want to be taken seriously by the dominant group. They have given themselves licence to disrespect all white people and yet demand absolute respect themselves. And when some (too few to be sure) in white society attempt to include or at least respect us, they have ended up being attacked even more than if they had walked away. I know for a fact that those running Emily's List and the Fawcett Society, and individuals such as Lesley Abdela, have tried hard to enlist co-operation but have not succeeded to the extent they wished. I also know that the received wisdom about white women involved in these important initiatives is that they 'don't care'. Let me give an example of how easy it is to fall into this trap. When Natasha Walter was researching her book, she tried many, many times to arrange a meeting with me. For all kinds of reasons which are always with us, I could not put aside any time for this. I then found myself fuming over the fact that she had 'neglected' black and Asian women's experiences. This was very unfair and I admit to it.

This leads to other issues that do need to be confronted. We never gave white women the right to feel free enough to comment and have a proper exchange with us about the choices we were making and the ways in which our communities worked. Every query, every mild piece of criticism was/is taken as racism or colonialism, even when human rights were being violated. Little wonder then that we have been left alone in our struggles for such a long time. Many white women do patronize and misrepresent our lives. But we retaliate in kind, and by making all white women equally culpable and homogeneous we fail to use proper judgement on those individual white women who are genuinely egalitarian and interested in breaking from the narrowness that has blighted the women's movement in Britain since the beginning.

One of the most depressing conclusions I reached after extensive interviews with black and Asian women was that the more politicized they were, the more likely they were to stereotype white women and to mistrust them indiscriminately. Maya, who works for an Asian women's refuge, is still enraged about how she thinks it was when she first went to women's group meetings in her local area.

> I would walk in and most of them would look surprised. Some would smile in that way which said, very pointedly, that I was welcome because I probably needed their support. You know? That kindness which is really insulting but you can't say it because it is better than unkindness and prejudice.

I remember feeling just as alienated when I first arrived in this country. Germaine Greer's *The Female Eunuch* was all that feminists would talk about at meetings. I could not see the point of the book and remember my sense of violation (quite overdone when I look back) that no one took any notice of this point of view. Yet there was much I wanted to talk about. How my African women friends at university had been gang raped by Amin's soldiers and how they had watched their men tortured and killed. No, the big thing was orgasms on demand and the rest be damned.

When you feel surrounded by injustice, you begin to get self-destructive, and listening to Maya rant in this way I at once felt guilty about how I too similarly maligned white women and how cheap and easy such petulance is in the end. The battles of our lives as Black women are exhausting and demoralizing. This is why so many of us hope never to be part of these exchanges again and want instead to snuggle up with other black and Asian women where we can complain loudly and at will without a problem. Or a solution.

Racism – a real and pernicious force which blights our lives – has made us blind and defensive. We have too often felt unable to relate properly to white people, or to exercise any kind of objective evaluation, of self-criticism or judgement about ourselves, for fear that racists would add more venom to their stings. This was in part the reason we lost our way. In making the rooms our very own, we inevitably kept out the light that others would have brought to bear to make us grow and flourish. Nearly a decade ago that peerless feminist writer and film-maker Pratibha Parmar wrote wistfully:

> It seems difficult to fathom where the optimism and stridency which
> many of us had who were active in the black women's movement has
> gone, and why. Where are the diverse black feminist perspectives
> which we felt were in the process of growth? And where, indeed, is the
> movement itself? In moments of despair, one wonders if those years
> were merely imagined.[28]

It is interesting that now Parmar spends more and more quality time
in the United States with black feminists such as Alice Walker who are
not sectarian in the way they think. Of course there are differences
and assumptions to challenge. Back in 1985 a member of a Brixton
black women's group said:

> What Samora Machel had to say about women's emancipation made
> a lot more sense than what Germaine Greer and other middle-class
> white feminists were saying. It just didn't make sense for us to be
> talking about changing life-styles and attitudes, when we were dealing
> with issues of survival, like housing, education and police brutality.[29]

This was true then and is even more true now. But poor whites are
also going through at least some of these problems, and an allied
approach is surely stronger than an enclosed, embittered one? In order
not to disappear into our own heads and become more divided and
more ineffectual, we needed to have alliances with and exposure to
those who were not line-by-line exactly like ourselves. It is outrageous
that we should only dip into the white world in order to see no good
in it or that we should dismiss the views of white women without even
knowing them, like Maya (above) does. She thinks part of the battle
is to disengage completely from white women:

> I never read them. These people like Suzanne Moore and Polly
> Toynbee. None of their writers either. I had to in school but now I
> have no books written by whites. Reading them is a betrayal, like
> sleeping with the enemy. I don't care how clever they are. I will not
> read anything by white women, ever.

At least Maya has made it her business to inform herself fully about
non-white feminists. This is barely true of the rest. How many black
and Asian women know of the extraordinary Indian feminists Madhu

Kishwar and Shabana Azmi? Or the Human Rights Commission in Pakistan which is run by Asma Jehangir and other middle-class women? These women have a clarity of vision when it comes to women's rights which is not available to western Asians surrounded as they are by racism. They are able to fight for women's rights without self-doubt. That is why we need to know their work. And although it is intensely irritating for us black women to be automatically relegated to cheap seats every time an African-American woman is in town, it is foolish not to acknowledge that women such as Toni Morrison and Alice Walker are truly inspirational and essential to our own growth. There is in the end no difference between those who worship blindly and those who reject influences because they are not 'British' and 'Black'.

We have a long way to go but the dawn will, I am sure, come. Perhaps what we should have done was to produce people like Alice Walker, June Jordon and bell hooks, black feminists who never took the easy way into shady enclaves but instead confronted white feminists, fought them, cajoled, persuaded, wrote so brilliantly that they became irresistible to the whole world. It may not be too late, with the emergence of young, gifted and black writers such as Aminatta Forno and Heidi Mirza. But at this point we are confused, riddled with contradictions and responding to this crucial moment in diverse ways. Some people have ended up despising their own race and communities and have in effect abandoned both. You can easily turn white in your thoughts without even knowing it.

Rita (previously known as Rashmi, a name she now considers disagreeably ethnic) personifies what I am describing here. A Punjabi woman with a Master's degree in sociology, she refuses to describe herself as an Asian any more.

> **I can't stand these folk any more. They are backward idiots and the sooner they are forced to change the better. They treat their women like shit and pray to plastic gods they buy in cheap stores. I hate it. I am a feminist and for me the Asian community is the very antithesis of what that means. I don't care about my so-called culture. I am British and this is Britain.**

At the other end of the spectrum are black and Asian women who have thrown themselves wholeheartedly on the pyres of 'culture' – a static never-to-be criticized culture. A by-product of this is the throttling demand that no one who is black or Asian, even our most powerful or most corrupt people, will be criticized because that is racist. Suppression of truth (sometimes important but never to be encouraged or expected) and the protection of cultural groups as if they were some kind of nearly extinct species, is part of this protocol. Breaking it in any small way can lead to extraordinary viciousness.

I have had a number of encounters on this front. My autobiography, *No Place Like Home*, which attempted to describe my painful childhood and to examine how Asians remained racially prejudiced in Uganda which is why our expulsion was so popular, raised fires all around my personal and professional life. Another unforgettable fracas arose when I wrote an article in the *Guardian* on one of the few ethnic minority women who had achieved a position of real power, not in the field of race. She was an Asian and the piece was a critique of how this was working both for and against her. I was also critical of her leadership. The reaction to this was salutary. For years afterwards I was regarded as a traitor by some of the more conservative members of the Asian community. She was one of us, and whatever she did she was to be protected. Many influential white people – some of them wives of politicians who have always enjoyed nurturing black and Asian individuals in their own image – who had in fact promoted this particular woman, were also incensed. This was a no-go area. As I am writing this, a similar story of bad leadership by a black woman is being defended on the same grounds. Such tolerance is indefensible. It seems to be absolutely imperative that we should challenge these codes of behaviour. We need bad black and Asian leaders like we need thorns in our eyes. And worst among these are those who will do nothing but defend the *status quo*. Too many black and Asian women are having their lives destroyed by their own for us to pretend not to notice. Fourteen-year-old British Asian girls are locked up, beaten, exported to Pakistan, India or Bangladesh to marry men they don't know and don't want. Hundreds of black women are abandoned by the fathers of their children and dare not speak up too loud because that is treacherous. And all the while the cultural bands play on, deaf to these cries.

In *Charting the Journey*, one of the most beautiful, lyrical expositions of this terror and silencing that has been imposed on black lives, the editors asked, way back in 1988:

> For where are we at present? Instead of at least the semblance of a Black women's movement, the futile 'politics' of victim and guilt tripping runs rampant and is used to justify actions that any self-respect would deem impossible. Or there is the tendency towards the collective adornment of moral and political superiority which is supposed to derive from the mere fact of being a Black woman. That this is so gives rise at least to a wistful sigh and more often a scream from the far reaches of the soul – the only way to express one's disbelief and bewilderment that we could have got here from there.[30]

These experiences, the internal and external restrictions, mean that the questions we ask ourselves, the stories we tell and the dreams we have, can never simply be about gender and inequality. Even when black women – such as the Southall Black Sisters – have absolute confidence that the approach they take when helping women in distress will not be muddied by concepts of cultural rights, the work that they do, how they are perceived and received, is always going to be different from that of a white domestic violence help centre. On the other hand, as Rozina says below, each generation that grows up here moves in the direction of the white, hegemonic, Anglo-Saxon value system, making it increasingly difficult to extract cultural diversity from hard common experience.

> I am Muslim, a doctor educated here and a mother of two children who are primarily now British. They go to private schools; they have aspirations and their father who grew up here wants them to aim high too. So what is the difference between white families and us? I think we overplay it so that we can get this grant or that.

But, talk on with Rozina and ask her about her daughter and her relationships with boys and a chasm opens between her and the Joneses next door.

> No, in that our culture must be kept. I don't want sex education, contraception for my girl. I don't want her to have sex before marriage or to know too much. She will find out everything afterwards from her

> husband. I can't bear to see these lesbians, free-sex girls, doing it
> with someone they speak to for five minutes, this is degenerate.

The really interesting question here is whether Rozina has a point that white feminists would take seriously (at least enough to be the subject of ten columns, as we get when Fay Weldon speaks out against feminism), if they did not immediately file away her thoughts under 'cultural difference'. I too am afraid that my daughter will pick up the sexual freedoms of the west which have done us no good at all. Germaine Greer has recently pointed out that 'In 1968 women had the right to say no without apology . . . now they have a duty to say yes.' Instead of saying no all the time, women and girls are now pushed – from the age of ten – to sell themselves in the market-place. Young women must, therefore, show all their wares, proffer up pierced navels, wonderbra boobs, slits and slashes, perfect bodies displayed for uptake by randy boys and men who seem more and more addicted to the idea of sex everywhere and any time, on tap. And now we will have to cope with Viagra men. Rozina's concerns are not 'cultural' if one looks beyond her own restricted description of them.

This illustrates the tensions between multiculturalism and freedoms and reveals too that grappling with the true complexities of these tensions might enable an essential interrogation of established views on many issues. Take the issue of the *hijab*. There are a number of reasons why so many young women are using it today. Many young, strident Muslim girls are taking up the garment as an assertion of their identity, as a protest against their demonization and exclusion; others do it to pacify their parents or as a challenge to young men who would have it all. As Bhikhu Parekh wrote when describing the episode in France in which schoolgirls decided to wear the *hijab*:

> [They did this] partly to reassure their conservative parents that they would not be corrupted by the public culture of the school and partly to reshape the latter by indicating to white boys how they wished to be treated. The *hijab* in their case was a highly complex autonomous act intended to use the resources of the tradition both to change and to preserve it. To see it merely as a symbol of their subordination . . . is to miss the subtle dialect of cultural negotiation.[31]

But this garment is also an imposition by families and sometimes the excuse to kill 'liberated' women as in Iran and Algeria. Many young university students not wearing the *hijab* have been murdered in Algeria. In 1994, Homa Darabi, an Iranian child psychiatrist in Iran, burnt herself to death in a public square in Tehran by setting her *hijab* alight because, like other educated women, she objected to being imprisoned in it.

We can never be white. Yet there is no going back to some pure 'ethnic' culture. The third way is what some of us are grappling with: how we can connect with mainstream issues and powerful white people – especially feminists – without being appropriated, embittered or silenced. And how we can remain true to our difference while judging our own communities using universal human rights standards. We need to get white feminists to be as self-critical and open as some of us are now prepared to be. And indeed this is possibly a period in which we can be uniquely optimistic about new developments in this area. There is no doubt that a new, more confident black and Asian intelligentsia is emerging and challenging ideas in institutions of higher education in particular. Many intellectual women are coming up. They are less interested in being good girls or being professional grousers. Even those who are still committed to their own spaces want those spaces not to be in the suburbs. They are rightly more excited by the possibilities of generating a dynamic, black, feminine intellectual firmament which has been missing here but which is taken for granted in America, India and elsewhere. An excellent example of this intellectual energy is to be found in a newish collection of essays on black British feminism written by ethnic minority women and edited by Heidi Mirza. She says emphatically that in 'this place called home, named black feminism' black women can collectively mark their presence and, more importantly in a world which still denies them their voices, affirm their identity and uniqueness to each other.[32] Such an emotional club (in both senses of the word) may be necessary for many for a good while longer. And the intellectual aspirations are absolutely right and worthy especially as black feminists are embarked on a mission of re-entering a relationship with white feminists on an equal footing, however hard that turns out to be.

These new Black feminists give us a sense that these experiences are

217

important not because they allow insight into hidden worlds but because they enlarge the concepts which have dominated and prevailed in Britain. Razia Aziz, one of these impressive new feminists, says clearly that she will not play the game by the rules set down in the past whereby

> the energetic assertion of black/white (or any other) difference tends to create fixed and oppositional categories which can result in another version of the suppression of difference. Differences *within* categories – here black and white – are underplayed in order to establish it *between* them. Consequently, each category takes on a deceptive air of internal coherence and similarities between women in different groups are thus suppressed.[33]

It is important to realize that stresses and strains have meant that we have developed strategies, mechanisms, ways of being which are important for all our futures. Long before David Blunkett and Jack Straw 'discovered' the effective social tool of naming and shaming, the Southall Black Sisters led the way in singling out families which violated the rights of women. In doing so then, they were using something which is fundamental to the Asian community – the notion of *sharam* – shame. Now, of course, this tool is used in all sorts of other areas. Black and Asian women perceive their own lives in hugely symbolic terms – something that Gayl Jones, the African-American writer, recognized a few years ago when she was writing a book about black women in the United States. She realized how, at an individual level for a black woman,

> her attention is mostly directed outside of herself and her life is described in terms of social rather than personal or intimate implications. Women seem to depict essential mobility, essential identity to take place within the family and the community.

These two observations – the lack of space or time given to the inner lives of such women even by themselves, and how their functioning is located within a sphere outside their individual selves – would be true of the many black and Asian women living in Europe today. But this perspective is not automatically to be scorned or pitied. There is something admirable in this ability not to be entirely self-obsessed and over-intimate with one's own thoughts at the expense of broader concerns. Charlotte Raven is quite right to point out that

> [t]he ethical hole in modern feminism is its failure to generate anything but self-justification. Desire itself is politicised, self-gratification a right. This has led to an abdication of social responsibility in favour of almost libertarian licence. 'I want it so it must be all right.'[34]

As yet, thank God, we do not have many black or Asian women writers producing self-indulgent (best-selling) tracts on too big bums or how to be a right old bitch. Zarah, twenty-five, an aspiring actress, puts it like this:

> We seem to be less superficial and less obsessed about ourselves. I just read that book *Bitch* by Elizabeth . . . and I thought most of the women in my life would not want to be like the heroines in this crazy book. Theirs is such a me, me, me world. I tried to read Helen Fielding and I just couldn't stand that self-absorption. We are so much more conscious of the whole world and about our place in that world. They see themselves as the globe and the rest of life as dots. We do the exact opposite. I also find it difficult to sympathize with white women who simply want more of everything.

But it is in that central experience of motherhood that links and possibilities are most clearly revealed. Motherhood has been a key issue not only because of all the dynamics, the gains and losses which preoccupy traditional white feminists, but also because it is so central to the lives of dispossessed minorities in this country and in the two-thirds world. You watch Doreen Lawrence's face displaying at once tenacity and impossible pain as she seeks justice for the killers of her son, Stephen, and you see what hopes were killed on that day at the bus stop – the hopes that drive immigration, the hopes of a young black woman who felt strong enough to risk procreation in a racist society, and the hopes of a mother who felt that the future was worth all the troubles and sacrifices that motherhood brings. Motherhood here cannot only be examined through the white, gender perspective because such an analysis fails to explain or understand what a woman like Doreen Lawrence has gone through. It ignores the fact that for many women of colour, motherhood is an enclave, a source of safety and joy from constantly demeaning lives in a hostile environment. Children are often a mark of defiance against oppression and destruction, and also terrible victims of the wrath which their very existence can generate. This is why motherhood is rated so high and why few black and Asian women, whatever the personal costs, would be unlikely to take the radical anti-procreation position of some white feminists. I remember being horrified when I read Jill Tweedie saying that she had advised her children never to have any kids. When you talk to white women from deprived backgrounds you see how differently they view parenting. Two women, Marilyn black, Debbie white, lone mothers and close friends living on a horrendous housing estate in Harlesden, talk to me over a cup of sugary tea. Marilyn says:

> You know posh women don't understand what children mean to us. We love them and want them not because we are so stupid and sex mad, but because they are something to be proud of, and I hate it when I watch those programmes when women say that children stop your careers and that. They are so cold like their wombs dried up. As a black woman I cannot afford not to have kids. Where will the community be without kids in the future? We are too few already.

Debbie adds:

> Yeah. Right. I know I am not working and that. But I love my kids so much I wouldn't trust anyone else with them. All those people – like that woman with five children with millions of pounds who had all those nannies. I couldn't do that. I don't want to. I am sure the government would sterilize us if they could. They hate us.

What possible sense can simple feminism make of these views? One thing is certain – there are many more women like Debbie and Marilyn than there are self-defined feminists in Britain, and their lives – impoverished, made impossibly hard by the terrible problems caused by the arrival of children – have often also been brightened and enhanced by children and not diminished by them. Neither our past nor our present is necessarily their future and what binds them is their motherhood.

To conclude this chapter, then: black and white women, whether feminists or not, must develop a new relationship beyond individual friendships. White feminists need to listen more, show greater humility and courage and also check out their own non-negotiable principles because increasingly women of colour are as likely to question them as are many men of all hues. White feminists have infinitely more power and influence than do black women and must take responsibility for changing the way the world treats black women. Black feminists and women in general also have decisions to make: are black women a part of womanhood or are they apart from it in some exotic imagined place of their own? Have they played a part in their own marginalization and do they now have to break free from a culture of separation to a more equal, participatory and difficult relationship with their white sisterhood? We have so much to talk about. And feminism surely lies at the heart of these conversations even if most women these days wouldn't be seen dead wearing the label. The vision is described by Heidi Mirza:

> The black feminist critique engendered a guilty paralysis among white feminists for over twenty years and this needs to be intercepted if feminism is to move forward. Feminism as a term, a movement, is not impervious to change. If feminism changes to embrace differences rather than be preoccupied with difference, then its meaning will change and strengthen black and white feminist activism through a unified and cohesive and strategic identity.[35]

8
Me, Myself, I and Mine

For the past two decades the sites for struggle, rage and fundamental
social encounters have moved from the floor of factory and Parliament
to the family. This is something accepted now even by structuralist
and high-minded feminists like Ann Oakley who said in 1994 that the
family had become a dangerous 'battleground' for women, causing
them mental and physical illness and in many cases destroying them.[1]

That over-rated world guru, Francis Fukuyama, having arranged the end of history, has gone on to declare that the new challenges are all about the 'Great Disruption' to family life and values.[2] Perhaps this is an inevitable stage which had to follow, something that was bound to happen as feminism began to shift power relationships outside the home. But there are other reasons too. The personal is replacing the political because cynicism, complacency and self-interest have so infected the mainstream political domain, and because of an increasing (totally unsubstantiated and convenient) belief that governments are powerless to affect the big brute forces of environmental disasters, globalization and ethnic wars. We should legitimately ask why we elect governments any more. Perhaps it is in order to fend off such disturbing and fundamental questions that the government relocates and increasingly begins to intervene (or interfere, if you are right wing) in family matters.

Having privatized large chunks of the public sector and surrendered to multinational business, our governments are now, with some enthusiasm, nationalizing private lives. Since the days of the cold, disturbing calculations of people such as Keith Joseph who, in the eighties, started the unsavoury debates about whether the poor were reproducing too much and bringing down the material stock of the nation, to the interventions by the Social Exclusion Unit which is advocating the teaching of parental skills to those defined as the overlooked, what was once considered private terrain is increasingly perceived not to be. This is not a value judgement but an observation, and obviously there are huge differences between the punishing values of Joseph and Thatcher and the more empathetic policies of the Blair government. What is interesting, however, is that many of the people who are targets of such cyclical national concern, believe there is little difference. Josephina, black, 22, and Ella, Irish, 23, are neighbours, living on a council estate in Acton. They have six children between them by six different fathers. They despise what they feel is state control over their private lives – Josephina especially.

> Yes I have three kids and their fathers are long gone. I know I am only
> 22. I know I have no qualifications and that I am taking state cash.
> But I am a damn good mother. My eldest could read at the age of 3

because I taught her. Her school couldn't believe it. I want to stay
with my kids while they are young because I am all they have. But
middle-class children have bad bad lives, I'm telling you. Who looks
after your kid while you are running around doing this? Is your book
more important than your children? That woman Nicola Horlick. Five
kids and three nannies – they are like children in care. My kids are so
well behaved, so kind, you should see for yourself. Why doesn't the
government leave us alone?

Governments may feel more in control if they are able to determine
the choices such people can make. But if such interventions are to
work, there needs to be a better understanding of what is going on in
British family life. There is ample evidence that existing assumptions
about values are no longer settled. Those fighting for changes are as
guilty of presuming to know what people are and what they want.
The new divorce laws introduced in 1999 are despised by many ordinary people because they institutionalize the concept of a no-fault
divorce. Almost all the people I spoke to for this chapter felt that in a
world already without any moral anchors, these changes give licence
for people to behave badly in marriage. Many facets of life we thought
we could take for granted are resurfacing with controversies and
questions stuck all over them.

The national ferment over family life means that other sectors too
are jumping on to the back of the crisis. Voluntary organizations built
around panic over the family are now one of the few growth areas in
the non-profit-making sector. In the professional middle classes, a
growing (and growing rich) band of pundits churn out 'How To' books
which are overwhelming people from all classes. Whither and wither
the family is an obsession with media folk too. A casual check of the
broadsheet press from June to December 1997 revealed 245 separate
articles and comment pieces on the subject.

But speaking a lot about something does not mean we speak with
more sense. On the contrary. What such attention does do is reveal
the inadequacy of leaders and politicians on these issues. While Conservatives have lived out (and sometimes been publicly shamed for it)
the utter hypocrisy of their political position on family values, liberals
(more intent on not being taken to be Conservatives than on doing

the right thing) have chosen to ignore vital evidence on the cost of disintegrating families to human beings. They have, instead, spent decades snipping away to alter morality to fit the situations which require ethical assessments and actions. Adultery, for example, is no longer something that is wrong but something that just happens. At a conference on the New Left in June 1999 Polly Toynbee, Will Hutton and Anthony Giddens argued that moralistic frameworks were out of date in modern family life, and that people had a right to make and re-make their families.[3]

The statistics are now outstripping excuses. Forty per cent of marriages in Britain end in divorce. The rates are the highest in Europe. In 1961, 30,000 divorces were registered and in 1995 the figure was 155,000. Lone-parenting figures which include divorcees and those who are separated from relationships, are also among the highest in the western world, as are increasing numbers of teenage parents. It is always important to remember, though, that these are overall figures and that within different visible communities the figures can be much lower. Statistics in a multicultural society can be very much more complex than is often realized. Attitudes in these communities are also vastly different from those generally assumed. I often wonder why it is, for example, that all the white friends I made at university are divorced. And that almost none of my Asian friends – those with whom I was at school in Africa and later at university in Uganda – have gone down this road. The trends that people describe seem alien to this group of people. And it is when you start looking at the cross-currents of race, class and relationships that you begin to get at least a hint of how little consensus there is about men and women in this country today.

This consensus has been under even more pressure in the post-Clinton era. When the most powerful man in the world begins to lose his authority because he failed to keep his penis in order, sex suddenly becomes a whole lot more political. All those who have made clean divides between the private and the political have to swallow (!) their theories and grapple with difficult lessons arising out of the Clinton scandal. Here a private relationship (one of many others previously) depended on the political might and power of a man. Whether they were victims or predators, none of the extra-curricular women in

Clinton's life would necessarily have done what they did if he was a local plumber. His incontinence and dissembling in one area might be repeated in another. How do we know his bombing of Sudan did not come out of the same recklessness that enabled him to seduce an intern while he was doing world business on the telephone? Clinton saying that a politician and a bishop must also have a private life suddenly sounds feeble and unsustainable, particularly in the context of Britain and the United States where there has been such indecent interest taken by politicians in the family values of others. After the Clinton implosion, family troubles are even more at the heart of politics. Generally people seem to be expressing the view that leaders need to be more self-controlled and to honour their family obligations more, as do the rest of us. People feel that even if they fail, there is a point in having moral codes. In contrast to this the hysterical rejection of such 'oppressive' codes by feminists and liberals comes out looking like the reactions of adolescents who drown out the voices of adults warning them of the perils of free sex, drugs and rock'n'roll.

There are various moods of dissent out there. And sometimes the dissent is within our own souls too. We who were so all-knowing in the sixties, seventies and even early eighties find ourselves rebelling against our own inventions and ideas.

Look at the abortion issue in Britain. After thirty years, there is still a minority in this country which believes that a needs- or demand-based abortion law militates against humanitarian principles. These objections to abortion have leaked into the hearts if not the minds of those who are intellectually committed to the right to abortion. I include myself. Where once we had the op., came home and got on with our lives, these days we grieve even though most of us would never surrender ourselves to the bad old days here or to the appalling situation faced by women in countries which don't or can't have easy access to safe abortions. But the ghosts of the babies we never saw haunt us, and increasingly so.

Vanessa is a deputy editor on a magazine. She has had three abortions in her life and is now pregnant again at the age of 39.

I hate myself now for what I did to those babies. It was like nothing to us. We behaved worse than animals just dropping these

inconveniences and walking off to the next party. I was so promiscuous, I cannot even bear to think about it in the dead of the night. The pregnancies were not sinful, but our reactions to them were.

What are so often dismissed by the liberal left as traditional right-wing values are today being proudly asserted in the most unexpected places. And we must listen to and respect these positions. Take another example. Bel Mooney is a self-confessed 'sixties person'. She is a liberal and a firm believer in free speech and tolerance. Today she is anxious and prepared to take on her libertarian friends because it seems to her that there need to be some 'limits of freedom of expression'. She is taking a stand 'against the seemingly endless downward spiral of sex and violence in books, films and on television'. She argues that unless we take charge, our children will be condemned to inherit a moral vacuum instead of a civilized community.[4] I think Mooney is absolutely right and I have been appalled at the number of liberals I have met who now dismiss her as 'looney Mooney'.

When I was exploring family values, my research revealed this to be an area of exceptional confusion. There was much talk about the family and the death of it. Myth has taken over here even more powerfully than in the realms of romance. But look around. How can anyone claim that the family is dead when one looks at the numbers of people who give up everything to take care of family members in need? When all our abiding cultural images and longings are still built around the idea of the family? Equally, how can people argue that the family is the nest of security we all need, when so much evidence daily appears about the physical, emotional and sexual abuse of children within families?

Liberal views often imposed on society by an arrogant elite are becoming questionable too when one looks at the eternal triangle of children, work, and male/female relationships. Josephina and Ella, and many other interviewees who were not or did not consider themselves to be middle-class professional women, did not share many of the stridently anti-father, anti-man positions even now being put forward as the norm by women in public life. In spite of all the betrayals, disappointments, violence even, most kept their faith in the family and the ever more elusive good man.

And yet in the nineties our main feminist commentators have suggested the very opposite of what I found. Just two examples: Suzanne Moore has often written about how it remains unclear what it is that fathers do that is so important. Bea Campbell has concluded: 'To reveal the redundancy of men is the real crime of mothers.'[5] And these views have influenced those involved in family policy and practical work too. Sue Slipman, when she was Director of the National Council for One-Parent Families, often reiterated this idea of the unwanted father.

When it came to male–female relationships, the same tidal wave approach has dominated. Germaine Greer reaches majestic form when she attempts to interpret the widening fissures between men and women and the backlash against feminism:

> **Male hostility to women is a constant; all men hate all women some of the time; some men hate all women all of the time; some men hate some women all of the time. Unfortunately, women cannot bring themselves to hate men, possibly because they carry them in their wombs from time to time.**[6]

My research was qualitative and as such not statistically instructive. Nevertheless, it was extraordinary that such grand disdain was not reflected even in modest ways among the majority of the women I spoke to, and especially not among the poorest ones who were all too aware of the way unemployment, racism and other forces had diminished the ability of some men to be good fathers and partners. Leroy, black and a father of two small children, is quite clear about this.

> **How can I be as good a father as someone like Kilroy. I mean he had me on his programme and started having a go at me. If I had his money I can be a great dad. But with no job, no car, nothing man. How can I look my kids in the eye? Why did I have them? Because they are the only thing I have that I can be proud of.**

The more you talk to young lone parents, the more you realize that Leroy and his sort know that they will find any number of women who will understand their plight and carry on having their babies. There was a touching and sometimes frightening solidarity expressed by men and women from poorer groups (two of the women I interviewed defended their men even as they were nursing terrible domestic-violence injuries) than ever was manifested by the better-off couples. They were not only standing by their men; they were letting the men stand on them. As Ella said:

> I feel let down by these men, but I can't feel as if it is all their fault. Ian, my last one, will buy a lottery ticket every week with my name on it so that one day, maybe, we can be together and be happy. If life wasn't so shitty he would be kinder to me I know.

There was also brutality freely expressed in the family. Lisa, a 10-year-old who has been taken into care at least once, has three other siblings in her family, all with different fathers. Sad beyond her years, she spoke to me at great length on the phone one evening when she was left babysitting:

> They are all so angry. She hit the baby today. And then she was crying. I love my mum but she's upset all the time. I don't go to play because after school she is very tired and she hits the kids. My dad hits her. He broke her tooth. Will you come again?

But her mother still dreams of getting married to the last man who walked out on her. She wants that white wedding, the Persil home, and is waiting for him to return. But if dispossessed women are clinging on to traditional roles, women with an endless flow of possessions seem increasingly to be pining for them too. Ally McBeal and Bridget Jones (described memorably by Yvonne Roberts as singletons desperate for any man as long as he can breathe in and out) must make Greer and others weep, if they allowed themselves such weaknesses.

There were other salutary lessons too. Like many others, I have been in a state of some panic over teenage pregnancies and the sexualization of young children in our society. But I found that many of these young mothers are not only very good mothers, but that if they had not had children, they would not have gone on to bigger and better things. They had already been marked out for educational failure by the 11-plus exams of life. Connie, for example is a 15-year-old mother. She looks after her child as if she is a jewel. The social workers are impressed, as is her own mother, Vera, who is an alcoholic. Vera says:

'Con is great, you know. She is really happy with the baby. I have never seen her getting angry or anything. She goes out with her mates and that but she comes home early now. She wants to. I think she thinks I can't babysit properly.' As a result of her research, Anne Phoenix believes that

> [c]ontrary to popular belief and the ways in which 'teenage motherhood' has been socially constructed, early motherhood does not constitute cause for general concern. The majority of mothers investigated in this study (as well as in many other studies) were coping with motherhood well. Their children, according to maternal reports and assessed on a standardised developmental test, were also faring well.[7]

Other strong beliefs need to be assessed. Work is no longer a panacea for women. And it is not only disenfranchised women such as Ella and Josephina who are troubled about the new orthodoxies which demand that mothers must go out to work. And both women were truly terrified that with new government regulations their children would have to be looked after by others while they were forced to go out to train and work. Both accepted that it would be better in the long run, but the love of their kids and their sensitivity to their vulnerability made them feel quite desperate.

In 1997 Harriet Harman, then a minister, claimed that nine out of ten women wanted to work. But research by the Economic and Social Research Council found that only 3–5 per cent of women looking after children at home were interested in getting jobs outside. In 1991 the Office for National Statistics showed that 73 per cent of women of working age were either in work or looking for work. In 1997 the figure had fallen to 69 per cent, the biggest fall then for twenty-five years. Melissa Benn writes convincingly about her own niggling worries about what she calls the 'new mantras':

> Once the fervent call of every woman who longed for freedom from domestic slavery it is now all about getting women, particularly poor women, into a job. Any job. Worse, child care today risks losing touch with locality and community and becoming instead a high-powered, educationally geared form of warehousing. Where is the liberation

in that? We need to think more seriously about what is involved in caring and how much we, as a society, are prepared to support it. It's becoming a dangerous heresy in these New Labour times to argue the legitimacy of anyone staying at home to bring up children, even for a short period . . .[8]

After talking to a number of stay-at-home mothers I have to accept – against my own instincts – that in many of these cases the children have a better life in some ways than do the children of those who go out to work on low (or even high) wages. Josephina's children were delightful and confident and incredibly responsible to one another and to their mother. What struck me most was the easy speech and comfortable silences between mother and children which seemed to come out of long periods of intimately shared time and space which is now no longer possible for working mothers. Neither the mother nor the children displayed that terrible panic about how little time there was to do the things which needed to be done. I was shocked at my own surprise that women like Josephina could teach professional women like myself a thing or two about motherhood – that actually there is something unnatural about constantly planning how you are going to usefully use every precious minute with your children. At the risk of idealizing these women (and why not?) I would say there was a passion too about wanting better lives for their children when they grew up which gave these mothers an edge over those of us who are now involved simply in reproducing advantage through our offspring, and dealing with the debris if this does not naturally happen. These women will never write best-selling books on how to bring up children. Ella's family on the whole seemed extraordinarily at peace. There were stresses and these too were obvious (but somehow contained), as was the lack of many of the toys and things one takes for granted in middle-class homes. Ella told me tearfully that she had slapped her eldest child that day because she could not bear to be asked for things she could not buy.

Black and Asian women were much more confident about their roles as mothers and home-makers, and even the most astoundingly high-achieving women, those who have made millions and are names in their own right, seemed gloriously proud of the men and the success in their lives. Parveen Warsi, the food magnate, says she sees herself first of all as a wife and mother.[9]

We need to be aware of these realities if only to assess properly just how feminism and womanism are working through our personal lives as we reach the end of the twentieth century, and more importantly how we may revive or at least save from extinction meaningful bonds between partners, children and other members of the family. Ironically, because we, Black women, have not been included among the striding feminists of Britain, we have not wholly fallen into the 'norm' of society. We can make choices with some hindsight. Most of us now wonder if the price to be paid to get to the top is what we wish to pay and we can see the clear connections between economic success and personal cost. Lorna is a black businesswoman whose business is just taking off. She is both excited and worried about this:

> I have a young son, Justin. I am a single parent and he means the world to me. My business at the moment is run from home and he is getting to see a lot of me, even if my head is down in paperwork or thinking about a million things. This could all change if those who are keen on investing in my idea have their way. My responsibilities as a black mother to a boy are different from most other people. We have seen a generation of men lost to us. Many were the latchkey children because, when they first came here, Caribbean couples had both to work long hours in low-paid jobs to keep up a basic standard of living. The kids meanwhile were dealing with racism, with bad schooling and all that. Now I have seen what that did even to my own brother. And Justin's dad. I have also seen how many white businesswomen simply don't have a real family life. I can learn from those examples and try not to fail the next generation.

Almost every one of the black and Asian women interviewed for this book felt strongly that though they agreed in principle with equality between the genders, in their own personal lives they did not want to enter the highest echelons of the workplace if that meant that they would have to learn to deny that they are real women at all, or pretend that real ambitious women have no wombs. I remember the grossly uncharitable things that were said around the time Linda Kelsay, erstwhile editor of *She* magazine, left her job. Somehow her private reasons and emotions became public property as men and women fought over whether women could have it all. Wrong question. 'Do women want it all?' would have been the more appropriate question. She was brave, I thought, to walk away and say in effect that she did not want it all and that that did not make her a failure or a victim.

Other women living in the hinterlands when it comes to power and influence also have a lot to say on these key issues. Jyoti Patel is 26, married, and a dentist. She has a toddler and lives in an extended family with her in-laws. She sees herself very much as a woman with a message for the future because so many white Britons have lost the way.

> Tony Blair talks about rights and responsibilities, about the community. He talks as if these ideas have only just been invented. We live out those principles. I live with my husband's family. They look after my child while I work and I look after their needs as much as I am able. All our possessions are jointly owned and I do feel it gives me more security in this country where every person is looking out for themselves. We have learnt, like drinking mothers' milk, how society needs control as much as freedom in personal lives. How we cannot take up top jobs as mothers and let our children suffer. That there must be sacrifices and if men can't make them, we must. Because if we don't we should throw away our children. And now we are being told that the Prime Minister of this country would like everybody to try to think like we do. They never give us credit, just take our ideas, our food and keep us on the outside. This will not do.[10]

Those who still ridicule these principles need to get a little humble. Today it is not only old world eastern women or educationally disadvantaged women such as Josephine, but a growing band of independent women who are moving back to the future. In their report, *Tomorrow's Women*, Demos predicts that 'the back to basics movement is likely to gain growing support'. Of women who are working, 3.2 million (most of them under 35) would rather be at home; 36 per cent of 24–34-year-old women believe that family life suffers if women work full time.[11]

Many more women are also prepared to be more self-critical. Why, asks Jyoti, if it is equality we seek, do we have such double standards as women?

If a man abandons his family, he is called a bastard. If a woman runs off and leaves her kids, this is a reflection of the search for freedom from the prison of home life and all the speculation is about how unhappy she must have been with him who must be left behind.

All the women's magazines extol the liberating virtues of affairs for women. In the film *Betrayal*, based on the real-life betrayal of Nora Ephron by her husband, we are left in no doubt about who is contemptible. But Isadora Wing in *Fear of Flying*, and Emma Bovary, are heroines. Women who wound other women by running off with attached men are never as severely condemned as the men. At least two of our most outspoken and famous feminists have done just this and then gloated about it in the press. In both cases, the wives responded with unspeakable pain. It makes you wonder what feminism really means. A man is always a bastard but a woman, even if she is bitchy, has all sorts of positive reasons assigned to her, automatically, on grounds of gender. Katy Roiph argues convincingly in an article in the *Observer*: 'When a man cheats, we assume it is all about a new naked body, but when a woman does it we assume it is for love.'[12]

There can be little doubt that these are becoming defining issues of our time and that is precisely why we should view with extreme caution anyone who presumes to drown out the complexity and diversity of experience and opinion. We may wish it were not so, but there is a very real crisis in family life although the manifestations of this are very different among the various tribes of Britain. Not one person I spoke to thought that all was well with this central unit in our society. So many questions remain unanswered. What happens when men are denied both the role of provider and the role of nurturer? Could it lead to them abandoning responsibility for both because these have become such thankless tasks?[13] Is female independence only possible at the expense of men? A report into fatherhood by the Institute for Public Policy Research described how modern fathers across the country are feeling increasingly troubled and marginalized.[14] For example, 1.6 million fathers are non-resident. And yet we have not really asked enough questions about all of this, as Andrew Samuels says: 'The good enough father has not been written about very much. Why not? Why do we prefer either to idealize or derogate the father? . . . Retheorizing the father is essential.'[15] Ros Coward, warning against 'virgin birth fantasies', reminds us:

> There have been real losses for fathers in the contemporary family and to say so does not involve harking back to outdated ideas of the father's role. Fathering has changed fundamentally in the past thirty years. The first changes happened in the 60s with the emergence of the modern egalitarian family emphasising equal partners and the welfare of children . . . More recently increased economic uncertainty for men and women's challenge to the authoritarianism inherent in the provider role have undermined the breadwinner role. Fathering has changed, but no new ideals have emerged to take account of those changes.[16]

Divorce affects around 150,000 children every year. The figures are going up all the time and this country has one of the highest rates of family breakdown in the western world. Whatever lies we tell ourselves, family breakdowns affect children adversely.[17] We went to a lunch party in 1997 where not one of the ten couples invited were original partners. Our children had thirty-six parental configurations between them. The older ones took some delight in this and were overheard recounting (between giggles) how complicated the weekend arrangements were in their convoluted lives. Anna, 9, put it something like this:

> You see I go to my real dad and his new wife, not the divorced one, I mean not my mum, who he is also divorced from, but Nina his second wife. She like, she is gone. But his new wife Donna and her son every Friday. Nina's son comes too. And then my step-dad comes to get me on Saturday so I can be with him and my half-sister and his daughter, who is also Lisa and my age.

A BBC2 documentary in May 1998, *Children of Divorce*, featured children talking about divorce in their own lives and showed movingly how, even years on when they are young adults, there is real pain, loss, anger. And yet, since the sixties, liberals have pretended to themselves that their children would not be affected by their own need to be free agents with few imposed or internal restrictions on that freedom, or an acceptance that others might be paying for it. Statistics have been enlisted for their cause just as they have by those with a fundamentalist family values agenda. There was an interesting drama in the summer of 1998 when a report on divorce funded by the Rowntree Trust, was claimed as a victory by both moral libertarians and moral authoritarians. Both exaggerate their arguments to a degree which makes them increasingly irrelevant to the lives of people. Men and women cannot and should not be imprisoned within truly miserable or abusive marriages. But to pretend that divorces and separations create only freedom and happiness all round is immoral.

Common sense and common sensibility should tell us that we may choose freedom over obligation and that sometimes such choices are essential, but that such choices often negatively affect those nearest to us. As Jyoti Patel, quoted above (pp. 233–4), suggests, if one wishes to understand the dynamics and the future of family life one source must be communities which have not been caught up in the major trends of mainstream society and which have been able, to an extent, to take what is best and reject the destructive developments of the last thirty-five years. Take this story.

Zahoora Khan is a bright and beautiful Muslim woman who was born and raised in the northern city of Huddersfield. As the eldest of five sisters and a young brother, from the age of 11 she had to carry huge responsibilities, especially after the death of her father, when the other children were very young. She found this hard, but what made the burdens harder to bear was the constant abuse she and other Muslim children were subjected to at school by their peers. Her intelligence marked her out, though, and her teachers persuaded Zahoora's mother to let her daughter carry on with her A-levels and then go to university. Zahoora, blinded by enthusiasm, did what she thought was a passing deal with her mother. After college, she promised, she would marry her cousin from Pakistan, an illiterate farmer, someone whose name had been floating around her life for as long as she could remember. Half-way through her course she was called back home. She arrived back to find her home swarming with people, a sullen man whom she did not recognize, and wedding clothes in her room. Three days later she was forced into the marriage she had promised. The ceremony took seven hours because she refused to say yes every time the mullah asked her. Finally her mother threatened suicide, so she had to agree. She was locked in her bedroom with her husband for the night. She refused sex. He knocked her out with an iron and raped her so violently that she bled with internal injuries for the next three days. He gave her a gold necklace he had bought for their wedding night. On the second night Zahoora broke the window, jumped out and escaped. The police and social services helped her to get to London, where in time she was able to settle down and complete her education. A black social worker became her lifeline. Three years later her brother found her and tried to kill her. By this time she was divorced and living with another Asian man, who loved her though she would not agree to marry him because he was not a Muslim. She loved night-clubs, shopping, modern city life. She was working and secretly communicating with her sisters, telling them not to surrender their rights.

Suddenly one day, she gave it all up and went back home and asked her mother and brother to find her another husband. A man was duly found. He believes that a woman should not work, drive or even laugh too loudly. Zahoora traded in her BMW, her job, her friends, her lover, her freedom and moved in with a family of twenty. She says she has no regrets. She says she found the responsibility gap impossible to live with. The human spirit needs to be under some kind of pressure and family life demands generosity and the surrender of liberties: 'How to live without any obligations, without any rules, no higher authority than my own needs? I could not enjoy it any more. I wanted to be a member of something bigger than me, me, me.' When she changed her life back again, it was at a time when she was, she felt, a feather flying but not on the body of a bird. 'Useless, but free.' But the difference is that she now feels she made her own choices not to be free. She is a willing prisoner. If she felt she was being forced into being one, even now, she would run off again. Do not pity Zahoora. Understand her. Understand, too, that there might be edification in this story.

Many women understand the need for duty and morality in this excessively individualistic world. For Vanessa, a happily married black family lawyer, moral relativism is the worst kind of self-justification:

> **I can live with people who try at least to live by some principles. What I cannot stand is those who have made excuses into morality. Black**

men saying that they have the right to be baby fathers because their
great-grandparents were slaves. Feminists stealing men from families
and then claiming that the grand sisterhood does not depend on their
behaviour. Is this what we want to teach our children? This is the
biggest mess and children are the ones paying for it.

There is something utterly defeatist and depressing in a life of never-
ending adjustment to reality. As if we have no strengths, only weaknesses which must needs be fed. Human beings have gone from being
conquerors of the earth, seas and skies only to end the second millennium being victims of their passions. This diminishing of our ability
to live by ideals has sapped our capacity for true and deep passion.
Instead we have all become the things of small gods; sexual adventure
and fancy; overblown torment over divorce settlements, nannies and
mortgages. We seem also to have lost the imagination to live with
other human beings without feeling diminished by the obligations that
imposes upon our lives, causing us to suffer a bit and learn through
that suffering.

One of the most depressing testimonies to this approach was a long
treatise on marriage and divorce which was published in 1998. The
author, the talented Deborah Moggach, feels that people need help on
how to make not better marriages but better divorces, because that is
the inevitable outcome for most people:

Many of us have lost the stamina for a long marriage. We've lost the
good will and the selflessness; we've lost the aptitude for compromise
and forgiveness . . . marriage has changed from a structure of defined
familial responsibilities to the pursuit of personal happiness. We
put ourselves and our needs first, *even before the needs of our
children.*[18] [My italics]

The first thing to say about this outpouring is that many women and
men would not agree with any of it. And therein lies some hope for
the children if they are not to end up even more disenchanted than
they are. All the Asian women I spoke to have not lost the stamina for
a good marriage or relationship. They might have had their hopes
dashed but they retain a profound belief in long partnerships and
motherhood. They are capable of great restraint, compromise and

selflessness. When not self-destructive, these qualities make a better, not a worse world. Most of the black women I spoke too were also keen on finding the perfect soulmate. None of them would say that she would put her own needs before those of her children – increasingly the norm among white metropolitan folk.

Sounding like a cross between a *Daily Telegraph* editorial and a rabid Christian fundamentalist, Moti, my friend, successful researcher and mother of three, says:

> It is all the women's fault. They have cut off the pride of men. They can't cook, sew, bring up children. All they want is to be men as if we can trade in our wombs for the private parts of men. We can never be men and that must be a cause for celebration. I would do anything for my husband as long as he treats me with respect. I don't mind the housework and all that. It gives me pride that I can work and keep a wonderful home. I cannot bear these resentful English women who do nothing for their men and expect everything from them. I know not all are like that and some are real victims of bad men like some of us are too. But too many of them never put down their weapons.

What Moti is clearly identifying here is one unpalatable truth: women are not natural born saints nor are they the solution to the world's problems. Neither can they still collectively be described as the most oppressed people in our society. And it will not do simply to move the goalposts and find new ways of 'proving' that men are still as unreconstructed as before and women are still their victims. Look at the way the 'new man' is constantly derided or described as a mirage of our craving hearts. Of course we could pile up evidence to show that new men still do not do the washing up as much as the women in their lives, etc. etc. But as Ros Coward, quoted above (p. 235), says, those of us who have egalitarian male partners know and delight in the knowledge that as lovers, friends and fathers, some men have changed beyond recognition within a single generation. Failing to accept and praise this is hardly likely to encourage men to commit themselves to a process which must appear to them at times thankless. And to suggest that there have been profound changes does not mean that we are unwittingly allowing a right-wing agenda to prevail.

Change is taking place in all the communities and it is sad but true that where this change is causing confusion, people tend to blame white feminists, convinced that their ways are being corroded by such women who have forgotten how to be women. Versions of black women as invincible hearth-makers may be grounded more in fiction than in fact. Only four of the twenty-five black men I interviewed felt that it was possible for black men and women to have equal and equally respectful relationships. For now. It is as if they retain hope but cannot produce the reality to sustain that hope. And instead of examining themselves, they have found it easier to blame white society. Several of the Afro-Caribbean men complained that they were being emasculated by their women who were too interested in middle-class lives. These men are among the most discriminated against groups in this country and a number of them were finding it hard to live with the fact that their children were being brought up by successful white men who were proving to be excellent step-fathers. One told me he had wept buckets when he saw *The Full Monty* because he knew how 'dickless' the young unemployed father must have felt when the mother of his son moved in with a man with money and a big house.

Other endemic fissures are revealing themselves in the British Asian family. Most of the young Asian men complained that their sisters, and other young women in the community, were learning the bad habits of their white sisters. Nineteen-year-old Hamid put it like this:

> I came here like my twin sister Hamida from Pakistan. I still think like my uncles and my father. Some things are better here, but the English women are just rubbish. You just use them for a fuck. They know nothing. Not cooking, not decent. Why should our girls want to be like them? They should stick to our ways. Be housekeepers and good wives and mothers like Allah says. My dad, like he used to beat up my mother and she would never say a word. She was an angel.

Hamida on the other hand (secretly in love with a white boy) treats her brother with utter contempt:

> He doesn't want to change because he will have a great time in the future with some young wife washing and cleaning up after him and giving him sex whenever he wants. What do young men like him have to lose? While I would have to be that young wife to some idiot who

would be upset at the idea that I have a brain. Our young Asian men
are soon going to realize with a shock that there are no British Asian
girls left who will marry them. We want more in life and they still want
to be their mummy's little spoilt boys with ladoos in their mouths.
They will have to go and find some virgin in India. I mean I don't
agree with those crazy white feminists but I don't want to be a
doormat either. We are finding a half way.

Within such emotional talk lie the genuine worries and seeds for future
developments. More and more people seem concerned that the way
to create the good life for children may entail some fundamental
reconsideration. What it might mean is that the expectations of such
women are radically different from those of family experts who speak
out on behalf of women. Talking this issue through with a small group
of young Asian women, I found that most of them felt that white
women often did not know an apple pie even if it landed on their
tongues. They thought white women were amazingly lucky to have
partners who were prepared to try and change. Nita Patel best represents this view:

> They [the men] shop, clean with their partners, bathe the children,
> change nappies, cook . . . and none of it is enough. What do white
> women want? They should try and live with some of our men.
> I sometimes feel very sorry for white men. In employment they are
> so powerful and I am against the way they discriminate and all that.
> But they are all paying in their domestic lives. Married three or four
> times. Does that show they are happy?

But nothing in this book should ever be taken to be the whole truth.
A minority of young Asian women (and actually some older ones too)
see the battles taken up by white women as something only to be
admired and envied. Asma runs an Asian women's refuge. She says:

> Look how much white women and black women have achieved for
> themselves. They used to be as dominated by their communities as
> us. But today they can do great things, take on society without
> anybody saying to them shame on you. This shame, *izzat*, guilt is used
> by our people only to imprison our hearts so that even if we think we
> are free to make decisions, we never feel good about that freedom.

> Only guilt. I have women here who have been destroyed and who still
> feel guilty because they have escaped.

Bhumika, a 55-year-old divorcee, also describes herself as a feminist
with no more space in her life for men.

> They destroy our lives, our bodies and our minds. Even at the point of
> our birth, as Indian girls, we are so unwanted that all sorts of things
> are done to kill us before birth. Our fathers and brothers first, then our
> husbands treat us worse than slaves. At least after a few hundred
> years slaves were liberated and their stories told. For thousands of
> years Indian women have been lower than slaves and we still worship
> the institution of marriage. We should learn from these white women.

A group of black women, on the other hand, thought that white
women were too soft and undemanding. Marcia who has 'lost' two
men to white women says:

> They are so easily fooled. Those men bring them some charm and
> they will do anything, fall at their feet because they have this idea
> about black men in their heads, you know. Black men do have a
> harder time with us because we want more than the best fuck in the
> world.

We have no hard evidence to indicate whether there are indeed
different rates of change among different ethnic groups of men. Or if
there is any change at all among some. One thing that is indisputable,
though, is that the New Man culture has not informed, inspired or
created an impetus for change among black and Asian men. Yet.
Anecdotally and in terms of what is perceived, some black women and
Asian women (often among the most ambitious, and high-achieving)
believe that white middle-class men are more likely to try and be more
equal partners. They accept that their transformation is not by any
means complete and will not be for many years, and that perhaps such
changes in any case are easier for white men who have not had their
pride emasculated through racism. The hardening backlash against
female equality worried many of the interviewees, especially as so
many Asian and black lads have already settled into the backlash
without moving an inch in the direction of progress. White men are

becoming God's answer to women again and in an unexpected way. These men, in turn, feeling that they have been made to feel wretched for too long (by 'white ball-crushing, bloody feminist cunts', as one of them puts it) are enjoying their moment in the sun. Shriti, a divorced doctor who has recently married Brian, also a doctor and divorced, gives the impression, when she describes her husband, that she feels she has found gold in the dustbin.

> Brian is one of the kindest, funniest, most caring men I have ever met. I have a son whose father has paid no attention to him since I conceived him really. All his reactions were built around pride that his sperm was excellent enough to produce a boy. If I had had a daughter it would have been the fault of my egg. But Sunil, my son, needed a real father; someone who would share in his life. And Brian has been that father. I still cannot understand what made his wife leave him. How she failed to appreciate a good man. We fight of course and he is not perfect. Nor am I. But compared to my first marriage where there was no communication, no equal respect, this is paradise.

Talk to Brian and the same sense of wonder and gratitude comes through.

> I think Shriti has something that has long been thrown away by white middle-class women. She is capable of making a man feel he is not on trial all the time. She can approach our marriage in an organic way, as something instinctive. I used to feel I had to pass tests all the time before. Had I done my half of the chores, remembered to be caring, been the new man. And the more I thought about it, the easier it became not to do it. Now I am under no pressure except that of love and respect. I am a better husband for it. I find a lot of Asian women have that quality.

But a minority of the ethnic minority women interviewed took a different position on this issue. They feel strongly that to go with white men is to join the enemy and anyway, they say, change there has been, among black and Asian men too, and in the direction we, as women, have been demanding. Elphina, a black woman accountant, says:

> I do get tired of the way we are all expected to be disappointed in our
> men and have a go at our men because we believe in equality. How
> can that be right? You have to see where we started from. My partner
> loves me like my mother couldn't even dream about. She brought us
> up on her own because my father came over here and got himself a
> white woman. She now lives with me and watches the way David
> cherishes me and the kids and she thinks she is on another planet.
> All these women going off with white men, do they know what they
> are betraying? How are our men ever going to survive if we now walk
> out on them? We should be ashamed that so many black men are
> turning to white women because we have become so impossible to live
> with.

Many black women also feel – surprisingly more than the Asian women
I interviewed – that racism makes it a duty for them not to have too
high expectations of black men in their personal lives. Josephina
certainly feels that deeply. Such a charitable view must in the end help
her to cope with her lot. Shirley Skerrit, a black woman activist talking
to the journalist Chinyelu Onwurak, typifies this position:

> In the west the relationship between black men and black women is
> distorted because of white oppression. But even if it could be proved
> that black men are sexist the struggle against racism would take
> priority.

But white women who are part of this web of race and sex are feeling
isolated and misunderstood by almost everyone, black and white men
and black and Asian women. Norma, the white partner of a black
man, and a university lecturer, is furious about the way white women
get it from both sides.

> I despair. What do you Black women want from us? How dare you
> knock us and defend white men who have been responsible for all the
> historical misery you have suffered? You will probably say I am a
> racist. But I have had it. Black women telling me I am too sweet with
> black men and Asian women saying that I am too hard. You should
> remember that if it hadn't been for the women's movement none of us
> would have been where we are.

Norma will I hope be reassured that not all Black women take such oppositional positions to the experiences and struggles of white women. Some are deeply grateful to them and the world they have managed to create. Sushna, a science teacher, is one of them:

> You know I am so happy my parents came over here to live. That is what gave me access to so much about how traditional relationships within families can be changed even in a short time. But we have to be careful how far to go and what we should preserve. I am always mediating between the old world and the new world without taking sides. Take my son who is 14. He was very rude the other day to his grandmother who lives with us. This would have been unthinkable in my day and it is wrong. I gave him hell for it. But in some ways his relationship with elders in the family is much healthier than mine was. I was so scared of showing disrespect I just kept away from my grandparents. My son talks to his granny like a friend. Now I believe in my heart that we learnt something good from this society and that we must give credit to the women in that society who started challenging old ways. We are picking up the fruit of their hard work.

Afro-Caribbean and white women appeared to have a much more individualistic approach to who they were and what they wanted to be. There were exceptions in all of these groups. Some Asian women envy the freedoms of their white and black sisters, and among the younger generation certainly there is a desire to escape into that freedom. In one refuge twelve young women talked about this envy they felt. Summa, a lovely young woman brutalized by her own and then her husband's family, said bitterly:

> What is so good about our lives? Why should we want to be angels? These English women have the right idea. Just give the bastards hell and throw out the bloody mother-in-laws. We make up all these stories about ourselves. Do you know what hell goes on behind those curtains in Southall, Handsworth? I am telling you if I could get a nice English man I would go away with him and to hell with our culture. I spit on it.

Belinda, on the other hand, a white professional woman, is just as tired of her freedoms. Pondering whether she should convert to Islam, she has found life as an independent, well-paid, single white woman a burden she now wishes to shed. Unprovoked, she has been writing to me for a few months. I have found her an engaging, bright and confident correspondent and perhaps this has given me a greater understanding of how individualism and feminism are failing to satisfy women who are born into a world where both can be taken for granted:

> I just want to be told the right way to be. I grew up with hippy parents who gave me no direction. There has never been religion in my life. I feel so rootless and unchallenged. I need community, I need hard choices, moral instruction, anchors. Islam gives me that I think.

Islam has become one of the most dramatic confrontations in our society for testing out the various value systems that determine how we live and how we think we should live. White feminists and liberals have inexplicably strong prejudices against this general and vague thing called a Muslim. They fear us, or beam some useless, generic commiseration in our direction and some use all their intelligence to justify these racist responses. Some Muslims (and an increasing number of them) do exactly the same in the opposite direction, except they at least know a bit more about hegemonic western values. What critics of Islam fail to understand is that when they see a young woman in a *hijab* she may have chosen the garment as a mark of her defiant political identity and also as a way of regaining control over her body. Safia, a pharmacist, explains:

> I am not covering up because I am oppressed. But because I want to show people I am not ashamed of my family and my religion. But more than that, I hated the way when I became a teenager, I became a piece of sex for the boys in the school. Like all the other girls. The way boys treat girls – like they are pieces of meat. And the way these stupid girls start changing their clothes and bodies to keep these boys interested. I was sickened by that. I want to be myself, not somebody's fantasy. And you know we have a much easier time. My brother adores his wife, really adores her physically and mentally. She is a size 18 and she never worries that he will run off with Kate Moss. I was talking to her the other day and she explained how sex with the same person becomes better as the years go by because your flesh becomes one. And yet all the time television and magazines tell us

that we must change our sexual partners like we must change our
hairstyles. I don't want to do either.

There is indeed extraordinary depth, sustenance and permanence of
family life to be found within British Muslim communities and other-
faith Asian communities too. There are low rates of divorce (though
high rates of misery among some); teenage pregnancies are still a rarity
and, on the whole, sex only within marriage is still regarded as the
norm even by the young. Marriage and not cohabitation is what is
expected and people still believe that you marry for life. Since these
are some of the outcomes everyone says are good for any nation, why
have Muslims, Hindus and Sikhs not been co-opted into the burgeoning
Better Families industry? Could it be that many in the political and
voluntary sector can only see Asian women as victims? And Asian
families as pathological? That they cannot see what they might learn
because for centuries they have looked down on these cultures and
religions?

These questions were asked on a BBC2 programme which showed
Ayisha Bhutta, née Debbie Rogers, a tough young Glaswegian who
converted to Islam when she married her husband. Ayisha then went
about converting the tough neighbourhood too. Thirty plus people
were persuaded, including her parents and her brother. One convert
was Trudy, a lecturer from Glasgow University who was carrying out
research into Islam in Scotland. Most of them gave family life and the
seriousness of marriage as key reasons for their conversion. Ayisha's
husband said on the programme:

> I feel as if I have known her for centuries. That we must never part
> from one another. According to our faith, you are not just partners for
> life but you can be partners in heaven too. For ever. It is such a
> beautiful thought.[19]

This is of course a family and a marriage which is working well and
in which the religious and cultural boundaries are enabling the couple
to make sense of their lives, to grow and to provide shelter from the
panic which sets in when things are not going too well. It doesn't
always turn out like this.

Through this most difficult of the areas I have tried to understand in the book commonalities between women also emerged. Domestic violence is one area where cultural difference and racial divides seem not to matter. None of the women I interviewed who had been victims felt that there was any group of men who was better or worse than the other. Even when excuses were being made that disenfranchised men had more cause to behave badly, the women concerned said that when it came down to it, male violence against women was universal and needed to be dealt with. On this issue, because it is that ultimate violation, like rape, sisters can share their pain and even engage in a search for solutions which don't divide them.

I visited a number of refuges. Mixed ones as well as those specifically set up for particular groups. The cries were the same. The mistrust of men was the same. The drive for survival combined with the tendency to blame themselves was present among most of the women. What is clear though is that refuges for specific groups are still supported, especially by Asian women because their sense of shame, guilt and failure is so profoundly different from that of other women.

Complicated or what? White women are at once feminist bullies who deservedly are being abandoned by their men for softer options with brown skin and are also inexplicably soft and undemanding when it comes to black men, according to black women who are finding it difficult to find the perfect partner from within their own community. Asian women, on the other hand, seem divided between those who feel that only white men can give them the freedoms and partnerships they crave and those who feel they want to stay within their own lives where the natural order of things still prevails. The latter group often expresses fears that unless they put up the barricades, they too will go down the destructive road taken by white feminists. White women on the other hand are of course dealing with the old and the new versions of their own struggles. Add men from all the broad categories to this mixture and, even with the heavy stereotyping, one is confronted with the real complexity of where we are at and where we wish to go next.

This awareness is important if only to assess properly just how feminism and womanism are working through our personal lives as we reach the end of the twentieth century and, more importantly, how we may revive or at least save from extinction meaningful bonds between partners, children and other members of the family. Ironically, because we, Black women, have not been included among the striding feminists of Britain, we have not wholly fallen into the 'norm' of society. We can make choices, knowing what the consequences of feminism are. Most of us now wonder if the price to be paid to get to the top is what we wish to pay and we can see the clear connections between economic success and personal cost.

At a conference organized by the Council of Europe where I was the chief *rapporteur*, white and non-white Europeans from twelve countries gathered to discuss the tensions between gender equality and cultural autonomy. One conclusion, overwhelmingly endorsed by the non-white women, was that many of them have been able to accommodate changed aspirations *within* their families without causing the kind of havoc they see in the wider community. The pity is, they said, that these strategies and skills are rendered invisible or incomprehensible because as 'immigrant' women they have so little power in the way society is run and understood.[20]

Mary Walker, who was on the team which produced the BBC2 series *Living Islam* in 1996, said this after they had completed the project:

> If my definition of equality was free will, then I could no longer define oppression as a symptom of Islam. The women all exercised their right to choose – to some extent they were freer than me.[21]

Talk to Chinese, Asian, Turkish and black women and you do not find an enormous sense of desperation to leave their communal settings. What you do find is the desire to change vital attitudes and behaviour from within – the number of cultural apologists has certainly fallen and now there is an emerging important gender divide between those who too readily proclaim the right to leave 'culture' untouched and those who insist on challenging the *status quo*. But almost all the women and men I interviewed from the Britons of colour seemed to feel that their attitudes towards family, work and marriage were different from mainstream attitudes and that they were better.

But there are some questions that apply to all the types of women I spoke to. Why is there such turmoil over the family and about masculine and feminine roles in it? Is part of the problem that people talk too long and hard about such issues? Could there be bliss in a little ignorance? Are books such as this simply adding to our sense of helplessness and weariness? And finally how is the inner self affected by all this?

Some facts are becoming uncomfortably clear. There are even biological indicators – if Oliver James is to be taken seriously – that our levels of unhappiness are higher than in the fifties. He has established that our levels of serotonin – the 'happiness brain chemical' – are lower than they were fifty years ago. Swimming energetically in this ocean of knowledge about how to get more out of life, we are more miserable than ever before. The inner self, the soul if you like, is unsettled, roaming, looking for itself. His explanation is that we are simply asking too much of our relationships and ourselves, and that unless 'our overheated aspirations as an individual cool', state policies will do little.[22]

One major problem is that nothing, nothing including the number of spasms one has during an orgasm, is left to individuals and their own instincts and inner life, strengths and beliefs. Too many experts seem to be cluttering up modern life. There is an addiction, especially among white Britons, to such experts and their advice. Does this show a lack or an abundance of confidence? Do we really need to consult outsiders – often charlatans – on how to make love all night long (a myth even bigger than the one that says a man is not anxious about the size of his organ), breathe, move, have conversations, flirt, have babies, bring them up, dress and feed them, play with them? Can we not make up our own minds about what time children must go to bed, what activities (that word which blights the lives of anxious, guilt-ridden working professional women) they need, where they go to school, how they learn, how you 'communicate' with them and with your partner and mother and his mother, how you balance work and home life, what you cook, eat, what nightdresses and bras you must buy?

We watch ourselves doing every single thing we do. We measure this against an ever more impossible set of standards. We look in the mirror and we look for what we should be, not what we are. One of the most reassuring moments when researching this book was finding enclaves of ignorance, resistance and indifference in the midst of this maddening, over-instructed life. Like Noor, the young Turkish woman, beautiful in her last days of pregnancy, who looked puzzled when I asked her if she had a birth-plan. I explained and she laughed loudly, saying:

> **It is up to Allah. Do you think I am going on a plane journey that I must have a plan, a timetable? I am a woman and I will have my mother with me. Then we will see what happens. I hope and pray I have a healthy child. But no thank you I do not want to have music or a swimming pool. What is this? Do we think we can do better than nature?**

The other side of the coin is just as important. If some ethnic groups have not discarded the skills essential to maintain parenthood and nurturing and learnt not to go with the crowd, in protecting themselves so much from the changing norms of society, they have ignored some important developments. They are worse off for this. The one lesson still to be imbibed is that of individualism and the self. I remember interviewing Asian women in prison a few years ago. All twelve of the women I spoke to said that they felt happier in prison than out because they had finally arrived at a notion of the self, the individual, personal choice and rights. Saira is a young mother who is now in a refuge. She has tried to kill herself at least three times because she cannot cope with those around her providing her with no space to be herself.

> **I just want someone from my father, mother, husband, son to see me as me. Not as their daughter, mother or wife. Just me. A person. A special person, you know? I don't want to be free. Just to be me. In the middle of the night I wake up and ask myself, Saira who are you; what are you? I have no answer. Like there is this big hole where my personality, my wishes, they should be there. But like they are drowned, you know. I have so many questions too. When does love for a daughter in our community turn to fear and hate and why? My father loved me so much until I was eleven. He hugged me, he spoke to me with such light in his voice. Then one day, just like that, it changed to anger and hatred because I was becoming a woman.**

Saira is one of hundreds of such women. Research by Dr Soni Raleigh shows that suicide in this group is much higher than the national average.[23] Black women have their individuality taken away by other means. They are always representative, as Dr Lola Young says. Always watched, judged for how they might be affecting the well-being of the black community.[24] But talk to black men and they also feel that they are too often called upon to be perfect for the sake of something beyond their own lives. And though most Asian men feel content within their family structures, alcoholism and depression is rising in this group too.

At least two of the white men with black partners that I interviewed found this minimal sense of individualism at once reassuring and irritating. Sam, a high-powered City accountant, married to an Asian woman who is also an accountant, explained:

> **Shula, my wife, is wonderful with me, the kids, my family, even my distant aunts. There is nothing she will not do for family members. But I find it makes me feel awkward. I wish sometimes she could just be herself, be bad, be selfish, like the rest of us. She is so full of duty there is no room for anything else.**

For Craig, the values of Vron, a black businesswoman, are actually affecting their marriage:

> **I will not be able to stand this for much longer. Everything is political in our lives. Every damn thing is an illustration of racism or colonialism. And we always have to be careful of what Vron calls 'the black community' will think. I want to understand why she is the way she is, but I can't live with it.**

So having walked through this thicket what can one conclude about our personal lives today? Beyond the indisputable conclusion that things are terrifyingly complicated, there are some trends which did emerge. An overwhelming sense that I got at the end of the long interviewing process for this book and from much of the research I have carried out in my journalism over the years, is that women still believe in the family as something they like or would have liked to have had in their lives. Even the most disillusioned did not all declare that men were so useless and damaging that they should be kept out. Where some of these sentiments did crop up was over the issue of divorce. Melanie, 38 and in the process of getting divorced, says for example:

> I hate men today the way I never did and never wanted to. This divorce, the utterly disgraceful way my husband is behaving. His lies, his greed, his total disregard for the way I have serviced him now makes me think that there is no future in any of this. So many of my friends are in the same position. And you begin to question this family thing. You have the kids but that is not a family, is it?

But even Melanie felt, like most of my interviewees – male, female, black and white – that to demonize all men is wrong and unfair. And yes, maybe I seek these views because I still love sleeping and living with the so-called enemy and I love my son as much as I love my daughter. But I did not know what people were going to say. There seemed agreement too that we should worry more that boys are doing badly, that many men are suffering from a crisis of masculinity, and that structural changes are leaving so many without career paths. We can't, as is too often the case, simply ask them to stop whining and to grow up. Too much is at stake simply to take on the revenge strategy.

Talking to men and women of colour, I felt that their need for family and community networks in a society still so racially exclusive was much stronger and that the reality often matched their high expectations. It was in the Asian, Turkish and other 'eastern' groups that I found the most flourishing children. One reason was that they were taken care of within the family networks. There is much that mainstream Britain could learn from these models. But the lives of many of these children went downhill as they reached adolescence when they started to assert their rights, and there are too many women whose lives have been turned into one long, endless obligation. Men are also beginning to suffer as a result of the social pressures in many ethnic communities which affect the well-being of their children and partners. What is essential is for those men and women who have had few rights of self-determination and selfhood to acquire some of the individuality and courage that changed mainstream British society from the sixties onwards.

So where do such conversations take us? They show us that no one group has all the answers; that the torment felt by women and men of all ethnic groups comes out of an irreversible and changed world. Previous generations of women – across the world – expected to be underlings. Although this expectation still survives in far too many parts of the world, the presumption is increasingly challenged and rejected. We might find better solutions if we learnt, one from the other. Too much freedom has created as many (more, some would say) victims as has too much restriction. Only screaming to defend these freedoms is to show the foolishness of mountaineers going on with an ascent because doubt cannot be admitted. What is going to make things harder is not only that things are very far from what they have been made to appear, but that they are incredibly difficult to comprehend; and that they reveal the breaking up of orthodoxies – old and new. But from that confusion, says Morwena Griffiths, must come something more alive and meaningful. I agree.

> Fragmentation is the ordinary condition of human selves . . . Not only does [fragmentation] show us difference, but it impels re-assessment and change as we both act in the present, as we are now, and at the same time reflect on our own incoherence. This dual process of action and reflection is a source of insight and further change. The acknowledgement of the complexity of ourselves is a pre-condition for self-transformation in so far as transformation is needed.[25]

And It Does Not End Here

9

Reflecting ourselves in each other's eyes, we will
move forward and
create our own worlds,
speaking in tongues which will resonate our unspoken dreams
. . . Rising, rising, rising from yesterday's silence to tomorrow's dreams.

Pratiba Parmar, in Storms of the Heart, 1988

A stone's throw out on either hand
From that well-ordered road we tread
And all the world is wild and strange.

Rudyard Kipling

I have crossed an ocean
I have lost my tongue
from the roots of the old one
a new one has sprung.

Grace Nichols, Holding My Beads, 1984

How do you conclude a book such as this? It is only one exploration of enormous issues, each of which could sprout a dozen different books. I am all too aware of this. I will not pretend that my long trek has ended (can it ever end?) or that I have all the answers to make this imperfect country live up to its glorious self-image. But what I do know is that there are many other areas of our national life, beyond those inescapable ones already covered, which need to shake themselves out of their complacency. I will touch on a few of these here in this last chapter. And I also believe that unless people in positions of power, white primarily, but black too, play their part in this process, another century of possibilities will be lost.

The scope of this book is limited. I have not been able to go into crucial national activities such as the law, science and technology, and academia, all of which can be and should be scrutinized in terms of how much adaptation there has been to a modern, multiracial population. We know that over 20 per cent of doctors working in the National Health Service are not white, but that fewer than 1 per cent are consultants. Similar disparities can be shown when it comes to lawyers and judges or lecturers and professors. Such employment profiles are not only unjust but unwise because they lock out the potential for widening horizons and incorporating diversity. The same iniquities, lack of ambition and imagination are found in these areas as in the government, the media, schools and elsewhere.

But before this particular journey is completed, I do want to look briefly at that self-important sector, the creative arts, which portrays itself as an indispensable barometer for the state of a nation and which is presumed to be bold, unconventional and internationalist. In his book, *Creative Britain*, Chris Smith, Secretary of State for Culture, Media and Sports, wrote: 'Cultural activity can help us with the development of our sense of who and what we are. It can help therefore to set a sense of direction for our society.'[1]

So let us look around at British 'cultural activity'. What do we see? Take publishing. It is a good year to be doing this because bets are that the top literary awards in 1999 are predicted to go either to Salman Rushdie for his new book, *The Ground Beneath Her Feet*, or to Vikram Seth for his, *An Equal Music*. I remember the day Salman Rushdie was described as a British writer and how that made me feel. I recall too the terrible personal sense of betrayal I felt when, during and after the *Satanic Verses* quarrels, he left us, his people, and surrendered himself to the easy, adorable charms of Hampstead. But he was the first and the best and he (without, I imagine, thinking that this is what he was doing) changed the literary terrain so others could grow. We have seen the wonderful flowering of writers like the unpredictably clever Hanif Kureishi, and others such as Meera Syal (*Anita and Me*) and Shyama Perera (*Haven't Stopped Dancing Yet*) or Courttia Newland (*The Scholar*), Diran Adebayo (*Some Kind of Black*), Andrea

Levy (*Fruit of the Lemon*), Ferdinand Dennis (*The Sleepless Summer*), Farhana Sheikh (*The Red Box*), Gbenga Agbenugba (*Another Lonely Londoner*) and Atima Srivastava (*Transmission*) – whose books are about life here, in this essentially hybrid land. Trade is picking up and may one day be unstoppable.[2] Almost as important is the increasingly confident creativity of writers exploring history and the immigrant's story. Caryl Phillips, Fred d'Aguiar, Abdulrazak Gurnah, Joan Riley, Ruksana Ahmed, Buchi Amecheta, Beryl Gilroy, Merle Collins, David Dabydeen, Pauline Melville and Laurence Scott are among the finest of these. Yet they are judged by innocents. Dabydeen's first novel was praised by Penelope Lively, who went on to say, 'We badly need good novels about the immigrant experience in Britain.' As Maya Jaggi pointed out in response to this patronizing pat on the curly black head: 'Far from interpreting the "immigrant experience" to curious outsiders, these novelists shatter myths of identity at Britain's heart. To read them is not simply to understand "them" it is to understand "ourselves".'[3] Rushdie once said that the immigrant is not only transformed by his new world, he also transforms this world.

What has been a huge barrier is the reality that it is still easier to be taken seriously if you are an 'eastern' writer like Arundhati Roy or an 'African' like Ben Okri. Best of all is to be fortunate enough to be an African-American writer for then you can get limitless access to the literary world. However, most of these celebrated writers are themselves embarrassingly ignorant of black Britons. When Marsha Hunt established the Saga Prize, she had the gall to say that there was hardly any good writing in this country because she had not heard of it. What makes it worse is that the more you are part of the British world and black, the more likely you are to be painted out of the landscape by both whites and separatist blacks. On the other hand, Roy is now, for some reason, seen as a British writer although she lives and works in India,[4] and the Indian director Shekhar Kapoor who directed the wonderful film *Elizabeth* must also be surprised to have his film so uncompromisingly described as a 'British' success. For most actual and aspiring black artists, though, they are not yet of this place, not in its heart, not yet. As the novelist Mike Phillips told me:

> You know I am still described by many as 'British based' as if soon I
> will be returning to the Caribbean. Do people know anything?
> Caribbeans came here with the complete British heritage. Our
> carpenters back home could recite Shakespeare. Shakespeare and the
> King James Bible is buried in our cadences. If you speak fluent and
> educated English you are not considered authentic by whites, or these
> days by blacks. I despise that invented black culture which is stitched
> out of reggae rap and red, green and yellow caps.

This is then the spur which pushes more writers to come up and fight
for recognition. As the writer Andrea Levy says: 'If Englishness doesn't
define me, redefine Englishness.' And that is exactly the challenge posed
by that unique urban poet of our times, Benjamin Zephaniah. Neither
the *Daily Mail*[5] nor the *Independent* can understand how a Rastafarian
'ex-burglar' knows not his place. Writing in the latter paper, John
Walsh finds it 'a little hard to fathom' why this man ('semi-literate,
black ex-convict with dreadlocks') has become such a darling of British
literary circles, those who are literate, white uprights, without uproari-
ous hair.[6] Benjamin Zephaniah, one of our most popular and instinctive
poets, who can bring to this art form those who have never read a
word for pleasure, must feel like knocking these people about and
returning to prison. There are at least seventy-five published black and
Asian British poets today. Jackie Kay, John Agard (who in 1998 was
poet in residence at the BBC), Linton Kwesi Johnson, Grace Nichols,
Suniti Namjoshi are among the best known and best loved across the
races. But they never quite stay in the warm, continuous limelight as
does, say, John Hegley.

What is equally depressing is the lack of any knowledge of literary
history here. Do Walsh and others like him have any real sense of the
literary antecedents of these modern black and Asian writers? I suspect
not. Perhaps what we all need is a massive publication venture which
presents to all Britons the work of previous black and Asian writers
such as George Lamming, Andrew Salkey, Sam Selvon, E. R. Braithwaite, Edgar Mittelholzer, Wilson Harris, and – of course, of course
– Nirad Chaudhuri, Attia Hussian, V. S. Naipaul and Derek Walcott.
We do now have that sense about the contributions of Irish writers
past and present. The Jewish British heritage is more than well estab-

lished and deservedly so. But black and Asian writers remain without a publicly recognized pedigree. Individuals are slowly being excavated. In 1997 the life of Ignatius Sancho, known in the eighteenth century as the black 'Dr Johnson', was celebrated in an exhibition at the National Portrait Gallery and the publication of an extraordinarily vivid book, *Ignatius Sancho: African Man of Letters.*[7] But these drops cannot make that fundamental connection, that my heritage is their heritage too.

The British film industry has been similarly myopic. Black actors have few opportunities in British films and most of the time the roles are stereotypical. Look at films such as *Four Weddings and a Funeral*, which is meant to be about young metropolitan folk. Was there a black wedding, or even funeral for that matter? The sequel to this over-rated film is even more of an insult. The producers, writers and directors could not have tried harder to whiten the most famously Black area in London, Notting Hill Gate. The film is even called *Notting Hill*. Writing in the *Guardian* Ferdinand Dennis observes:

> [the film] represents a huge failure of imagination to miss out those two days in August when the neighbourhood celebrates its fantastic diversity in the carnival. Instead it concentrated on characters who were too familiarly British, white and middle class. Movies like this fill you with despair like Ralph Ellison's Invisible Man, who shouted 'they can't see me!' Me, in this instance, being peoples of colour without whom Notting Hill would be as bland as yesterday's salad.

Dennis is being too benign if anything in his analysis. It is not that they don't see us, but that film-makers don't want us to litter up their olde worlde landscape. In this country 99 per cent of films are written by white, middle-class people for and about white middle-class people. It takes a Mike Leigh or Ken Loach to give us the alternative view, and here Black characters appear as a matter of course, as complex, real individuals. We have no Spike Lee yet or Denzel Washington because the much applauded British film industry has done nothing to make them happen. *Bhaji on the Beach*, a film about a gang of Asian women going to Blackpool for the day and interacting with the locals and each other in unexpected ways, was a huge success. But it was Robert Redford who gave Gurinder Chadha, the director, the opportunity to go to his famed screen-writing school and learn more about her craft. *My Beautiful Launderette* made Kureishi, but none of the Asian actors have become stars like Daniel Day-Lewis who got his big break with this film. One of the stars of *Secrets and Lies*, Marianne Jean-Baptiste, was shortlisted for an Oscar in 1997 but not considered good enough to go with the team of young British actors to Cannes, invited there to represent the best of British talent. Paul Barber, the black actor in *The Full Monty*, was similarly excluded from the array of award nominations. Not only that but if you look closely at the film it becomes clear how racism informed the script. 'Mr Horse' (a name given to him because, as everyone knows, black men have big ones) is a role which would not be created in the United States. Black women are used within the set sexist/racist iconography. Look at *Mona Lisa* and *Peter's Friends*. Asian women are simply not there unless James Bond is using them to show how sexy and bold he is by unwinding their saris and jumping off a balcony, or unless they appear as servants and other menials in Raj movies. Films by independent directors such as Isaac Julien and Julian Henriques break these moulds, but where do you get to see their films if you are not some crazy late-night film buff? Channel Four has played a major role in financing films by black and Asian people. *Bhaji on the Beach* and *My Beautiful Launderette* came out of this spirit of risk-taking and nurturing. In his detailed, painstaking account of black people on the screen in Britain, Stephen Bourne shows clearly how, unlike in the United States, black actors here are kept in their place. Yet images of black people have been a part of films shown in this country since 1896.[8] The charming Earl Cameron has been acting in this country since 1952. How many people would recognize him as they do, say, James Mason? Perhaps the next time the boys and girls in the British film industry gloat about their films and show off to Hollywood they should say: 'The white British are coming.'

That connection between us and us tends to be made even less in the world of the traditional arts. In the 1970s we were treated to the dubious charms of *Ipi Tombi*, described by David Benedict as 'basically a tits 'n' feathers show'.[9] The first all-black non-musical production in the West End was only seen in 1987 with James Baldwin's *The Amen Corner*. It was, like the more recent *Five Guys named Moe*, a black American success, hardly anything to do with Britishness. Even more tragically, the glory days of well-funded fringe theatre have gone, taking with them at least twenty black theatre companies expressing new artistic truths. Talawa survives, as does Tamasha, both of which need to be taken much more seriously than they are. Yvonne Brewster continues to be one of our most innovative directors and Tamasha has an Asian/white team in Sudha Buchar and Christine Landon Smith who together have not only stormed the preciously inward-looking Radio 4's drama departments, but have produced some of the best theatre I have seen in London for years. Their shows are always sold out and the audience is completely mixed in terms of age, gender, race and ethnicity.

These companies find fertile temporary homes in the successful fringe sector. Watermans Arts Centre, the Battersea Arts Centre, the Lyric Theatre in Hammersmith, have plays and shows by the various tribes of Britain as a matter of course, an everyday occurrence. The emerging skills of a Barv Bancil or Anu Kumar are often first seen in these places, as are stand-up Asian comics. I first saw Nina Wadia, now a star in *Goodness Gracious Me*, at the Watermans Art Centre. But none of this is as well known as it should be. One frustrated Asian dancer and choreographer feels it is 'easier for an obscure Russian or Polish group to be embraced by the white middle classes than it will ever be for us'.

The central obstacle here is that these companies are seen as 'ethnic'. As Felix Cross, director of the Black Theatre Co-operative, reminded the top folk in theatreland: 'The day that Adrian Noble turns up to a conference on black theatre will be the day we can really have a debate.'[10] The prevailing philosophy among arts funders has been to fund 'ethnic arts' as if they are a tourist distraction and to assimilate black and Asian people into mainstream areas – only a few at a time you understand. Just think of the number of hot debates about boring integrated casting that take place as predictably as rain on a summer party day. Even after one of the most unforgettable performances by David Harewood as Othello at the National in 1998, all that critics could discuss was the fact that he was black. The third space, the most important space, still has to be argued for an uncomprehending world. Hopes remain high, though. The hugely talented classical actor Hugh Quarshie said at a confernece:

> I'd like to believe that the arts, especially the theatre, can bring a
> splintered society together and remind us that what we have in common
> is of greater value than that which appears to divide us . . . classical
> theatre establishes a massive authority on forms and meanings but
> there is little discussion of the morality of the theatre. Whom does it
> benefit? Does the theatre have any social responsibility?[11]

The theatre director and critic, Jatinder Verma, pointed out how the
lack of such a vision diminishes us all:

> We've come from nowhere and we're going nowhere. We are devoid as
> a nation of our true history, of mythology. The day for release will
> come when black arts has broken into places like the National Theatre
> and the RSC. The day the National Theatre produces an Indian
> classic it will deserve to be called our national theatre.

This statement was made more than a decade back. Today Verma has
been produced in the National. His version of Molière based in India
was a wonderful production. He is regarded by those who know, such
as the *Guardian* theatre critic Michael Billington, as one of our cleverest
directors. And yet Chris Smith's eager and enthusiastic book, *Creative
Britain*, about the cultural life of this country, made no mention of
Verma, nor of Gurinder Chadha, Meera Syal and many other Black
artists. Pop music features much in Smith's book because the distinction
between high and low art is being demolished and yet even here barely
a handful of names appear.[12] In fact, quite disgracefully, ten names of
non-white Britons appear in this book and they are crowded together,
like passengers in a third-class carriage in some impoverished country,
in two sentences. Again and again, you get the same pale picture of
white people of influence who are either unable or unwilling to represent
the world we live in, and choose instead to feed us the same old-world
diet. Every single media profile of the phenomenally gifted Verma
describes him as 'Asian', as does every description of me in the public
arena. Meera Syal is still only asked to do curry paste adverts, not
those for cars and vodka, and even now has to battle against the image
of her as an Asian woman rather than as a successful British actress.
This puts us in our place, tells us emphatically to cut our ambitions to
size, and to realize that we are only ever a minority.

And it was, it seems, ever thus. Even in popular culture. It was shocking for me – an ardent fan who spent so much money on records even as a hard-up teenager – to discover that the Beatles totally wrote out of their success and their story the amazing contribution of Allan Williams and Lord Woodbine. These were black musicians who were followed around by the Beatles (like orphans, says Woodbine – they were even known as 'Woodbine's Boys'), and who played an enormous role in the first burst of success which came their way. I wonder how many times Sir Paul McCartney calls them today, and if he realizes how important it is for someone in his position to pay his dues in gratitude if not in kind to these black musicians. Again and again you see appropriation and negation. By 1989 Heera, the bhangra band, had earned three gold discs for the numbers of records they were selling. They were never featured in popular music programmes. As Nadhir Tharani, the radical architect who eventually left this country out of despair, wrote: 'The Eurocentric cultural discourse in this country locates the east as despotic, stagnant and stranded in history . . . the major characteristic of this tendency is to pose a false dichotomy between tradition (the East, South) and modernity (the West). This has led to South Asian artists retreating into a position which upholds South Asian art forms as immutable.'[13] Black artists respond by removing all standards by which judgements must be made. Everything that is black or brown cannot simply be applauded. Such indulgence creates a different and pernicious racism.

I do feel compelled to ask why so few black and Asian Britons go to the mainstream theatre. Should we not be as turned on by Chekhov as we expect white Britons to be by Ayub Khan Din's play, *East is East*, which eventually transferred to the West End? It can happen. When Tom Stoppard's play *Indian Ink* was put on in the West End, not only was this the first play to feature a number of young Asian actors, but a huge number of British Asians loved it. But the self-imposed exile from other kinds of theatre is foolish. The irony is that our black and Asian youngsters are much less inclined to go to the Royal Shakespeare Company than are their middle-class parents, who, if they were educated under the imperial sun, have strong attachments to western drama. Even now, you always meet intellectuals from India or South Africa, but not from London, at the RSC.

But I do find this willed ignorance less forgivable among the white elite, especially as the more influential they are, the less they seem to be able to understand the importance of this and how much catching up with new modernities they have to do. Sometimes they are the worst of the lot. Roy Hattersley tells a story of how Fay Weldon went to his constituency – after having expressed concern about the rights of Asian women – and then disgraced herself by assuming that young Sikh boys with top-knots who were playing football were actually Muslim girls.[14]

The same processes of exclusion are seen among others in that team of the great and the good. The Groucho may be more trendy than the Garrick, but it is only another club of the white glitterati. The few blacks who are allowed in look as if they are tourists in their own kingdom. All this means that the real cultural personality of Britain remains unrecognized. We have not even begun to have the fundamentally important discussions which have gone on in the United States – the so-called culture wars – even if they are frightening and upsetting and sometimes foolish. Here we got the anti-Political Correctness backlash but not the political correctness debates. Even Isaiah Berlin was unable, in the end, to cross over into the new cultural landscapes and worried about the 'problems' of multiculturalism until his death. In an interview with Stephen Lukes in *Prospect* magazine, Berlin spoke of how

> immigrants have only become a problem now. [Immigration] was not a problem in the nineteenth century because then most immigrants were not that different . . . but cultures which have grown up with no contact with each other have now collided. That is a serious problem. One hopes for assimilation.[15]

This interview might have been more revealing if the interviewer had been black and someone who did not so deeply identify with the idea of immigrants as a problem. And it is worrying to accept that even Berlin seemed to have lost track of how connected the histories of colonized peoples once were with their indifferent masters. At a seminar held in August 1998, Eric Hobsbawm expressed similar views about assimilation, as if that should be the only road left open to a diverse nation.[16]

We need to contemplate our culture, values and excellence. Extra-ordinarily, white intellectuals in this society know the United States of America more intimately than the United Races of Britain. Without the fundamental discussions about new histories (which don't need to negate the old histories because, as Mike Phillips says, they are ours too), artistic output and theatre for all our futures, how can this society begin to connect its parts and grow organically *and* bear fruit? For years now individuals such as the historian Christopher Hill have been urging a more complex and less nationalistic sense of history for this island. Most intellectuals, book editors and critics are unaware that there are now black and Asian thinkers, such as Mike Phillips, Dr Lola Young, Onyekachi Wambu, Ziauddin Sardar and Rana Kabbani, engaged in important quests for the future voice of this land. Even internationally famous intellectuals such as Stuart Hall, Paul Gilroy or Bhikhu Parekh remain unknown to those who are paid to know better. These voices are extraordinary because they are not interested in the comfortable assimilationism of a Naipaul, or the metropolitan hybridity of a Kureishi which asks for nothing but to be allowed to roam free in the land, unbeholden to anyone. Some of the people listed above are engaged in the most fundamental struggles about art and standards and excellence and judgements and the soul of the nation. They are fighters, grappling in the most energetic way with the place they will claim, for better or worse, in the next century. They are post-decolonization artists with little simplistic idealism. They are not desperate to be approved of by white opinion, while knowing full well that it is the white world which has the power to make them matter – even to their own people. Most important of all, these people are the urgent voices of Britain, not just Black Britain.

There are now a number of people in high enough places who are profoundly aware of this willed ignorance and the dangers of it. This may help liberate the spaces occupied by art. Philip Dodd, director of the ICA, is one of those attempting to break down old fences. He put together a season of Bollywood films at the ICA so that white Britons could see – for the first time – what the biggest film industry in the world (if you count audience figures) is all about. Many learnt for the first time that the playback singer Lata Mangeshkar is the highest selling singer in the world. Even more impressively, young British

Asians went to the ICA in droves – the first time this has happened. Deborah Swallow, one of the curators at the Victoria and Albert Museum, is another key player in this important development. She has set up wonderful exhibitions from Pakistan and India and done it in a way which indicates that this is not free tourism but a showpiece of multicultural Britain. Swallow and Dodd are rarities. The cultural elites are not up to the task of imagining who we are or might be. And they have been blind and deaf for decades. Remember that it was George Orwell who wrote, in *England, Your England*, that Britain would never agree to rebrand itself as a nation of immigrants. Even when it clearly was. The establishment was fixated on the notion of a noble continuous ancestry which could transform the cultures of others and yet remain imperiously impervious herself. Yet, as Mark Leonard says, 'creativity is a state of mind that is restlessly looking for new ways of doing things . . . Cultivating that creativity requires us to remain a diverse, challenging society.'[17] The only way this is happening at present is through consumption of the 'other', the food, the frocks and the exotica.

Here, perhaps, it is time to deal with the biggest thorn in the garden of diversity: the failure of liberalism itself to cope with change, movement, flights of fancy which fall outside the norms of post-Enlightenment societies. It might help to remember that J. S. Mill himself was unable to think beyond the imperial model, and that within the heart of liberalism lies a deep racism. After all, liberals approved of colonialism and from the beginning, as Bhikhu Parekh says: 'Liberalism became missionary, ethnocentric and narrow, dismissing non-liberal ways of life and thought as primitive and in need of the liberal civilizing influence.' Mill himself divided human societies into two – the 'civilized' with people who were in the 'maturity of their faculties' and were European and the rest, who were in a state of backwardness and infancy. Mill then went on to proclaim neatly that this difference of status meant that the first had a right to rule over the second.[18]

The point at which, in recent times, all this was laid bare was the ten-year battle over *The Satanic Verses*. The issues raised by this book have barely been understood even by the most educated in our communities. They went far beyond the issue of a single book, or author, or the religious sentiments of a community.[19] This event, more than any other, made white Britons confront the fact that multi-culturalism was not merely about happy-clappy festivals and world music, or even the exciting expansion of literature. Nor was it about cricket tests. Fundamental values were now being contested in a public arena. Freedom of expression could not always prevail unquestioningly. It is an argument that has since been taken up by those wishing to control publications such as *American Psycho* or novels about the sexual degradation of young children. It changed the lazy beliefs about freedom. As the writer Edward de Bono wrote with reference to this fiasco:

> Civilization is not solely defined by freedom but by the way freedom is limited by responsibility, duties, compassion, and, when these prove inadequate, by the law. The jungle is free. Civilization is not. The freedom to insult is matched by the freedom to feel insulted. Those who exercise power without restraint are bullies.[20]

It was because of the anger against *The Satanic Verses* that people began to accept that speech could be an action, that some things were still sacred even in the midst of post-modern confusion. We started to get the first ever debates over what we mean by censorship, a word which was carelessly used by the pro-Rushdie camp. Censorship is something enforced by powerful people and their institutions. The *fatwa* was censorship. The book-burning was the exact opposite. As one young Muslim academic at Bradford University explained to me:

> We showed them their own dodgy values and how imperialist they were. All those lefties are really imperialists and fundamentalists. Once they forced us to lose our languages and be ashamed of our culture. Today they terrorize us with the objective to get us to become white and like them. The way Rushdie has obliged them. Or Naipaul. We will not be flattered so easily or forced. The changes we make will come from within and for reasons which make sense to us. We are not fools to go and die under the wheels of some slogans of total freedom of speech.

Asian people of faith were no longer just clamouring for access but for influence and power in cultural and political life. For many white liberals, especially those who expected and had previously received praise and gratitude for doing the right thing, such conflicts were disheartening. This coincided with a sense of loss and failure that many were already experiencing as the left began to collapse across the eastern bloc and in the west itself. The affair created the first Muslim intellectual movement in this country but we had hard questions to ask ourselves. If there were only two sides in the blazing conflict, where did people like me fit in? We became orphans, simultaneously losing liberalism – until then the rock of our education – and Islam because of the insane way it was manifesting itself.

Reassessment is leading to a rather too crude reassertion of liberal values. Too many writers to mention have been putting forward their beliefs in forms which have been described by some as 'liberal fundamentalism'.[21] And it is worth repeating what Ziauddin Sardar and Meryl Wyn-Davies boldly asserted in their book, *The Distorted Imagination*:

> 'Civilization as we know it' has always meant Western civilization. Civilized behaviour and products have been measured by the yardsticks of the West. Europe and now North America has always contemplated itself as the focus of the world, the axis of civilization, the goal of history, the end product of human destiny. Colonial history and colonial Christianity did their utmost both to annihilate non-Western cultures and obliterate their histories. Now secularism in its post-modernist phase of desperate self-glorification has embarked on the same goal.[22]

One is quite spoilt for choice when choosing these soldiers for the liberal cause. Michael Ignatieff, with proud free will, stands up to be counted:

> There is nothing sacred about toleration – we're not obliged to tolerate those who threaten us because of our opinions. But it does commit us to a habit of mind and a way of life: to listen when we don't want to listen, to endure offence when we would rather retaliate, to struggle to understand when we would rather fight, and to fight, as a last resort, when intolerance will not listen to reason.[23]

There may be more trouble ahead, as the song says, and we may not be able, any longer, simply to face the music and dance. Not in separate dance-halls anyway. Life in the next century in this country is likely to be more challenging and promising than we can yet imagine. We will soon have third- and fourth-generation white and black Britons who have known no other reality but that of a multiracial Britain. These younger people will need to feel that this is something to be optimistic about. They can then, we hope, be enabled to take each other for granted but also make more demands from one another. The leadership – whether political or cultural – has shown itself so far to be unnecessarily cautious and self-limiting (or lacking in imagination and vision perhaps). This can't do. It won't do.

Globalization is likely to accelerate, causing not only economic instability but increasing mistrust and disorder. This is a spreading infection which cannot be stopped.[24] Leaders in this country have never mined the huge reserves of knowledge and perceptions which reside with Britons whose origins lie in the countries which are now experiencing the pains and gains of economic liberalization policies. There cannot be globalization of big business and international finance without a global consciousness in which the citizens of this country feel deeply for those across the world. We can see this with the recent unprecedented flood disasters in Bangladesh. Because we have such a large and vocal British Bangladeshi community in Britain today, this crisis was felt more powerfully and this led in turn to politicians such as Oona King making heartfelt speeches and appeals for help. Globalization also leads to pan-national virtual communities. You can see this most clearly with the growth in pan-Islamic identity in the past decade. Such developments obviously produce new perils but, on the whole, positively interconnected lives are better lives whether we are talking about domestic or international politics.

Too many people do not see the potential but only the crises produced by globalization. This is why we now have so much evidence of fear and uncertainty in the world, causing many to dislocate, to withdraw, to get into hatefully narrow politics. India, once a proud secular democracy, is in danger of disappearing behind the foaming madness of Hindu fundamentalism. In many areas of the United States, cells of disenchanted citizens are planning (or, in the case of Oklahoma, carrying out) violence and havoc, ostensibly to defend their rights to be free and to be different from the whole. The Nation of Islam is succeeding in answering the desperate cries of many black men who feel there is no respectable place for them in this brave new world. Here in Britain, much of the consensus that was built up over the past three decades about values, freedom, equality, access, justice and nationhood has all but disappeared. Liberalism, religion, feminism, socialism, the British identity, the monarchy, love, sex and marriage, child-rearing and human rights, which once could be safely understood and where common ground within limits did exist, are now far from settled. There is no package deal any more. Previously, if you were on the left or right, you knew what your thoughts should be on all of the issues listed above. Now there is no such safety.

Anodyne mainstream politics in which everything settles around whether Mrs *Daily Mail* will smile or frown is creating an illusion which will do the country great harm in the long run. We might as well move the editors of such papers to Downing Street if politicians have lost the will and the stomach to take on the fights that are essential in a democracy. When there appears to be no political choice any more – just as in the United States – even the most involved begin to give up on the political process. This is highly dangerous. When politicians say and do the things that will win them further elections rather than the things which would be better for the country, everyone loses out in the end. Let us take just one example. *The Economist*, to its credit, has for years argued that the country needs to think through its restrictive immigration policies and to open up to the idea that immigration may actually be extremely important for the next century. Today our health service managers go on ignoble shopping sprees for nurses to Finland and Australia because shortages are so acute in some areas of Britain. Who, in all three political parties, has the courage to raise the point that this is madness? That this country loses more people than it gains each year and that it might soon need a positive immigration policy?

There are so many other issues too. The soft political centre is creating more and more constituencies on the fringes where people are full of rage, impotence and anxiety. This binds them in ways they do not themselves yet realize. Swampy and Kalim Siddique would never have shared a tree house, but both were driven by an inconsolable sense of injustice and exclusion.

Add to this, then, at least 252 known languages and dialects; hundreds of small and large ethnic and religious groupings; mixed-race communities too; class and income differentials; the growing elite and underclass; diasporic connections – and you can see how unruly society appears. Remember too that we are at the beginning of the devolution process and in the middle still of identity politics. It is astonishing to hear pundits and politicians speaking of the 'four nations' of Britain. *Windrush* and its aftermath is not even an afterthought in this discourse. So when Scotland has got kilted up and the English have established their homelands far from the Welsh and Irish, where do we, the black Britons, go? Perhaps we can put in a bid for London, please? When ethnicities are created on the back of bold political decentralization, and identity is tied to history and territory, the results are not always what you would want. Within the first months after the referendum in Scotland, racism there against blacks and the English appeared to be increasing. The managing of this break-up is going to require much work. As Robert Hazell and Brendon O'Leary warn in their brilliant book on constitutional change:

> **The government needs to understand and articulate clearly a sense of the wider loyalties which bind us together at the level of the nation state and to foster a sense of loyalty to the Union . . . It will require an acceptance of multiple identities and indeed a celebration of them . . . and it will require a clear statement of the common core of rights and responsibilities.**[25]

This in itself may be more than enough to drive Black Britons into that catastrophic hall of mirrors which is what the politics of purified identities has become in the United States.

The good news is that a number of key thinkers and doers are beginning to appreciate that with this scale of change and problem-solving, clinging on to the past is no longer an option. We need a new future where we are a better integrated society and better at managing our responsibilities in the world. In order to achieve these dreams, all Britons will need to be enlisted and involved. There can be no further talk about 'ethnic minorities' and the 'majority community' tolerating each other. We need our collective skills, wisdom, experiences, trust and faith to build a better nation, where we learn from each other and discard (even if it is painful) ways of seeing and acting which are damaging us or our country.

There are several key areas where an integrated approach must, as a matter of urgency, be instituted to provide better solutions to the issues that are causing concern across the various communities which make up the nation. Remember, though, that this is only the beginning of the road to mend the broken attachments and create the co-operation that Oliver James says quite rightly is essential for our emotional survival.

The first would be to introduce a wide-scale public debate on how this nation defines itself in the next century. We might even think of creating a new British flag which has black in it. All public policy-making bodies must have able people of all backgrounds, not to fulfil some mechanistic duty based on a numerical understanding of diversity, but with a passionate commitment because the end result will be better for cross-cultural consultation. The political parties and the government must make similar moves. They should be competing with one another to entice the best among us Black Britons, not begrudgingly performing some soulless duty in letting many of the weakest among us hang in the shadows of where they are carrying out their business. Black Britons for their part should give up the habit of ingratiation and of being prepared only to be big fish in small ethnic minority pools. What happens to this country is our business.

The media – whether private or public service – needs to take up this challenge too and set about examining the way they have carried out the task of interpreting the country and the world beyond. We need many more kinds of lives and views orchestrating and feeding into the key political slots, and many more able Black Britons need to be in gate-keeping positions such as those occupied by over-powerful critics and commissioning editors.

Education needs a complete overhaul. It is serving neither white nor Black children at all well. Silly fears about being labelled 'loony' seem pathetic in the face of the enormous challenges facing us. If we had a curriculum which valued all Britons, we could then begin to ask difficult questions about black male under-achievement. Racism may be a fact of life, but it has really succeeded when it makes Black people never strive, or if they use it as an excuse.

Feminism must put itself in order before it is taken seriously again. Feminists have to stop regarding theirs as the only valid issue in the world. Black women must make alliances and resist the temptation to disappear into their own moans. We must talk; we must fight with respect and as equals, and in the end we must produce something that all our daughters and sons can support.

Family life must be saved, and it can be if all of us – those with questions and those with unorthodox answers – can come together. There are ways of empowering an individual without destroying the family or the community. There is a way of learning how not to pine for the impossible, and to nurture new possibilities. None of this is achievable without creating a new morality which is neither so absolute that lives are destroyed by it nor so relative that it offers no anchors as we toss about.

All of the above depends on a new understanding. As Fred d'Aguiar writes:

> The last twenty-five years in Britain and the USA have confirmed that race issues are central to British and American definitions of themselves, if only because of the pain of witnessing a denial by most whites on this aspect of their sense of nationhood.

He goes on to show that without connections all will be lost, suggesting that now even slavery (or maybe especially slavery) is a story which should be embraced by everyone;

> This is part of the power of the story. In essence it denies the exclusivity of any one group or individual experience. It seeks to communicate against that privatising zeal in us all, that impulse to say, 'this is mine and no one else's'. It posits ways of linking one person to the next, one group to another by revealing aspects thought exclusive in one to be resident in the other and by showing difference as bridgeable.[26]

Bhikhu Parekh comes near to the vision which is now needed:

> If a plural society is to hold together, it clearly needs a shared self-understanding, a conception of what it is and stands for, a national identity. And if that society is to ensure both unity and

> diversity, its national identity should affirm both what unites and
> distinguishes its constituent communities.[27]

I come to the end of this book, which is the most heartfelt account of
how much has been wasted and how much has been lost since my
people first came to join the British nation, and the dreams that must
now come true. The Stephen Lawrence Report has been published. As
a nation we have had to listen and watch with anger and shame as all
that we value and ought to take pride in has shown itself to be poisonous
dust. A young black man with so much left to do is cut down in his
prime. His parents, who made that risky, often disappointing journey
from the Caribbean to this country to have their children and give
them a better future, are now coping with the reality that the journey
took away the life of their son. Do not look at their dignity; imagine
instead their rage, undeserved guilt too perhaps, and the pain which
is still fuelling their will not to see this murder disappear under the
deceptive sheets of official denial and self-protection. These are people
of this nation who have held a mirror up to our society to look at itself
and despise what is reflected back. And to take stock. What was it
that made white thugs kill a man simply because of the colour of his
skin, in spite of having grown up and been educated in intimate
proximity with Black children? What do the parents of these white
men do when they learn about the Inquiry? Do they celebrate that
they have raised such fine boys? And how dare the Metropolitan police
still deny that race had anything to do with the facts of their shockingly
indifferent investigation? But go beyond the obvious signs of personal
and institutional racism and something else shows up. A substantial
number of white Britons today see Stephen as their son. The *Daily
Mail* saw him as their cause. We have a Home Secretary who decided
that the nation should hear the truth. I feel that every time another
such story unfolds (and sadly it will) acceptance of such behaviour
will be less and less forthcoming. Racism has been lethally damaged.
The blood of Stephen Lawrence has changed something for ever. Many
more Britons today are convinced that the difference between the tribes
is bridgeable, must be bridged, and shall be bridged.

Notes

A Note on Terminology

1. Alastair Bonnett, 'Culture, communication and discourse: negotiating difference in multi-ethnic alliances', Workshop paper, University of Newcastle seminar, 9 December 1994.
2. In my book *True Colours*, on the role of government in changing attitudes to multiculturalism, published in 1999 by the Institute for Public Policy Research, I make a policy recommendation that such research should be carried out.
3. Figures taken from the Commission for Racial Equality Fact Sheet No. 1, 1995.
4. See *Race through the 90's*, BBC Radio 1 and Commission for Racial Equality, 1993.
5. See my report, *Flashpoint Communities*, Institute for Public Policy Research, 1999.
6. The Muslim weekly magazine *Q News* has been running this campaign for five years.
7. A. Sivanandan, 'Fighting our fundamentalisms', *Race and Class*, Vol. 36, No. 3, 1995, p. 73.

Introduction

1. Speech made at the Runnymede Trust, 6 October 1989.
2. HMSO, February 1999.
3. Facts from a paper delivered by Tariq Modood at the TUC seminar on black women and the labour market, London, 19 February 1998.
4. In some areas such as Newham in London these figures are even higher. In some neighbourhoods the majority of residents would be from the visible communities.

5. For up-to-date detailed empirical evidence of the realities of multi-ethnic Britain, see T. Modood, R. Berthoud et al., *Diversity and Disadvantage: Ethnic Minorities in Britain*, Policy Studies Institute, 1997.

6. See Bhikhu Parekh, 'South Asians in Britain', in *History Today*, September 1997.

7. See the information pack, *Visible Women*, published by the Commission for Racial Equality, 1997.

8. See Mark Leonard, *Britain TM*, Demos, 1997.

9. Figure from *British Crime Survey*, HMSO, 1996. The UN Committee on the Elimination of Racial Discrimination (CERD) responded to a report on racial discrimination submitted by the UK government in 1996. The Committee expressed serious concerns about the levels of racial discrimination, deaths of black people in custody, and other issues.

10. For details of these changes, see Chapter 1 in my book, *True Colours*, which looks at race, public attitudes and the government, Institute for Public Policy Research, 1999.

11. Michael Ignatieff, lecture at the London School of Economics, 16 February 1998.

12. Francis Fukuyama wrote *The End of History* saying that the fall of the Berlin wall meant the end of the last major historical struggle between ideologies. The west had won and the rest would follow.

13. Broadcast on 14 August 1998.

14. In the colonies we used England and Britain interchangeably. To get a sense of how the mother country was incorporated into our lives and dreams, see my autobiographical account, *No Place Like Home*, Virago, 1995.

15. I refer here to his periodic outbursts, the last of which was at the Tory Party Conference in 1997 when he said that ethnic minorities could not be a part of this nation unless they imbibed British values and history. See press reports for 3 October 1997.

16. Hazir Teimourian, 'A Kurd's eye view', BBC Radio 4, September 1998.

17. Meera Syal, *Anita and Me*, Flamingo, 1996, p. 203.

18. See two surveys, one quantitative carried out by NOP and one qualitative by Opinion Leader Research, into attitudes towards racial minorities and multiculturalism, Institute for Public Policy Research, 1997, summaries in Y. Alibhai-Brown, *True Colours*, op. cit.

19. Salman Rushdie, 'The new empire within Britain', *New Society*, December 1984.

20. Charles Moore, 'Time for a more liberal and "racist" immigration policy', *Spectator*, 19 October 1991.

21. See Stephen Bayley's diary in *Esquire*, 16 April 1998.

22. Bernadette Vallely (ed.), *What Women Want*, Virago, 1996, p. xxii.
23. See Demos, *Britain TM*, op. cit.
24. Quoted by Rushdie, op. cit.
25. *Guardian*, 10 July 1998.
26. Germaine Greer, *Sex and Destiny: The Politics of Human Fertility*, Picador, 1985.
27. Personal communication, March 1998.
28. Isaiah Berlin, *The Crooked Timber of Humanity*, John Murray, 1990, p. 38.
29. *Independent*, 14 February 1996.
30. See report in *Muslim News*, 25 December 1998.
31. Carol Gilligan, 'Getting civilized' in Ann Oakley and Juliet Mitchell (eds.), *Who's Afraid of Feminism?: Seeing Through the Backlash*, Hamish Hamilton, 1997, p. 19.
32. *New Statesman*, 24 February 1995.

Chapter 1 The Context: Gales of Change

1. Sarah Dunant and Roy Porter (eds.), *The Age of Anxiety*, Virago, 1996, p. ix.
2. 'A sense of the sacred', speech made at Wilton Park in December 1996, text in *European Judaism*, Vol. 31, No. 4, Spring 1998.
3. See Martin Goodman, *In Search of the Divine Mother*, HarperCollins, 1998.
4. The network, based in Llanberis, has details of how even the National Trust seems determinedly colour blind.
5. See the texts of his 1999 BBC Reith Lectures.
6. *Guardian*, 6 January 1999.
7. *Independent*, 22 August 1998.
8. *Bright Futures*, report by the Medical Health Foundation, 14 February 1999.
9. Oliver James, *Britain on the Couch*, Arrow Books, 1998; quote from extract in *Prospect*, October 1997.
10. Ziauddin Sardar, *Post-modernism and the Other: The New Imperialism of Western Culture*, Pluto Press, 1998, p. 22.
11. Arundhati Roy, 'The end of imagination', *Frontline*, India, July 1998.
12. See my essay, 'PC = Power Challenge', in Susan Greenberg (ed.), *Mindfields*, Camden Press, 1998.
13. Prince Charles, speech at Wilton Park, December 1996, op. cit.
14. Kenan Malik, *The Meaning of Race: Race, Culture and History in Western Society*, Macmillan, 1996, p. 12.

15. Michael Ignatieff, 'British national identity: liberal fictions and ethnic realities', *Prospect*, November 1996.

16. ibid.

17. See 2020 *Vision: The Action Agenda*, report commissioned by the Industrial Society, 18 November 1997.

18. *Guardian*, 22 August 1998.

19. For an interesting, if flawed, book on what this country needs to change in order to dismantle these edifices of the past, read Jonathan Freedland's *Bring Home the Revolution*, Fourth Estate, 1998.

20. *Observer*, September 1997.

21. *New Statesman*, 24 February 1995.

22. See the letters page in the *Guardian* the week of 8 June 1998.

23. Clive Aslet, *Anyone for England?*, Little, Brown, 1997, p. 24.

24. Roger Hewitt, *Routes of Racism: The Social Basis of Racist Action*, Trentham Books, 1996.

25. Dr Rae Sibbitt, *The Perpetrators of Racial Harassment and Violence*, Home Office Research Study, No. 176, 1997.

26. Les Back, 'Racist name calling and developing anti-racist strategies in youth work', University of Warwick, 1990.

27. For some of the most perceptive essays on this see Sarah Dunant and Roy Porter (eds.), *The Age of Anxiety*, op. cit.

28. *Independent*, 30 January 1997.

29. Adrienne Burgess and Sandy Ruxton, *Men and their Children*, IPPR, 1996, p. 1.

30. Germaine Greer, *The Whole Woman*, Doubleday, 1999.

Chapter 2 *Long in the Root*

1. See the first page in his book *Staying Power*, Pluto, 1984, repr. 1991.

2. For a detailed account of this early history and beyond, there is little to match Peter Fryer's *Staying Power*, op. cit. The book should be on the national curriculum.

3. Christopher Hill, *Lies about Crimes*, South Place Ethical Society, 1989.

4. Fryer, op. cit.

5. Rozina Visram, *Ayahs, Lascars and Princes: Indians in Britain 1700–1947*, Pluto Press, 1986.

6. Kusoom Vadgama, *Indians in Britain*, Robert Royce, 1984, and *India: British–Indian Campaigns in Britain for Indian Reforms, Justice and Freedom*, Banyan Tree Publications, 1997.

7. James Walvin, *The Black Presence: A Documentary History of the Negro in England, 1550–1860*, Orbach and Chambers, 1971.

8. Ron Ramdin, *The Making of the Black Working Class*, Wildwood House, 1987.

9. A. Sivanandan, *Coloured Immigrants in Britain: A Select Bibliography*, Institute of Race Relations, 1969.

10. Quoted by Fryer, op. cit., p. 11.

11. *The London Gazette*, No. 2185, 25 October 1686.

12. Prologue to *The Prophetess*, in James Kinsley (ed.), *The Poems and Fables of John Dryden*, Oxford University Press, 1970.

13. *Diary of Samuel Pepys*, ed. Robert Latham and William Matthews, Bell & Hyman Ltd, 1972, p. 215.

14. Fryer, op. cit., p. 24.

15. See the introduction in the latest edition of *The Letters of the Late Ignatius Sancho, An African*, ed. Vincent Carretta, Penguin, 1998.

16. See Fernando Henriques, *Children of Conflict: A Study of Interracial Sex and Marriage*, Dutton, 1975.

17. Edward Long, *Candid Reflections*, 1772, quoted in Henriques, op. cit., p. 137.

18. Y. Alibhai-Brown and A. Montague, *The Colour of Love*, Virago Press, 1992.

19. Rozina Visram, op. cit.

20. See Ziggi Alexander and Audrey Dewjee, *Mary Seacole: Jamaican National Heroine and 'Doctress' in the Crimean War*, Brent Library Service, 1982.

21. Vadgama, *Indians in Britain*, op. cit., p. 104.

22. See Yasmin Alibhai-Brown, 'The Commonwealth's cannon fodder', *Independent*, 12 November 1998.

23. *Financial Times*, 30 May 1998.

24. Yasmin Alibhai-Brown, 'Fighting for Blightie', *Independent*, 22 November 1993.

25. ibid.

26. For a detailed analysis, look in my report, *Attitudes to Multiculturalism: The Role of Government*, Institute for Public Policy Research, 1998.

27. PRO HO 213/244, 22 June 1948.

28. *Hansard*, 7 July 1948, col. 405.

29. Kenan Malik, *The Meaning of Race*, Macmillan, 1996, p. 19.

30. See Margaret Cannon, *Invisible Empire: Racism in Canada*, Random House, 1995.

31. Speech made in 1994 in London.

32. Cabinet papers quoted in the *Guardian*, 12 January 1986.

33. Paul Foot, *Immigration and Race in British Politics*, Penguin, 1965, p. 233.

34. Zig Layton-Henry, *The Politics of Immigration*, Blackwell, 1992, p. 67.
35. See the introduction in Y. Alibhai-Brown and A. Montague, op. cit.
36. J. Rose et al., *Colour and Citizenship*, Oxford University Press, 1969, p. 214.
37. Foot, op. cit., pp. 233–4.
38. For a full account see Z. Layton-Henry, *The Politics of Immigration*, op. cit.
39. Cited in *Hansard*, 5 December 1958, col. 1563.
40. *Racial Discrimination*, Labour Party, September 1958.
41. Layton-Henry, *The Politics of Race in Britain*, Allen & Unwin, 1984, p. 51.
42. Foot, op. cit., p. 232.
43. See details of this and other acts of racial antagonism in Fryer, op. cit., pp. 376–9.
44. See for example his essay, 'British racism: the road to 1984' in *Race and Class*, Vol. XXV, No. 2, Autumn 1983.
45. Cited in J. Rutherford, *Forever England*, Lawrence & Wishart, 1997.
46. 'Coloured people from British Colonial Territories', CP 50 113, 18 May 1950, para. 12, iv.
47. Layton-Henry, *The Politics of Race in Britain*, op. cit., pp. 28–9.
48. *The Politics of Immigration*, op. cit., p. 67.
49. This was described by many of those interviewed for this project. See the introduction. Two erstwhile white supervisors of factories in Walsall made it clear to the author that there were active recruitment drives by employers in the private sector to get 'good' workers from the Indian subcontinent.
50. For details of this see Fryer, op. cit., Chapter 11.
51. Paul Rich, *Race and Empire in British Politics*, Cambridge University Press, 1986, p. 200.
52. Quoted in John Solomos, *Race and Racism in Contemporary Britain*, Macmillan, 1989, p. 50.
53. Samit Saggar, *Race and Politics in Britain*, Harvester Wheatsheaf, 1992, p. 175.
54. Foot, op. cit., p. 172.
55. Layton-Henry, *The Politics of Race in Britain*, op. cit., p. 55.
56. ibid., p. 57.
57. R. Crossman, *Diaries of a Cabinet Minister*, Vol. 2, Hamish Hamilton, 1975, p. 149.
58. ibid., p. 299.
59. Colin Brown, 'Ethnic pluralism in Britain: the demographic and legal background', in Nathan Glazer and Ken Young (eds), *Ethnic Pluralism and Public Policy*, Heinemann/PSI, 1983, pp. 48–9.

60. W. W. Daniel, *Racial Discrimination in Britain*, Pelican, 1968.
61. Rose et al., op. cit., p. 736.
62. *Spectator*, 1 March 1968.
63. *Hansard*, 4 March 1976, col. 1605.
64. See A. Dummett and M. Dummett, 'The role of government in Britain's racial crisis', in L. Donnelly (ed.), *Justice First*, Sheed & Ward, 1969.
65. See the *Hansard* report of the debate on the Bill, in Parliament 23 April 1968.
66. Speech made to the West Midlands Conservative Political Centre in Birmingham, 20 April 1968.
67. Layton-Henry, *The Politics of Race in Britain*, op. cit., p. 71.
68. See D. Spearman, 'Enoch Powell's postbag', *New Society*, 9 May 1968, pp. 667–8.
69. See the debates in the press in mid-February 1995.

Chapter 3 *Rebranding Britain and the Weeds of Multiculturalism*

1. Printed the day after William Hague made a major speech on the need to create a new cosmopolitan identity for Britain.
2. T. Benn, *Against the Tide: Diaries 1973–76*, Hutchinson, 1989; entry for 16 January 1974.
3. Layton-Henry, *The Politics of Race in Britain*, 1984, p. 73.
4. This is what Heath said to Yasmin Alibhai-Brown in November 1997 in an interview for BBC Radio 4.
5. For a 'fictional' account of this theory see Peter Nazreth's *The General is up*, Tsar, 1991.
6. See my book *True Colours*, IPPR, 1999, pp. 76–80.
7. D. Smith, *Racial Disadvantage in Britain*, Penguin, 1977.
8. *Hansard*, 4 March 1976, col. 1601.
9. *Hansard*, 15 January 1976, oral answers, col. 560–1.
10. See Lord Lester of Herne Hill, *The Politics of The Race Relations Act 1976*, Runnymede Trust, 1997.
11. S. Saggar, *Race and Politics in Britain*, Harvester Wheatsheaf, 1992, p. 117.
12. J. Twitchin in *Five Views of Multiracial Britain*, Commission for Racial Equality/BBC, 1978, p. 6.
13. See T. Russel, *The Tory Party: Its Policies, Divisions and Future*, Penguin, 1978.
14. *World in Action*, Granada Television, 30 January 1978.
15. Russel, op. cit., p. 117.

16. Saggar, op. cit., p. 120.
17. Full quote in the *Independent*, 20 March 1991.
18. P. Dodd, *The Battle Over Britain*, Demos, 1995, pp. 26–7.
19. For examples see P. Gordon and F. Klug, *New Right, New Racism*, Runnymede Trust, 1985.
20. K. H. Proctor et al., *Immigration and Repatriation*, Monday Club, 1981, p. 5.
21. See for example, Natasha Walter (ed.), *On the Move*, Virago, 1999, which has an essay on this by Helen Wilkinson.
22. N. Murray, *Anti-racists and Other Demons: The Press and Ideology in Thatcher's Britain*, Institute of Race Relations, Race and Class Pamphlet, No. 12, 1989, pp. 2–3.
23. For a detailed description of how this happened see Gordon and Klug, op. cit.
24. Saggar, op. cit., p. 193.
25. See C. Searle, *Your Daily Dose: Racism and the Sun*, Campaign for Press and Broadcasting Freedom, 1989.
26. Research carried out by Opinion Leader Research and published by the IPPR, 1997.
27. For an excellent detailed analysis of this, see the section 'Racism and equal opportunity policy' in Peter Braham et al. (eds), *Racism and Anti-racism*, Oxford University Press, 1992.
28. See Saggar, op. cit., pp. 129–34.
29. Lord Scarman, *The Brixton Disorders 10–12 April 1981; Report of an Inquiry*, HMSO, 1981.
30. See the relentless attacks on the Lawrence Report in the *Daily Telegraph* and the *Daily Mail* in the last week of February and the first week of March 1999.
31. C. Brown, *Black and White Britain*, Policy Studies Institute 1984, and C. Brown and P. Gay, *Racial Discrimination: 17 Years after the Act*, Policy Studies Institute, 1985.
32. Paul Rich, *Race and Empire in British Politics*, Cambridge University Press, 1986, p. 206.
33. Mike Phillips and Trevor Phillips, *Windrush: The Irresistible Rise of Multi-Racial Britain*, HarperCollins, 1998, p. 81.
34. ibid., p. 13.
35. See my essay 'Living by proxy', in Sarah Maitland (ed.), *Very Heaven*, Virago, 1989.

Chapter 4 And So to Now

1. *Guardian*, 26 February 1996.
2. See various reports on rural racism by the CRE published in 1996, and press reports of racial violence in Yeovil in February 1997.
3. See *Strangers and Citizens*, a collection of essays by experts on immigration edited by Spencer, IPPR/Rivers Oram Press, 1994.
4. *New Internationalist*, September 1998, p. 19.
5. *Spectator*, 27 May 1994.
6. See Chapter 2 in my book *True Colours*, IPPR, 1999.
7. *Observer*, 13 October 1991.
8. *Guardian*, 12 November 1998.
9. Salman Rushdie, 'The Indian writer in English', in Margaret Bucher (ed.), *The Eye of the Beholder*, Commonwealth Institute, 1983.
10. Philip Dodd, *The Battle over Britain*, Demos, 1995, p. 13.
11. Bidisha Bandyobadhyay, 'Young and anxious', in Sarah Dunant and Roy Porter (eds.), *The Age of Anxiety*, Virago, 1996, p. 198.
12. Chris Smith, *Creative Britain*, Faber & Faber, 1998.
13. Keith Vaz, 'The glass ceiling', October 1997, and 'Whitehall remaining white', May 1998, both privately published by Vaz.
14. Speech at the Labour Party Conference, September 1997.
15. Ian Grosvenor, *Assimilating Identities*, Lawrence & Wishart, 1997, pp. 185–6.
16. See my comment piece 'The challenge remains', in the *Independent*, 25 February 1999.
17. Bhikhu Parekh, 'National identity and the ontological regeneration of Britain', in A. Gilbert and P. Gregory (eds.), *Culture, Markets and the Nation*, Avebury, 1995, p. 94.
18. See my piece in the *Guardian*, 'Whose food is it anyway?', 28 August 1998.
19. Broadcast on 22 January 1998.
20. Seminar held at IPPR on 9 February 1998.
21. Like the reports already mentioned in previous chapters (see p. 000), e.g. *2020 Vision: The Action Agenda*, Industrial Society, 18 November 1997.
22. *Daily Telegraph*, 7 May 1998.
23. Unmesh Desai, 'Community flashpoints', in Yasmin Alibhai-Brown (ed.), *Emerging Issues for the Millennium*, IPPR, 1998, p. 18.
24. For an excellent discussion of this see Peter Aspden in the *Financial Times*, 16 August 1997.
25. See text of his speech made in Calcutta to the Confederation of Indian

Industry on 9 January 1997.

26. He made this speech at the twenty-fifth anniversary of the *Gujarat Samachar* on 7 May 1997.

27. Ziauddin Sardar and Meryl Wyn-Davies, *Distorted Imagination*, Grey Seal Press, 1990, p. 276.

28. *Attitudes to Race* surveys published by the IPPR, 1997.

29. *Racial Equality in School*, Association of Teachers and Lecturers, July 1998.

30. Dr Rae Sibit, *The Perpetrators of Racial Harassment and Violence*, Home Office Research Study, No. 176, 1997.

31. Mark Leonard, 'The Empire's new clothes', *Guardian*, 21 November 1998.

Chapter 5 *Distorted Mirrors*

1. One of the clearest illustrations of this was in the BBC2 fly-on-the-wall series following Gordon Brown as he went about his official business. His personal advisor, Charlie Whelan, suggested throughout the programmes that he could make the media dance to his tune.

2. John Pilger, 'Distant voices of dissent', *Guardian*, 19 February 1990.

3. Harold Evans, 'A positive policy', in *Race and the Press*, Runnymede Trust, 1970, p. 45.

4. Karen Ross, *Black and White Media*, 1996, p. 87.

5. Stuart Hall, 'The whites of their eyes: racist ideologies and the media', in Gail Dines and Jean M. Humez (eds.), *Gender, Race and Class in the Media*, Sage, 1995, pp. 19–20.

6. Cherry Erlich, *The Erlich Report*, BBC, 1986, p. 3.

7. Joe Harte (ed.), *Black People and the Media*, London Borough of Lewisham Conference Report, 1988.

8. *Television in a Multicultural Society*, Commission for Racial Equality, June 1986, p. 2.

9. Speech at the Black Media Workers Conference, London, June 1988.

10. Zeinab Badawi, 'Reflections on recent television coverage of Africa', in John Twitchin (ed.), *The Black and White Media Book*, Trentham Books, 1988, p. 134.

11. Jim Pines (ed.), *Black and White in Colour*, British Film Institute, 1992, p. 160.

12. Tony Freeth, 'Race on television: bringing the colonials back home', in Phil Cohen and Carl Gardener (eds.), *It Ain't Half Racist, Mum*, Comedia, 1982, pp. 24–5.

13. BBC2, 1985, 1986.

14. *Television in a Multicultural Society*, CRE, June 1986.
15. For an excellent analysis of this see 'How could Corrie get it so wrong?', *Sun*, 11 December 1998.
16. Glasgow Media Group, *Race and the Public Face of Television*, 1997.
17. ibid., p. 1.
18. Guy Cumberbatch, *Channels of Diversity*, Commission for Racial Equality, 1996.
19. Chris Searle, *Your Daily Dose: Racism and the Sun*, Campaign for Press and Broadcasting Freedom, 1989, p. 49.
20. Nancy Murray, *The Press and Ideology in Thatcher's Britain*, Race and Class Pamphlet No. 12, Institute of Race Relations, 1989, p. 2.
21. *Sun*, 10 June, 16 June 1986.
22. 'In plain black and white', *Independent*, 1 December 1998.
23. Yasmin Alibhai-Brown, *Independent*, 26 April 1995.
24. *Daily Mail*, 15 November 1996.
25. *Sun*, 18 September 1992.
26. *Sun*, 4 March 1999.
27. Leon Wieseltier, 'Witness to intolerance', *Guardian*, 8 January 1992.
28. *Daily Telegraph*, 2 March 1999. See also Polly Toynbee in the *Guardian*, 3 March 1999.
29. The *Runnymede Bulletin*, December 1995/January 1996.
30. See my analysis in the *Independent*, 9 February 1999.
31. This was presented at an all-day conference organized by the Southall Monitoring Group and London Borough of Hounslow in November 1997.
32. *Guardian*, 25 August 1998.
33. Quoted in *Race and the Public Face of Television*, op. cit., p. 1.
34. Samir Shah, in Jim Pines (ed.), op. cit., p. 162.
35. See coverage in the week of 19 November 1998.
36. Ross, op. cit., p. 131.
37. *Independent*, 17 August 1993.
38. See Gary Younge in *Guardian Weekend*, 6 February 1999, for a full discussion of this success story and white audiences.
39. 9 January 1999.
40. Ross, op. cit., p. 178.
41. Fay Weldon wrote a number of articles in 1989 denouncing Islam and the idea of multiculturalism which protected Muslims who wanted to ban Rushdie's book. See also Melanie Phillips's essay, 'Illiberal Liberalism' in Sarah Dunant (ed.), *The War of the Words*, Virago, 1994.
42. Tariq Modood, 'Goodbye Alabama', *Guardian*, 22 May 1989.

43. Quoted by Yasmin Alibhai-Brown in 'The great backlash', in Sarah Dunant (ed.), *The War of the Words*, Virago, 1994, p. 70.
44. ibid., p. 77.
45. *Independent*, 27 June 1996.
46. *People*, 5 May 1996.
47. *Independent Magazine*, 4 March 1989.
48. *The Times*, 11 May 1989.
49. *The Times*, 21 April 1995.
50. *Guardian*, 10 July 1998.
51. See Mike Marqusee, 'Fear and fervour', *Guardian*, 4 July 1995.
52. Philip Dodd, *The Battle Over Britain*, Demos, 1995.
53. Glasgow Media Group, *Advertising and the Ethnic Minorities*, November 1996.
54. *Sunday Telegraph*, 25 February 1996.
55. The report, *Advertising and the Ethnic Minorities*, was published by the Race for Opportunity on 19 November 1996.

Chapter 6 *Learning Not to Know*

1. This was shown to me by a black mother whose child had tried to rub off his black skin with a Brillo pad. She had a little book where she collected these racist comments in children's classics.
2. *Independent*, 30 January 1999.
3. *European Youth Survey*, MTV, 6 February 1997.
4. See the *Mirror* and the *Daily Star*, 16 January 1999.
5. See the *Evening Standard*, 9 February 1999.
6. Quoted in the *Guardian*, 8 October 1996.
7. See report in the *Daily Mail*, 18 July 1995.
8. Poem published in *Without Prejudice*, a booklet on racism by the Commission for Racial Equality and BBC Radio 1, 1994.
9. In forthcoming publications from the Department of Applied Social Studies and Research, Oxford.
10. Personal communication, August 1992. See also J. Eggleston, D. Dunn, M. Anjali and C. Wright, *Education for Some*, Trentham Books, 1986.
11. See for example A. H. Halsey, *Educational Priority: Problems and Policies*, HMSO, 1972.
12. Ali Rattansi, 'Racism, culture and education', in James Donald and Ali Rattansi (eds), *'Race', Culture and Difference*, Open University, 1992, p. 14.
13. ibid., p. 15.

14. For details see D. Kirp, *Doing Good by Doing Little*, University of California Press, 1979.

15. Roy Jenkins, 'Race equality in Britain', speech made on 23 May 1966, to a meeting of voluntary liaison committees of the National Committee for Commonwealth Immigrants, in Anthony Lester (ed.), *Roy Jenkins, Essays and Speeches*, Collins, 1967, p. 26.

16. Department of Education and Science, 1981.

17. *Sunday Times*, 25 October 1998.

18. Quoted in the *Guardian*, 6 September 1996.

19. *Sunday Mirror*, 22 March 1998.

20. Tony Sewell, *Black Masculinities and Schooling*, Trentham Books, 1997.

21. See ibid.

22. See Jenny Bourne, Lee Bridges and Chris Searle, *Outcast England: How Schools Exclude Black Children*, Institute of Race Relations, 1995.

23. David Gillborn and Caroline Gipps, *Recent Research on the Achievements of Ethnic Minority Pupils*, HMSO, 1996.

24. The kind of material one could use is exemplified by a series of textbooks published by Waylands Publishing in the late eighties. They include books on racism written by myself and Colin Brown and others by authors such as Rozina Visram. The books were non-dogmatic and open to discussion.

25. Keynote speech made at the tenth anniversary conference of the Institute for Public Policy Research, 11 January 1999.

26. See 'Religious Studies', *Daily Telegraph*, 9 January 1999, for some interesting insights into how separate schools are faring.

27. Ziggi Alexander and Audrey Dewjee, *Mary Seacole: Jamaican National Heroine and 'Doctress' in the Crimean War*, Brent Library Service, 1982.

28. Kusoom Vadgama, *Indians in Britain*, Robert Royce, 1984.

29. A. Sivanandan, 'Race and the degradation of black struggle', *Race and Class*, Vol. 25, No. 4, 1985.

30. Ahmed Gurnah, 'The politics of racism awareness training', Critical Social Policy, Issue 11, 1984.

31. For a complete description of this see Colin Brown and Jean Lawton, *Training for Equality*, Policy Studies Institute, 1991.

32. See my article 'The reality of race training', *New Society*, 29 January 1988.

33. It is extraordinary that highly regarded publications on race and culture by the Open University and others avoid an examination of some of the education policies of boroughs such as Brent and prefer to read

what happened purely in terms of New Right assaults on progressive education.

34. David Milner, *Children and Race*, Penguin, 1975; *Children and Race, Ten Years On*, Ward Locke Educational, 1983.

35. David Smith and Sally Tomlinson, *The School Effect*, Policy Studies Institute, 1989, p. 307.

36. See John Rex, 'New vocationalism, old racism, and the Careers Service', in *Racism and Anti-Racism*, Peter Braham, Ali Rattansi and Richard Skellington (eds), Sage/Open University Press, 1992.

37. 'Tribal dances', *New Statesman*, 22 July 1988.

38. Ian Macdonald, Reena Bhavnani, Lily Khan and Gus John, *Murder in the Playground: The Report of the Macdonald Inquiry into Racism and Racial Violence in Manchester Schools*, Longsight Press, 1989.

39. ibid., p. 401.

40. Interviews in Barry Troyna and Richard Hatcher, *Racism in Children's Lives*, National Children's Bureau and Routledge, 1992, pp. 168–70.

41. 21 January 1991.

42. See the excellent essay by John Annette, 'The culture wars on the American campus', in Sarah Dunant (ed.), *The War of the Words*, Virago, 1994.

43. See Jardine's essay, 'Cannon to the left of them, Cannon to the right of them', in Dunant, op. cit.

44. 30 January 1994.

45. 8 March 1996.

46. Roger Hewitt, *Routes of Racism: The Social Basis of Racist Action*, Trentham Books, 1996, p. 33.

47. ibid., p. 40.

48. Figures in the *Sunday Telegraph*, 11 January 1998.

49. Quoted in an excellent article by Barry Hugill in the *Observer*, 15 September 1996.

50. An excellent report, *Recent Research on the Achievements of Ethnic Minority Pupils* for OFSTED by David Gillborn and Caroline Gipps, HMSO, 1996, gives other details.

51. A report on this was produced by the Independent Schools Information Service in July 1996.

52. Quoted in the *Guardian*, 6 September 1996.

53. David Gillborn, 'Natural selection? New Labour, race and education policy', in *Multicultural Teaching*, Vol. 15, No. 3, Summer 1997, p. 7.

54. Bernard Crick, *Education for Citizenship and the Teaching of Democracy in Schools*, Qualifications and Curriculum Authority, March 1998.

Chapter 7 *Ain't I a Woman?*

1. See my autobiography, *No Place Like Home*, Virago, 1995.
2. Yasmin Alibhai-Brown, 'Burning in the cold', in Katherine Gieve (ed.), *Balancing Acts*, 1988, p. 24.
3. Quoted by Susan Benson in her book *Ambiguous Ethnicity*, Cambridge, 1981, p. 4.
4. Beth Day, *Sexual Life between Blacks and Whites*, Collins, 1974, p. 8.
5. Diana Seabright, *Prospect*, July 1998, p. 74.
6. Rosemary Crawley, Unpublished MS, 'Be (a) ware black women at work', 1998, p. 12.
7. To see how some of this became received wisdom among some activist groups see Beverly Bryan, Stella Dadzie and Suzanne Scafe, *The Heart of the Race – Black Women's Lives in Britain*, Virago, 1985.
8. Lecture given at Spellman College, 25 June 1987, text in Margaret Busby (ed.), *Daughters of Africa*, Jonathan Cape, 1992, p. 573.
9. *Observer*, 2 April 1997.
10. *Guardian*, 13 May 1997; 20 January 1998; 5 January 1998; 9 September 1996.
11. *New Statesman*, June 1998.
12. In the *Guardian*, 2 February 1998. These arguments are lucidly tackled in greater detail by Mirza in *Black British Feminism*, edited by her and published by Routledge, 1998.
13. *Guardian*, 20 January 1998.
14. Sheila Rowbotham, *A Century of Women*, Viking, 1997.
15. As in the University of Hull where the courses run by Kathleen Lennon do this as a matter of course.
16. Morwena Griffiths, *Feminisms and the Self*, Routledge, 1995, p. 182.
17. Kate Figes, *Of her Sex*, Macmillan, 1994; Patricia Hewitt, *About Time: The Revolution in Work and Family Life*, Institute for Public Policy Research, 1993.
18. Natasha Walter, *The New Feminism*, Little, Brown & Co., 1998, p. 187.
19. Heidi Mirza (ed.), *Black British Feminism*, Routledge, 1998, p. 5.
20. Published respectively by Virago, 1978; Virago, 1985; Women's Press, 1997; Sheba, 1998; Virago, 1994; and Runnymede Trust, 1988.
21. Delia Jarrett-Macauley, *Reconstructing Womanhood, Reconstructing Feminism*, Routledge, 1996; Mirza (ed.), *Black British Feminism*, op. cit.
22. See the UNISON report, *Black Women's Employment and Pay*, March 1997.

23. Spinder Dhaliwal, *The Silent Contributors*, Roehampton Institute, 1998.
24. *Guardian*, 3 June 1997.
25. See her essay 'Is multiculturalism bad for women?' in the *Boston Review*, October 1997. See also the various responses to her ideas in the same issue.
26. See her *Women and Gender in Islam*, Yale University Press, 1992.
27. Filomena Chioma Steady, *The Black Woman Cross-Culturally*, Schenkman Books, 1985, p. 36.
28. Pratibha Parmar, 'Other kinds of dreams', in *Feminist Review*, Spring 1989, pp. 55–6.
29. In Bryan, Dadzie and Scafe, *The Heart of the Race*, op. cit., p. 148.
30. Shabnam Grewal et al. (eds.), *Charting the Journey*, Sheba, 1998, p. 3.
31. Bhikhu Parekh, 'Feminism and multiculturalism', *Boston Review*, October 1997. The issue is devoted to this theme and is an invaluable discourse on some of the most up-to-date thinking in this area.
32. Mirza (ed.), op. cit., p. 4.
33. In H. Crowley and S. Himmelweit (eds.), *Knowing Women: Feminism and Knowledge*, Polity Press, 1992, p. 293.
34. *Guardian*, 9 September 1996.
35. Mirza, op. cit., p. 18.

Chapter 8 *Me, Myself, I and Mine*

1. Speech at the annual Social Services Conference in Harrogate, December 1994.
2. Francis Fukuyama, *The Great Disruption: Human Nature and the Reconstitution of Social Order*, Profile Books, 1999.
3. See my column in the *Independent*, 26 June 1999.
4. See her essay in the *Daily Mail*, 30 November 1996.
5. *Guardian*, 15 April 1996.
6. *Guardian*, 23 September 1992.
7. Anne Phoenix, *Young Mothers*, Polity Press, 1991, p. 247.
8. *Guardian*, 28 May 1998.
9. See Spinder Dhaliwal, *The Silent Contributors*, Roehampton Institute, 1998, pp. 42–3.
10. This refers to a speech made by Tony Blair to Asians at an event to celebrate the *Gujarat Samachar*, an Asian newspaper, in 1997.
11. Report by Helen Wilkinson et al., *Tomorrow's Women*, Demos, 1997.
12. 19 October 1997.
13. I think that some of these questions have been put most effectively by

Melanie Phillips in her columns on the family through 1996 and 1997. The problem is that because many of her arguments on this and other issues appear to be close to Tory ideology, not enough attention has been paid to what she is arguing. She has also become so set and fundamentalist in her opinions that she is in the process of discrediting herself.

14. Adrienne Burgess and Sandy Ruxton, *Men and their Children*, IPPR, 1996.
15. Andrew Samuels, 'The good enough father', *Feminism and Psychology*, Vol. 5, No. 4, 1995.
16. *Guardian*, 12 April 1996. See too my column in *Community Care*, 10 September 1998.
17. See, for example, L. Burgess, *Lone Parenthood and Family Disruption*, Family Policy Studies Centre, 1994, and also P. R. Amato and B. Keith, 'Parental divorce and the well-being of children: a meta-analysis', *Psychological Bulletin*, Vol. 110, No. 1.
18. Deborah Moggach, 'Kiss and break up', *Guardian*, 6 June 1998.
19. *Divorce and Children*, BBC 2, 9 May 1997.
20. *Women and Migration: Establishing the Fundamental Right to Equality in a Setting of Cultural Diversity*, Council of Europe, Strasbourg, 5 July 1995.
21. Quoted in *Islamaphobia, a Challenge for Us All*, Runnymede Trust, 1997.
22. Oliver James, *Britain on the Couch*, Arrow Books, 1998, p. 342.
23. Soni Raleigh, 'Asian women and suicide', *British Journal of Psychiatry*, 1990, Vol. 156, pp. 46–50.
24. Lola Young, on *Diverse Perspectives*, Radio 4, 21 August 1998.
25. Morwena Griffiths, *Feminisms and the Self: The Web of Identity*, Routledge, 1995, p. 183.

Chapter 9 *And It Does Not End Here*

1. Chris Smith, *Creative Britain*, Faber, 1998, pp. 22–3.
2. See Robert Lee, *Other Britain, Other British*, Pluto, 1995, and the journalistic writings in the *Guardian* of Maya Jaggi, literary adviser to the London Arts Board.
3. Maya Jaggi, *Guardian*, 13 July 1996.
4. See, for example, Jonathan Freedland on the British national character, *Guardian*, 18 September 1997.
5. See the *Daily Mail* attack on him on 5 February 1998.
6. 'Poetry in Motion', *Independent*, 22 March 1999.

7. Reyhan King, *Ignatius Sancho: African Man of Letters*, National Portrait Gallery, 1997. *The Letters of the Late Ignatius Sancho, an African*, ed. Vincent Carretta, were republished by Penguin in 1998.

8. For a fascinating account of this see Stephen Bourne, *Black in the British Frame*, Cassell, 1998.

9. See his excellent article in the *Independent*, 1 April 1997.

10. Quoted in ibid.

11. Paper given to the German Shakespeare Society, Weimar, 1997.

12. Smith, op. cit.

13. Nadhir Tharani, 'Heads under the sands', *Artrage*, No. 16, 1987.

14. In the *Analysis* programme 'One land, many cultures', BBC Radio 4, 22 January 1998.

15. See *Prospect*, October 1997, p. 52.

16. I took part in this dicussion organized by *Marxism Today*.

17. Mark Leonard in *Britain TM*, Demos, 1997, p. 52.

18. See Bhikhu Parekh, 'Superior people', *TLS*, 25 February 1994.

19. See my account of this in *Prospect*, May 1998.

20. Letters to the Editor, *Guardian*, 12 February 1990.

21. For one of the most challenging expositions of this see Richard Webster, *A Brief History of Blasphemy*, Orwell Press, 1990.

22. Ziauddin Sardar and Meryl Wyn-Davies, *The Distorted Imagination – a Response to the Rushdie Affair*, Grey Seal Books, 1990, p. 276.

23. *Independent*, 4 March 1989.

24. The 1999 Reith Lectures by Professor Anthony Giddens were extraordinarily sanguine about the negative effects of globalization on the third world.

25. Robert Hazell (ed.), *Constitutional Futures*, Oxford University Press, 1999, pp. 45–6.

26. Fred d'Aguiar, 'The Last Essay about Slavery', in S. Dunant and R. Porter (eds.), *The Age of Anxiety*, Virago, 1996, pp. 143–4.

27. Convocation Lecture, University of Delhi, 1997, p. 9.

Index